Practical Debugging at Scale

Cloud Native Debugging in Kubernetes and Production

Shai Almog

Apress®

Practical Debugging at Scale: Cloud Native Debugging in Kubernetes and Production

Shai Almog
Tel Aviv, Israel

ISBN-13 (pbk): 978-1-4842-9041-5   ISBN-13 (electronic): 978-1-4842-9042-2
https://doi.org/10.1007/978-1-4842-9042-2

Managing Director, Apress Media LLC: Welmoed Spahr
Acquisitions Editor: Jill Balzano
Development Editor: Laura Berendson
Coordinating Editor: Jonathan Gennick

Cover photo by Joel Filipe on Unsplash

Distributed to the book trade worldwide by Springer Science+Business Media New York, 1 New York Plaza, Suite 4600, New York, NY 10004-1562, USA. Phone 1-800-SPRINGER, fax (201) 348-4505, e-mail orders-ny@ springer-sbm.com, or visit www.springeronline.com. Apress Media, LLC is a California LLC and the sole member (owner) is Springer Science + Business Media Finance Inc (SSBM Finance Inc). SSBM Finance Inc is a **Delaware** corporation.

For information on translations, please e-mail booktranslations@springernature.com; for reprint, paperback, or audio rights, please e-mail bookpermissions@springernature.com.

Apress titles may be purchased in bulk for academic, corporate, or promotional use. eBook versions and licenses are also available for most titles. For more information, reference our Print and eBook Bulk Sales web page at http://www.apress.com/bulk-sales.

Any source code or other supplementary material referenced by the author in this book is available to readers on GitHub via the book's product page, located at www.apress.com/. For more detailed information, please visit http://www.apress.com/source-code.

Printed on acid-free paper

Dedicated to Selma, Maya, Tara, and Tao.

Table of Contents

About the Author

Shai Almog is an entrepreneur, open source hacker, speaker, author, blogger, Java rockstar, and more. He is a former Sun (later Oracle) developer with more than 30 years of experience. Shai has built JVMs, development tools, mobile phone environments, banking systems, startup/enterprise backends, user interfaces, development frameworks, and much more. He speaks at conferences all over the world and has shared the stage with luminaries such as James Gosling (father of Java). Shai is an award-winning, highly rated speaker with deep technical experience to share, and he has a knack for engaging his audience.

About the Technical Reviewer

**Alejandro Duarte** is a software engineer working for MariaDB Corporation as a Developer Advocate. He has published several books on web development with Java and served as a technical reviewer for different programming-related books. Alejandro started to code at age 13 using the BASIC programming language on a black screen with a blinking cursor. He quickly moved to C and C++ – languages he still loves and enjoys – and then to Java during his computer science studies at the National University of Colombia. Alejandro moved to the UK and later to Finland to foster his career in the open source software industry. He became one of the well-known faces in the Java, MariaDB, and Vaadin communities, having published articles and videos with hundreds of thousands of views and presented technical topics at international Java conferences and Java User Groups. Alejandro splits his free time between his passion for the electric guitar, exercising, and the Finnish language. You can contact him through his blog at `www.programmingbrain.com`.

Introduction

It is a capital mistake to theorize before one has data. Insensibly one begins to twist facts to suit theories, instead of theories to suit facts.

—Sir Arthur Conan Doyle

This isn't a typical programming book. In a typical book, we build a demo, then slowly enhance it as we go through the chapters to learn a new tool. There's no single demo we can follow for debugging. When conceptualizing this book, I wanted to create a reference that not only covers the theory but also gets its hands dirty with the practicality. Debugging means chasing a bug wherever it leads you, and as such it requires agility and a wide set of skills.

I wrote this book for developers with some experience. I expect you to know debugging and even be good at it. This book is about making us great at it, getting out of our metaphorical box of debugging tools and practices and familiarizing ourselves with newer approaches.

Debugging is a skill that universities skim over since it isn't a testable skill. Despite spending a lot of time in the debugger, many developers treat it with the same fondness as one treats taking out the garbage – a necessity that we try to avoid. As a result, we spend more time in the debugger and often reach the wrong conclusions in our debugging sessions.

The book is divided into three distinct parts where we gradually work our way to a uniform skill set.

Part 1 – Basics

In Part 1, we discuss the basics and make sure everyone is on the same page. We learn the tools that power debugging and their individual value. This part gives us the "lay of the land" when debugging locally.

- Chapter 1: "Know Your Debugger" – We spend 60% of our time debugging problems, and a lot of this time is within the debugger. Yet most of us limit ourselves to "step over" and "continue." In this chapter, we will discuss dozens of powerful debugging features that most of us are sadly unfamiliar with.

- Chapter 2: "The Checklist" – Debugging theory is relatively simple. We encapsulate most of the principles within this chapter.

- Chapter 3: "The Auxiliary Tools" – Other than the debugger proper, we need to understand the tools from the operating system and third-party tools for debugging issues. In this chapter, we'll discuss tools ranging from git *bisect* to *strace* to *wireshark*. We discuss how we can use these tools as part of our investigating journey when tracking some issues.

- Chapter 4: "Logging, Testing, and Fail-Fast" – Logging and testing are precognitive debugging. We guess the areas where bugs might present themselves and prepare ourselves for future debugging sessions.

- Chapter 5: "Time Travel Debugging" – Time travel debugging isn't new. It's a system that records the execution of the program and then lets us play it back and forth similarly to a debug process, but with the ability to view everything taking place.

Part 2 – The Modern Production Environment

In the second part, we discuss the problems of debugging in a modern polyglot, highly distributed environment. We cover the types of failures we can experience at scale and how they differ from our local issues.

- Chapter 6: "Debugging Kubernetes" – This isn't a DevOps book. When a container runs out of memory, the DevOps team is on that and can fix that problem. However, if the code in the container is leaking memory, the DevOps team can't do anything.

- Chapter 7: "Serverless Debugging" – Serverless is notoriously hard to debug. This chapter can't change that fact. It does lay out the options and tooling we can use to mitigate the situation.

- Chapter 8: "Fullstack Debugging" – We discuss the tools and techniques to debug web frontend as well as database backend. This is essential when closing in on an issue that crosses tiers.

- Chapter 9: "Observability and Monitoring" – DevOps have had deep insight into the performance and stability of our servers for a very long time. These tools provide a deep level of insight that R&D should be a part of and should use to gauge the "real-world" behavior of our production environments.

- Chapter 10: "Developer Observability" – Developers have been left in the dark when it comes to observability. Newer tools are changing the dynamics in this industry and are offering new ways to debug production.

Part 3 – In Practice

In this part, we apply everything we learned in the book to real-world use cases and scenarios.

- Chapter 11: "Tools of Learning" – When we're new to a project or new to a portion of the code, it's often hard to understand the dynamic relationship and usage between the various pieces. We can use debuggers to study the way the different pieces fit together.

- Chapter 12: "Performance and Memory" – Profilers give us great information, but we're often left in a lurch by an unclear result. Debuggers can take us the rest of the way and pinpoint the issue.

- Chapter 13: "Security" – One of my first interactions with a debugger was as part of a hack. They have long been a tool for hackers; it's time to use them to improve the security of our systems.

- Chapter 14: "Bug Strategies" – In this chapter, we review past issues and lessons learned from the field.

Summary

I hope you find this book helpful. It's meant as a practical "hands-on" tool that you can reach to when struggling with a difficult bug. A common Israeli military axiom is "training is rough, combat is easy." I believe that if we train our debugging capabilities to their full extent, we will massively improve overall.

Debugging provides a deep level of insight into the runtime of an application. No modeling software or other tool provides that. It's a therapeutic system that puts us face to face with our insecurities and doubts. It's an investigative process that challenges us and rewards us. I hope this book will help you see the bigger picture around this underdocumented task that takes up so much of our time.

PART I

Basics

CHAPTER 1

Know Your Debugger

If debugging is the process of removing software bugs, then programming must be the process of putting them in.

—Edsger Dijkstra

In the mid-1990s, I was an overconfident developer. I knew "everything," and senior developers constantly sought my consultation, despite my young age at the time. Then I got lucky. I was debugging an issue with a senior developer, and the way he wielded the debugger nearly knocked me off my seat.

The experience was both amazing and embarrassing. My ego was bruised, but I persisted and learned everything I could about debugging techniques. I was lucky enough to see a master at work, to discover that there's a better way. I hope this book will pass that luck to you. That's why I chose to open with this specific chapter. It might seem basic at first glance; that's deceptive.

Most developers aren't deeply familiar with some of the more subtle capabilities of the debugger, a tool we use daily. It's a force of habit we developed over the years. We often perceive debugging as taking out the garbage; we hold our noses and try to "get it done." In that rush, we barely take notice of the tools we use. When you're struggling, you don't "check out the scenery." In this chapter, I will try to create a common baseline we can build upon. We need these capabilities to build a foundation of debugging tools as we move through the book. The techniques illustrated in this chapter will prove their value in your day-to-day job.

© Shai Almog 2023
S. Almog, *Practical Debugging at Scale*, https://doi.org/10.1007/978-1-4842-9042-2_1

Basics

The goal of this chapter is teaching the capabilities of the debuggers. I don't intend to turn this chapter into an IDE tutorial. I keep screenshots and deep IDE samples to a minimum, but still had to use some for this specific chapter. Please check Appendix A for the resource section of this book where you can find additional resources that are kept more up to date.

It's important to make sure our terminology is similar. Figures 1-1 and 1-2 show screenshots of the two leading IDEs in the market. Elements in each figure are labeled with the terminology that I use in this book.

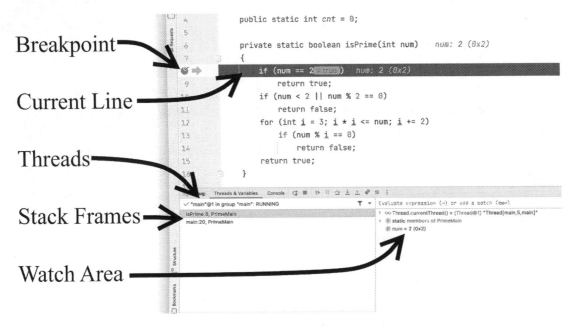

Figure 1-1. *Basic terms in IntelliJ/IDEA by JetBrains*

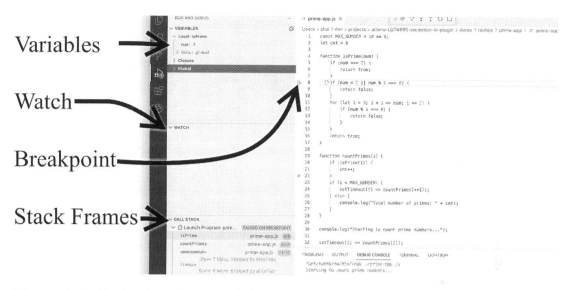

Figure 1-2. *Basic terms in VS Code by Microsoft*

As you can see, there are many features in common when debugging across IDEs and even across programming languages. There are some differences in layout, for example, IntelliJ/IDEA places elements at the bottom by default. I want these screenshots to illustrate how similar these features are between IDEs. Notice that, during the time of this writing, VS Code still doesn't have some features discussed in this chapter. However, the functionality we discuss here is universal and supported by many mature IDEs/tools. Beyond that, I'd like to point out two interesting differences as follows.

Watch and Variable Areas

VS Code separates the watch and variable areas. IntelliJ/IDEA uses a single area but uses different icons to signify the difference. Throughout this book, I will talk about the watch area as a single area to keep things simple. Keep in mind that this should apply to both.

Threads

There's no thread section in the VS Code IDE. In this case, we're debugging JavaScript code. As such, the list of threads isn't applicable. Notice that if we were debugging Java code, such an area would be available there.

Breakpoints

We all know breakpoints. They break. They stop the execution of the program so we can "step over" (or "step into"). Even this basic axiom isn't always true, as you will see in the section "Tracepoints and Suspend State".

We assume the stack trace we see correlates to the calls leading to the breakpoint. Again, that's something that isn't always true. We will discuss when talking about asynchronous stack traces.

In this section, we'll go over some basics related to breakpoints and cover some of the more esoteric things you can do with them.

Line Breakpoint

The line breakpoint is the workhorse of the debugging process. It's so common that we usually drop the word "line," so you might know it by the name "breakpoint." It's the most basic type of breakpoint, and most of us should be familiar with it. It's the breakpoint we saw in Figures 1-1 and 1-2. We see it when placing a breakpoint next to a line of code that isn't a field or method declaration.

Method Breakpoint

We can add a method breakpoint by clicking the gutter area next to the method or function. Method breakpoints aren't supported by every runtime or every IDE and for good reason.

The implementation of method breakpoints is often quite slow since the debug API stops for every method entry or exit. This includes the JVM implementation. As a result, modern debuggers, such as the one in IntelliJ/IDEA, place line breakpoints to simulate method breakpoints when possible. This is seamless to us as developers, but it's important to know since some dogma states (correctly) that they are slow.

In Figure 1-3, you can see the different breakpoint type representations in IntelliJ/ IDEA,[1] specifically watchpoint, method breakpoint, and a line breakpoint.

---

[1] VS Code represents all breakpoint types in the same way visually.

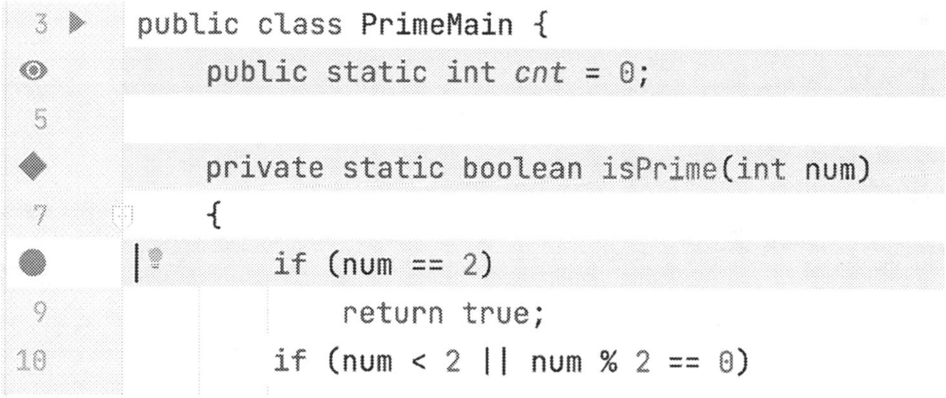

```
3  ▶      public class PrimeMain {
👁                public static int cnt = 0;
5
◆              private static boolean isPrime(int num)
7        ⊕        {
●          ╎💡         if (num == 2)
9                         return true;
10                    if (num < 2 || num % 2 == 0)
```

Figure 1-3. *Different breakpoint types in IntelliJ/IDEA*

We can configure a method breakpoint to stop at the method entry/exit or both. A method breakpoint on entry is functionally equivalent to a line breakpoint. An exit breakpoint is harder to simulate as a method can have multiple exit points, and it might be impossible to place line breakpoints that simulate that behavior from within the IDE.

Ultimately, a method breakpoint doesn't appear very useful. This is indeed the case, and very few developers make use of this feature. There's an interesting use case that makes sense for method breakpoints, which we'll discuss later in this chapter.

Field Watchpoint

A watchpoint is a breakpoint placed on a field. We can configure it to break when the field is read from, written to, or both. This is a remarkably useful tool to detect the code that changes a value or shifts it around.

This feature is even more useful when combined with tracepoints, which we'll discuss soon enough.

Exception Breakpoint

Missing from Figure 1-3 is the exception breakpoint. This breakpoint type stops execution when an exception of a given type is thrown. We can define whether to stop on exceptions that are caught, uncaught, or both. We typically add an exception breakpoint in the breakpoint management UI. In IntelliJ/IDEA, we can open this UI via the Run ➤ View Breakpoints menu option, which you can see in Figure 1-4.

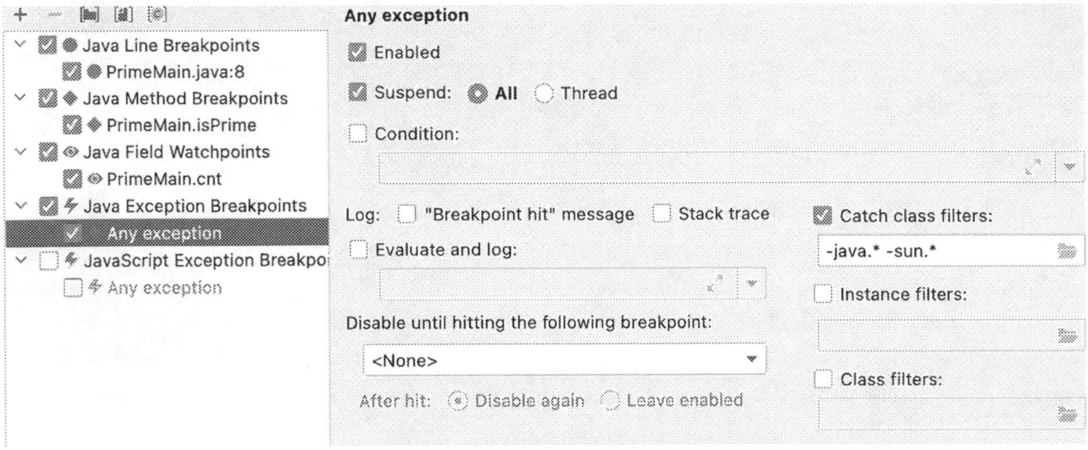

Figure 1-4. *Breakpoint management window in IntelliJ/IDEA*

In the breakpoint management UI, we also have the ability to break on all exceptions. This isn't a popular feature for JVM languages. The problem is that the JVM throws exceptions as part of normal execution. The solution for this is "Catch class filters" that let us ignore exceptions that are caught by specific classes.

We can ignore all exceptions caught by the JVM packages by adding the exclude statement:

```
-java.* -sun.*
```

Conditional Breakpoints

We can attach a boolean expression to a breakpoint; when the expression evaluates to true, the breakpoint will stop. Otherwise, it will be ignored. This is an important tool that lets us narrow down specific nuanced failures.

If we can determine the invalid state of the application, we can use conditional breakpoints to stop only when that invalid state occurs, and we can litter our code with breakpoints.

A good example would be the binding of a method breakpoint to a wide range of methods, then using a condition to stop when the application state is invalid. You will probably stop shortly after the application becomes invalid. At that state, there might still be valuable information you can extract from the application.

Tracepoints and Suspend State

A tracepoint is (a.k.a. logpoint, log message) a log we can add dynamically using the debugger. It's a breakpoint that doesn't stop the current execution and can print values of variables, methods, etc. Since it doesn't stop execution, it's very valuable in debugging concurrency issues. It has two major advantages over print/log-based debugging:

- You don't need to remember to remove them before committing.

- You don't need to recompile or stop execution to add a log.

If VS Code did one thing right, it's this: it brought tracepoints to the forefront by making them easily discoverable in the IDE UI. When right-clicking a breakpoint and selecting edit, "Log Message" is one of the options. We can enter a message directly on the following line as seen in Figure 1-5.

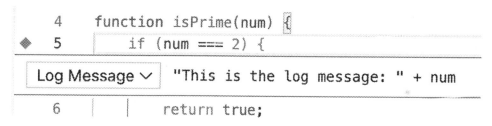

Figure 1-5. *Log message support in VS Code*

Notice that the log message accepts code expressions and not a plain string. This lets us write an expression where we can invoke methods or list variables. This log message will be visible in the "Debug Console" view.

This feature isn't as discoverable in IntelliJ/IDEA; we can reach it via the UI in several ways, such as shift-clicking on the gutter area. We can also uncheck the "suspend breakpoint" option to expose this feature. Tracepoints are mustard colored in IntelliJ/IDEA as seen in Figure 1-6.

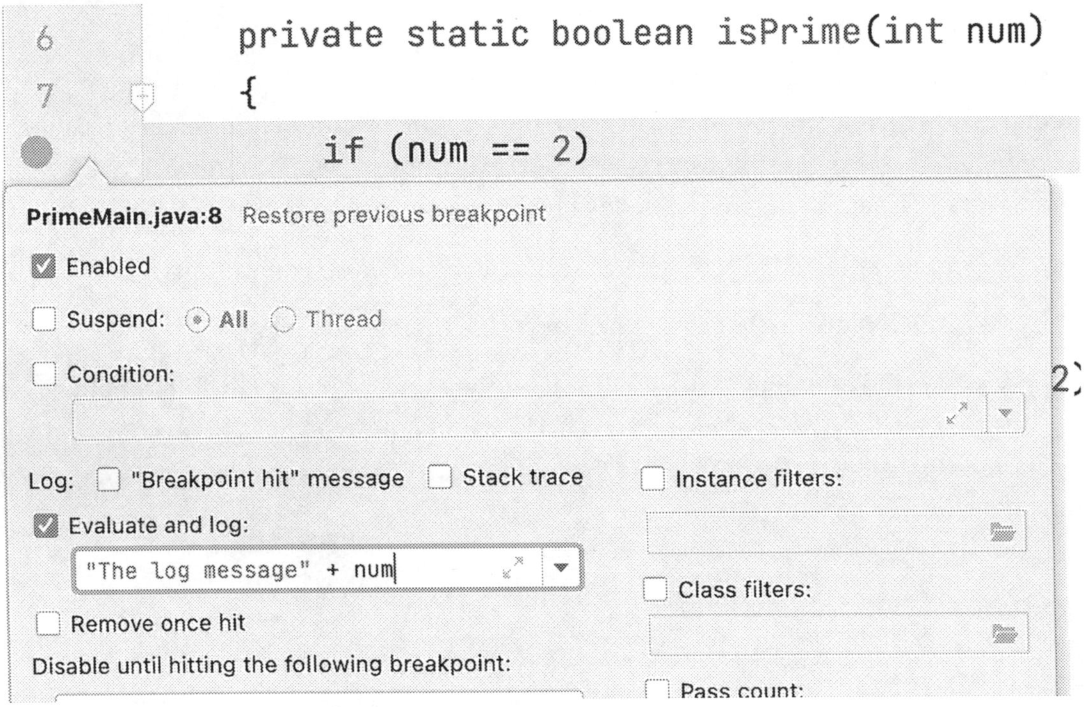

```
6        private static boolean isPrime(int num)

7        {

            if (num == 2)
```

PrimeMain.java:8   Restore previous breakpoint

☑ Enabled

☐ Suspend: ◉ **All** ○ Thread

☐ Condition:

Log: ☐ "Breakpoint hit" message   ☐ Stack trace   ☐ Instance filters:

☑ Evaluate and log:

```
"The log message" + num
```

☐ Class filters:

☐ Remove once hit

Disable until hitting the following breakpoint:

☐ Pass count:

Figure 1-6. *Tracepoint UI in IntelliJ/IDEA*

Once we do that, we need to check the "Evaluate and log" option and type our expression there. Notice that in IntelliJ/IDEA, we can create a conditional tracepoint. This means we can create a log that only appears if a specific condition is met. This can reduce potentially noisy logs to a manageable volume.

There are several other interesting capabilities we notice within the IntelliJ/IDEA advanced dialog. We can print a stack trace when we hit the breakpoint. This can help narrow down a message to a specific area of the code that printed it.

But the most interesting option is the suspend option. A typical breakpoint suspends all the threads when it's hit. A tracepoint disables that behavior and prevents suspension entirely. IntelliJ/IDEA also includes another option of only suspending the current thread. This is very useful for multithreaded applications where we might need the background threads running while debugging.

Asynchronous Stack Trace

In the past decade, reactive frameworks and functional programming have gained tremendous popularity thanks to many potential benefits. However, they have one major drawback: debugging is harder.

An asynchronous operation disconnects the stack trace and removes our ability to follow the chain of causality. As a result, when we stop at a breakpoint in an asynchronous callback, we might get a very short stack trace that doesn't help by much.

If you use a modern IDE to debug such APIs, this might not have been your experience. You might have seen a nontrivial stack trace for asynchronous calls. This is a feature of modern debuggers, which includes elaborate features to glue a stack trace. Some IDEs hide this "glued" aspect of the stack trace, while others, such as IntelliJ/IDEA, highlight it, as seen in Figure 1-7.

```
saveVisit:19, VisitAsync (org.springframework.samples.petclinic.owner)
invoke:-1, VisitAsync$$FastClassBySpringCGLIB$$aa549f3f (org.springframew
invoke:218, MethodProxy (org.springframework.cglib.proxy)
invokeJoinpoint:779, CglibAopProxy$CglibMethodInvocation (org.springframew
proceed:163, ReflectiveMethodInvocation (org.springframework.aop.framework
proceed:750, CglibAopProxy$CglibMethodInvocation (org.springframework.aop
lambda$invoke$0:115, AsyncExecutionInterceptor (org.springframework.aop.in
call:-1, 1196666227 (org.springframework.aop.interceptor.AsyncExecutionInter
run$$$capture:264, FutureTask (java.util.concurrent)
run:-1, FutureTask (java.util.concurrent)
Async stack trace
    <init>:132, FutureTask (java.util.concurrent)
    newTaskFor:108, AbstractExecutorService (java.util.concurrent)
    submit:139, AbstractExecutorService (java.util.concurrent)
    submit:348, ThreadPoolTaskExecutor (org.springframework.scheduling.concur
    doSubmit:290, AsyncExecutionAspectSupport (org.springframework.aop.interc
    invoke:129, AsyncExecutionInterceptor (org.springframework.aop.interceptor)
    proceed:186, ReflectiveMethodInvocation (org.springframework.aop.framework
    proceed:750, CglibAopProxy$CglibMethodInvocation (org.springframework.aop
    intercept:692, CglibAopProxy$DynamicAdvisedInterceptor (org.springframewo
```

Figure 1-7. Asynchronous stack trace in IntelliJ/IDEA

The glued stack trace consists of two or more stack traces attached to one another. This creates the semblance of a single, detailed trace. On the surface, it might seem like semantics, but it matters since the global state might change. There could be a big difference between the state of the application when between the two traces.

This system works by tracking all asynchronous calls and keeping a "shot" of the trace in memory. Then, when a callback occurs, the debugger uses a heuristic to "glue" the right stack trace instances together. The heuristic used could be the callback instance reference. If the reference is identical in both stacks, that means they belong together. As a result, this can add a lot of performance overhead to the debugging processes. The IDE supports disabling this feature in the preferences to keep the debugger performant.

Control Flow

Typical application execution follows a standard path that we can walk through when stepping over or stepping in. One of the most important capabilities of the debugger is the manipulation of this flow. In this section, we'll discuss the various tools to do that and their common use cases.

Return Immediately and Force Throw

Reproducing complex or edge case behaviors in the debugger is usually challenging. This is especially difficult when we need to debug things related to error recovery. To do that, we need to reproduce the error, then we need to go over the logic. With these tools, we can skip the "reproduce" part of the process. We can even simulate problems/behaviors that might be theoretical.

We can force throw an exception by right-clicking the stack and writing the exception allocation code into the dialog. This triggers a throw of that exception, and we can then follow the logic of the error handling code. In Figure 1-8, we can see the context menu for these operations.

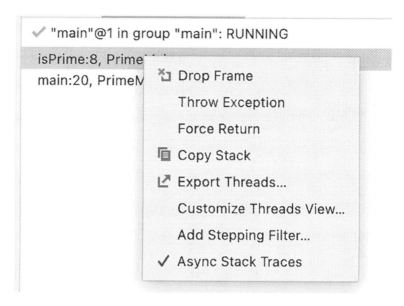

Figure 1-8. *Context menu of the stack frame*

In some cases, the behavior might be related to a different return value. In those cases, we can follow the same process and force a return with a different value from any location in the method. This lets us return a different value by typing in a custom expression. The expression can be anything, a method invocation or just a hardcoded value.

A big benefit of both approaches is the ability to skip the execution of some lines within the method. If we have code in the method that's currently failing, we can use one of these approaches to skip that code. This can happen in projects that are still a work in progress or at the edge of a long debugging session.

Drop Frame

I love undo. The undo shortcut is one of the most commonly used shortcuts on my keyboard. Undo in debugging is problematic though. How many times did we click the "step into" button by mistake and would want to undo the process?

Drop frame just removes the top stack frame and returns the application to the previous execution location. If you accidentally stepped into a method, you can use "drop frame" to return to the previous state. This typically works like force return by right-clicking the stack frame we wish to drop.

Jump to Line and Set Value

A common feature in the IDE is "Run to Cursor" where we can stand on a line and let execution reach that line. Jump to line lets us move the execution to a new line in an arbitrary location without executing the lines in between. We can move the execution pointer back to a previous location!

That is a remarkably useful feature. We can jump back and execute the same code over and over again while testing various scenarios. This works exceptionally well with the "set value" capability. Set value lets us modify variables dynamically and test different execution scenarios. Notice you can also use the "evaluate expression" capability to trigger a state change that would result in the same effect.

A great difficulty in software development is increasing the test coverage. The arguments passed to the unit test might be difficult to tune, so they will trigger the right branch/test. By tuning the values of variables and arguments to the method over and over again, we can verify instantly that a specific set of arguments will cover the right area of the code.

Not all runtimes and IDEs support this capability. To get this in IntelliJ/IDEA, we need to install a third-party plugin2. VS Code supports this only for some runtimes, such as C#, and at the time of this writing doesn't support it for Node.js.

Watch and Inspection

The watch area is our control center for the debugging process. It provides access to the variables and a view of their current state. Newer IDEs let you embed watch expressions right in the editor window and implicitly show variable values next to each line as we step over.

Rendering

IDEs display elements in the watch area using a renderer. Some debuggers provide deep rendering logic customizability. IntelliJ/IDEA provides the "Customize Data Views" UI, which you can access by right-clicking the watch area. In this dialog, which we can see in Figure 1-9, we can determine nuances on how elements are displayed in the watch area.

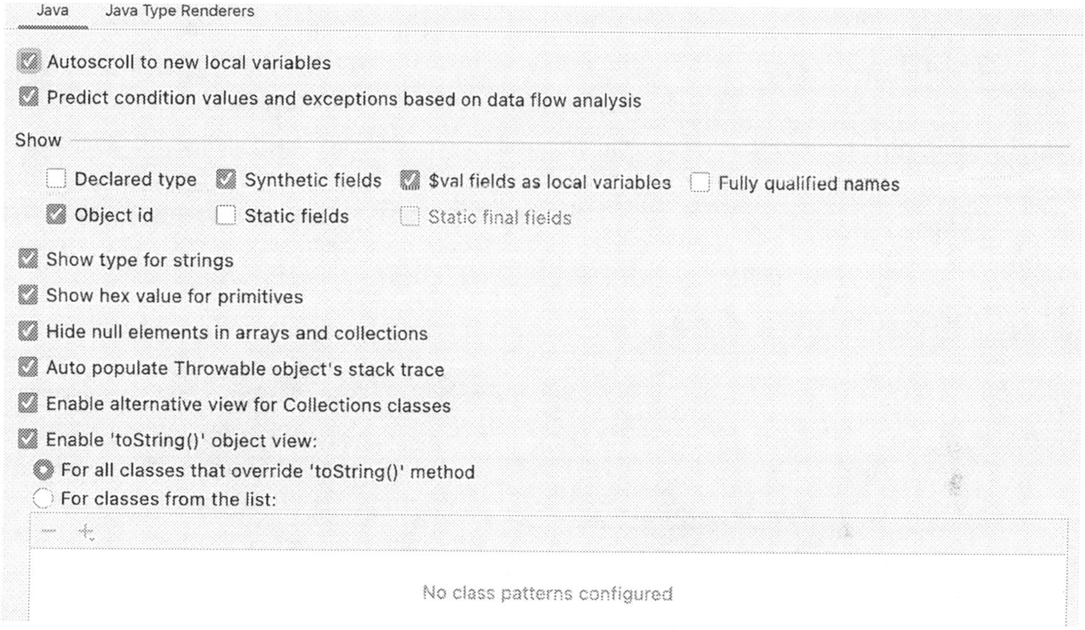

Java	Java Type Renderers

☑ Autoscroll to new local variables

☑ Predict condition values and exceptions based on data flow analysis

Show

   ☐ Declared type   ☑ Synthetic fields   ☑ $val fields as local variables   ☐ Fully qualified names

   ☑ Object id   ☐ Static fields   ☐ Static final fields

☑ Show type for strings

☑ Show hex value for primitives

☑ Hide null elements in arrays and collections

☑ Auto populate Throwable object's stack trace

☑ Enable alternative view for Collections classes

☑ Enable 'toString()' object view:

   ◉ For all classes that override 'toString()' method

   ◯ For classes from the list:

   − +

No class patterns configured

Figure 1-9. *IntelliJ/IDEA renderer customization dialog*

Custom Rendering

The "Customize Data Views" UI lets us perform much deeper customizations. By default, the IDE tries to show us the information we care about that's related to the object. For a language such as Java, the IDE will follow a process similar to this:

1. Is the element an array/collection?
   If so, it will render it as an expandable list.

2. Is the element a type that's known by the IDE?
   If so, it will use custom logic to display it.

3. It invokes *toString()* on the element and shows the result.

This works well enough for most standard cases. But the most interesting and complex objects are often quite problematic. Their *toString()* methods often include logic that makes more sense in a log than in the watch area. Their variable state might be too large and unreadable. So looking at them in the watch as we step over might not help.

Custom rendering lets us define how the object is presented as you can see in Figure 1-10. A good example is the *JpaRepository* from Spring Boot. The *JpaRepository* is an interface that to some degree represents a single SQL database table (this is a gross oversimplification). Its *toString()* method contains nothing of value.

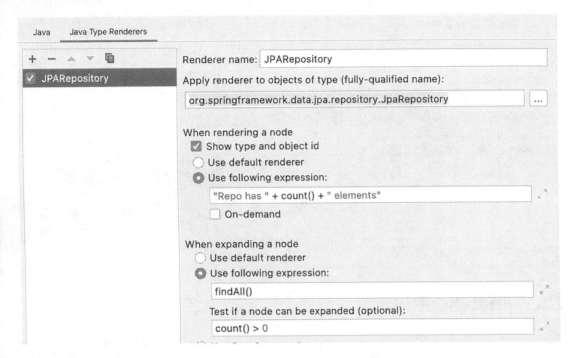

Figure 1-10. *Custom renderer for the JpaRepository type in IntelliJ/IDEA*

A renderer applies to a class (or base class) name. As you can see from Figure 1-10, we bind this renderer to the *JpaRepository* class. "When rendering a node" lets us define custom code to execute whenever the IDE needs to "decide" how an entry is displayed in the UI.

An entry roughly correlates to an "object." We use a different term here since it's the "projection" of the object into the watch area. An entry can be a primitive in the case of Java. It can be the elements within an array or the result of an expression you added to the watch. In this case, we can render this entry using the expression:

```
"Repo has " + count() + " elements"
```

Notice that the method invocation *count()* doesn't include a qualifier. It's executed in the scope of the object that's rendered. The same is true for the expressions when expanding a node. The *findAll()* method returns all the rows (collection of entities) within the table. By placing it in the "When expanding a node" section, we're indicating that it should be invoked to show the entries when the watched variable is expanded. This means a user can click the "+" sign next to the entry, and the results of the method will be shown, as you can see in Figure 1-11.

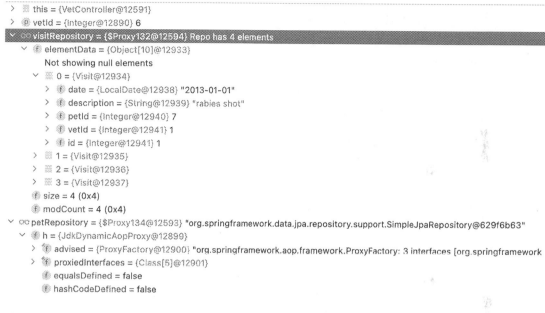

Figure 1-11. *Custom renderer and a typical renderer for the same type*

The result of the rendering process is a large volume of SQL invocations. The *count()* SQL operation is invoked to show the preview when we look at an entry. A full select call is made when we expand the actual entry UI. This can be an expensive operation, especially when debugging against a remote database. This would probably be reasonably performant for local debugging on a smaller dataset.

Mute Renderers

I sometimes click the step over button and have to wait several seconds for a response from the IDE. This is a major problem. Performance can be remarkably slow sometimes, and that can sour us on using debuggers altogether.

Renderers can have a significant impact on the performance and responsiveness of a debugger. To make the experience more responsive and flexible, IntelliJ/IDEA has the option of "Mute Renderers" on the right-click menu. When enabled, a renderer isn't shown by default, and instead we get a clickable area. Explicit clicking invokes the renderer on the entry.

Show Objects

When our program is running within a virtual machine, we have incredible access to the VM state. One such element of the VM state is the list of objects in memory. IntelliJ/IDEA lets you right-click any object in the watch and select the option "Show * Objects..."; for example, if you right-click an object of type *String*, you would see the option "Show String Objects...". Clicking that option will present you with every instance of a *String* object within the JVM as you can see in Figure 1-12 – including JVM internal strings!

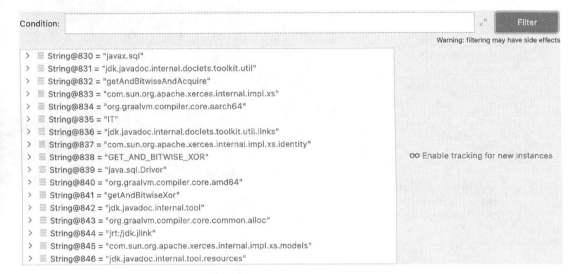

Figure 1-12. *String array objects in the Show String Objects... dialog*

We can filter this list with simple Java conditions so we can pinpoint a specific object of interest from memory. This is helpful for the common case where we wonder where a specific value came from.

Just use a dialog like this to find the right object and understand where the value is coming from. This is a remarkably useful tool for discovering duplication. A common source of bugs I encounter is one where we have multiple object instances with the same values. Using the filter, we can detect such duplication.

Memory Debugger

Memory inspection provides another way to get into the object list dialog and some amazing capabilities. We can enable this additional debugger view, and as we step over the code, we can see the differences from the previous allocations. Double-clicking of each entry seen in Figure 1-13 can show the list of VM object instances similar to the list in Figure 1-12.

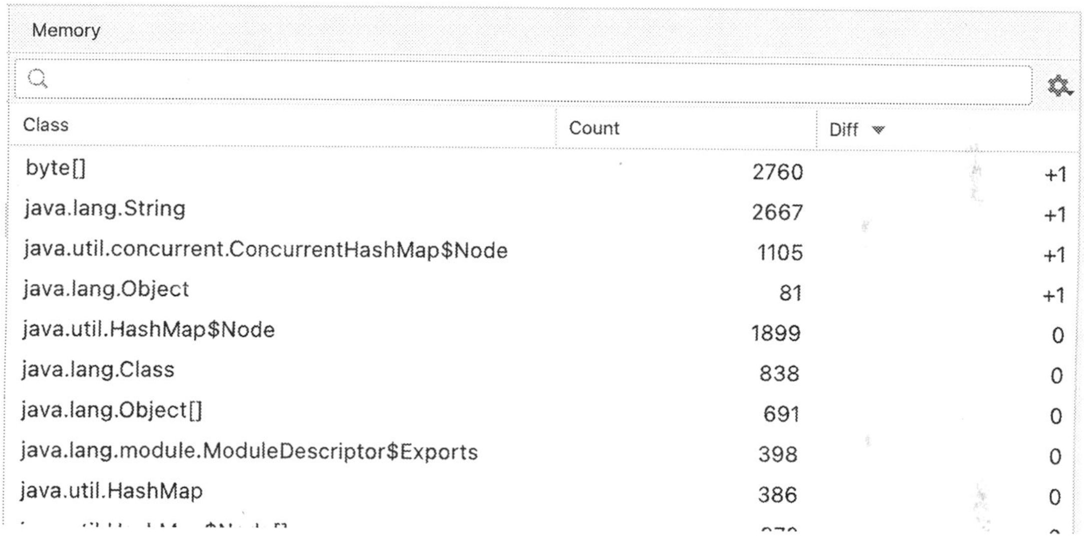

Memory		
Class	Count	Diff ▼
byte[]	2760	+1
java.lang.String	2667	+1
java.util.concurrent.ConcurrentHashMap$Node	1105	+1
java.lang.Object	81	+1
java.util.HashMap$Node	1899	0
java.lang.Class	838	0
java.lang.Object[]	691	0
java.lang.module.ModuleDescriptor$Exports	398	0
java.util.HashMap	386	0

Figure 1-13. *Debugger memory view in IntelliJ/IDEA*

We can see exactly how many objects we have of each type and the change for every step-over or between breakpoints. But we can take this much further...

On the right-hand side of Figure 1-12, you will see an option to enable tracking. Clicking this will cause the VM to track every allocation of this object type. The result is that we'll know exactly which objects were allocated between these two steps and the exact stack traces for each object!

We can show only the new instances of a specific object by clicking the context menu option "Show new instances." But an even more interesting feature is the ability to see the stack traces, as we can see in Figure 1-14.

Figure 1-14. Tracking instances in memory can show the stack for every allocation

Object Marking

Two of the worst types of bugs relate to object identity. The first I mentioned before: having two object instances with the same values within them. This can trigger painful bugs down the road.

The second relates to multiple threads accessing one resource simultaneously. Both are remarkably hard to detect and track. I used to pull out a pen and paper, write the object ID (or pointer) of each object, and compare this manually every time we stopped on a breakpoint. It's an error-prone and fragile process.

Object marking solves both problems in the most elegant way possible. We can select any object instance listed in the watch area and mark it from the context menu. Object marking creates a global label for the object which we can then use to reference it from anywhere. We can add a label to the watch, which is helpful, but we can do something far more powerful: we can add it as a conditional breakpoint as seen in Figure 1-15.

Figure 1-15. *Using object marking for a conditional breakpoint*

To create Figure 1-15, I watched the *Thread.currentThread()* instance. Then on right-click, I selected the option "Mark Object" which I named: *MyThread*. Notice that IntelliJ/IDEA appends an "_DebugLabel" suffix to named objects. I added the label to the watch as well, so it will be easy to see that this stores the current instance and is not just a label around the watch.

As you can see, the values of the two thread objects are different; both have similar names, but one is thread 1 and the other is marked as 2. It means that the second invocation of this method used a different thread than the first invocation. This means there's a theoretical chance for race conditions, deadlocks, etc., if we write risky code.

The amazing thing is that we can detect this situation almost seamlessly by using a conditional breakpoint and referencing the label object. We can do this within a tracepoint as well and log the information, which is a very useful tool for debugging thread-related issues.

This applies to the comparison of every object. APIs such as JPA can fail subtly when we invoke the API from outside the transactional context. This can implicitly create new object instances, which we didn't expect an intelligently crafted breakpoint such as this can instantly verify such a bug.

Filtering Collections and Arrays

I almost didn't include the following feature because I assumed everyone knew about it... After a debugging session with a relatively senior developer, I had some doubts. This is understandable, filtering on arrays and collections isn't a universal feature for debuggers.

We can add a filter to a list (collection) or array through the right-click context menu. This can be any expression that's performed on each element and should return true in order to show the element or not. Instead of sifting through a list of elements, let the watch condition do the work for you as you can see in Figure 1-16.

```
∨  ≡ vets = {Vets@76787}
    ∨  f  vets = {ArrayList@76801}  size = 10
            ▼ Filtered by: getFirstName().length() > 5 clear
        ∨  ≡ 3 = {Vet@76806}
            >  f  specialties = {PersistentSet@76828}  size = 1
            >  f  firstName = {String@76821} "Rafael"
            >  f  lastName = {String@76829} "Ortega"
            >  f  id = {Integer@76830} 4
        ∨  ≡ 5 = {Vet@76808}
               f  specialties = {PersistentSet@76831}  size = 0
            >  f  firstName = {String@76823} "Sharon"
            >  f  lastName = {String@76832} "Jenkins"
            >  f  id = {Integer@12756} 6
```

Figure 1-16. Filtering a list of vets in IntelliJ/IDEA

Stream Debugger

Java 8 was a revolutionary release that borrowed some ideas from functional programming into the Java language. Streams are one such notion for processing sets of elements in a more functional chain of responsibility approach. As an example, the following code can find prime numbers and print them:[2]

---

[2] Demo code from `www.jetbrains.com/help/idea/analyze-java-stream-operations.html`

```
IntStream.iterate(1, n -> n + 1)
                .skip(50)
                .limit(50)
                .filter(PrimeMain::isPrime)
                .forEach(System.out::println);
```

The problem with this code is that it's much harder to debug. We can easily step over a for loop and unwind it to understand the underlying failures, but a stream can be problematic.

To solve that, JetBrains introduced the stream debugger, which you can launch by clicking the button shown in Figure 1-17. Notice that this button is only visible when the debugger stack frame is pointing at a line of code with a stream within it. Also, keep in mind that the location of the button changes sometimes; it can appear directly in the debugger toolbar in some cases.

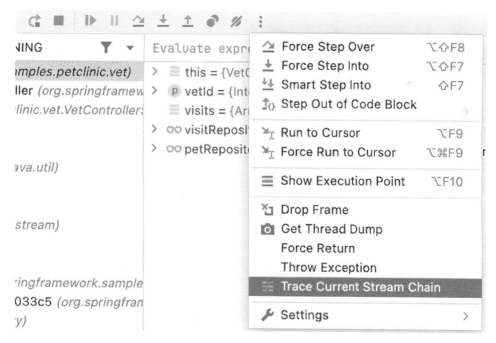

Figure 1-17. *Button that launched the stream debugger*

Within the stream debugger, we can follow each stage of the process and look at how the values mutate through the states. This works very well with object streams too, but the screenshots would be far more confusing as there are many details to sift through. As you can see in Figure 1-18, you can track the values as they move through the streams and follow the lines. The stream debugger takes inspiration from the realm of back-in-time (a.k.a. time travel) debugging.

```
IntStream.iterate( seed: 1, n -> n + 1)
        .skip(50)
        .limit(50)
        .filter(PrimeMain::isPrime)
        .forEach(System.out::println);
```

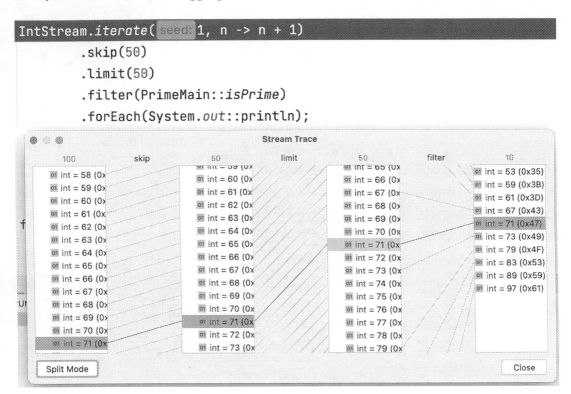

Figure 1-18. *Stream debugger showing how the list is processed to pull out only the prime numbers*

Debugger Annotations

Some tools I discussed in this chapter require skill, patience, and awareness of the tools. Unfortunately, we can't always educate our team about building custom renderers. We also can't ask JetBrains or Microsoft to build support within their tools for debugging our specific project – definitely not if it's internal to our company.

In the past, our only choice was to build an IDE plugin. This isn't a hard task unto itself, but it's got its challenges, and getting your end users to install the plugin is an even bigger hurdle. Thankfully, there's another way, and it's much simpler. We can add annotations to our code that provide crucial hints to the debugger. These annotations let us specify elaborate debugger information provided in our library/application code.

Dependency

To get started with the annotations, we first need to add a dependency. In Maven, we can add the following dependency within a typical JVM project:

```
<dependency>
  <groupId>org.jetbrains</groupId>
  <artifactId>annotations</artifactId>
  <version>23.0.0</version>
</dependency>
```

Custom Renderers in Code

The custom renderers I mentioned earlier are pretty amazing. If you have a similarly elaborate object graph, you might have such issues when rendering them in the watch. A "proper" renderer might make sense in this situation.

We can use some code annotations to represent the same sample we showed in the custom renderer section with no user interaction. Avoiding the UI is a small benefit, but the ability to define such renderers for teammates or customers seamlessly is the biggest benefit. This would be remarkably useful for any library with a complex object graph, for example, UI libraries, ORM, etc.

```
import org.jetbrains.annotations.Debug.Renderer;

// snipped code ...

@Renderer(text = "\"Repository has \" + count() + \" elements\",",
  childrenArray = "finaAll()",
  hasChildren = "count() > 0")
public interface VisitRepository extends JpaRepository<Visit, Integer> {
  // snipped code  ...
}
```

Stack Trace Hinting

As we discussed before, asynchronous code is one of the hardest debugging problems. We lose the context of the code. Stitching the stack trace to the original point where the binding was made is a great way to follow the causality of an operation.

IntelliJ/IDEA does that implicitly for common APIs, such as asynchronous calls in Sprint and similar APIs. However, if you implemented a custom API, such as a listener or an executor API, you might have a problem. You might get a callback with no context of execution. At that point, the original caller is gone, and we have no way of knowing how we reached this state. We can solve this by using custom annotations to indicate that we're interested in such stack trace stitching to occur and how we would like that carried out.

To implement this, we have two separate annotations:

- *@Async.Schedule*

- *@Async.Execute*

These annotations work in tandem where the schedule annotation marks the location where an element is added for later asynchronous processing, and the execute portion marks the code that's invoked to execute the process.

```
public void addMyListener(@Async.Schedule MyListener listener) {
...
}

public void fireMyEvent(@Async.Execute MyListener listener) {
...
}
```

The annotation triggers the storage of the reference pointer to the listener when we invoke the add method. Then when we invoke the fire method, the references are compared by the IDE, and the stack traces are stitched together seamlessly.

Summary

The debugger is the most basic tool in our debugging quiver. Yet, although most of us spend a significant amount of time within it, we rarely explore its full set of abilities. It's an amazing and versatile tool. Most times, we rush to solve or reproduce problems in a particular way without thinking about the unique ways in which we can leverage the existing tooling.

If you suspect a race condition, use marker objects to track the threads involved. Use tracepoints to see what's going on and get a deeper sense of the inner workings without disrupting the flow of our observed application.

If you have a problem that takes a long time to reproduce, use control flow techniques to isolate the area of the problem and repeatedly assault that specific problem. Use "set value" and "evaluate expression" to get a fine-grained reproduction of the problem.

If you have a memory leak, or similar memory issues, use the memory options in the debugger. We often rush into the profiler, but from my experience, it isn't very good for fine-grained issues. The ability to search through the entire set of objects using expressions is invaluable.

If you keep stepping over the code and digging through deep entries within the watch trying to find the stuff you need, spend some time building renderers to display information that's useful. Do it for your entire team with annotations and boost your productivity.

This chapter focused on practical actionable tools. In the next chapter, we will dig deep into the theory behind debugging. We'll review core concepts and debugging methodology we should have learned in university but probably didn't. I hope it will help you adapt a more "strategic" view of the debugging process.

CHAPTER 2

The Checklist

In another moment down went Alice after it, never once considering how in the world she was to get out again.

—Lewis Carroll, *Alice's Adventures in Wonderland*

Alice in Wonderland is the most wonderful analogy for debugging. Debugging is about observation, curiosity, experimentation, and adventure. Yet I often get the sense that people don't enjoy debugging. Antagonism toward debugging stems from the frustrating nature of the process and the often cringe-inducing results.

In my experience, most bugs are stupid. As we resolve the debugging process, our most common response is a groan. How did I miss that? This is normal behavior, but it results in shame. That plays to inadequacy and impostor syndrome. I can attest that after 40 years of programming, my bugs are still just as stupid.

But unlike most, I relish this feeling. It's a humbling feeling that keeps me grounded. Without that feeling, my ego might have inflated to unmanageable dimensions destroying my relationships with colleagues, family, and friends. It's a form of meditation. I feel that some CEOs could use debugging as a meditative process that would keep them grounded.

In this chapter, we tackle the scientific method that underlies the debugging process. We will also discuss the methodology we should follow when tracking and fixing bugs. By following this process, we can shorten the time spent debugging. Figure 2-1 is the path we need to go through when debugging as discussed in this chapter.

© Shai Almog 2023
S. Almog, *Practical Debugging at Scale*, https://doi.org/10.1007/978-1-4842-9042-2_2

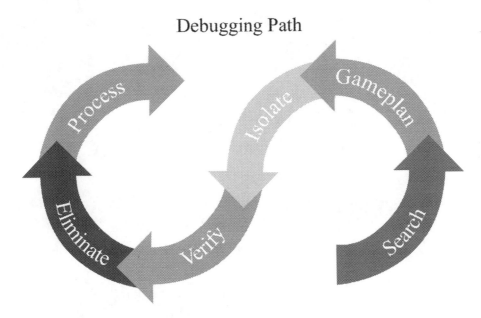

Figure 2-1. *The path of a debugging process*

Documentation

It's often said that "5 hours of debugging can save you 5 minutes of reading the docs." This is wrong. Don't get me wrong... You should read the docs when applicable. You should know the platform and system you're working on. That's part of why that saying sounds right to most of us at first glance. Every single one of us spent time debugging something, only to find out that the bug was due to misuse of an API that might have been documented.

Why Is It Completely Wrong?

There are several inherent problems with sending us back to the documentation. I'll start with the obvious: I never ran into useful documentation that could be read in five minutes. There's no such beast other than for trivial tools which are probably not the source of your bug.

Next is the documentation itself. Which documentation? The documentation describing the system, OS, language, frameworks, tooling, etc.? Where do we stop? You should read all of those as much as possible, but it isn't always practical or relevant at the scale we need.

Documentation doesn't point you at a bug or even at a general direction of interest. If you could hold the entire application source code in your head and the full set of documentation, then parse the whole thing to reach the conclusion within five minutes... Then you might have a useful alternative to debugging.

But here's the most ridiculous bit. I've wasted countless hours because of wrong and partial documentation. Back in the 1980s, reading the manual to understand a low-level architecture was essential. Modern systems move at a much faster pace and are far more fluid. Often, the only documentation we have is the source code. This isn't a good thing. Unfortunately, it's often the reality.

You Should Still Read the Documentation

Documentation isn't an alternative to debugging. However, it's still remarkably useful. Search engines revolutionized debugging, and with many issues, you can just search for the error message as a starting point. If you have documentation, search for the error and various keywords related to the error within the documentation; this can indeed save you some time.

Avoid the mistake of diving directly into an issue without first checking if someone else solved it first or if it's a part of the troubleshooting section.

Classification and Game Plan

Our strategy moving forward depends on the type of issue we're dealing with. Ask yourself the following questions before proceeding:

- Is this issue reproducible on the user's machine?

- Is it reproducible on your machine?

- Is it consistent?

- Is it a regression?

If the issue is a regression and ideally, you can reproduce it. I suggest checking out the section on `git bisect` in Chapter 3. It will let you narrow down the specific revision where the issue first appears.

If you can't reproduce and didn't "see" the bug, we already have an important data point: the bug itself might be incorrect. External factors might be the cause of the issue, for example, a plugin on the end-user machine. This should enter your list of assumptions.

At this point, you need to make a "game plan." There are two different paths you can follow to debug, and they vary based on the answers. If you have a consistently reproducible issue, you can move directly to the next stage of isolating the assumptions.

Story   Many years ago, I was trying to track an issue with the wrong number of elements in the results. I didn't use any method or strategy. I felt confident I'd find it. Two days later, it all boiled down to a "<" character that was facing the wrong direction. Impatience cost me two days of work. Had I worked patiently with an organized game plan, I would never have wasted so much time.

"It Works on My Machine"

I have a backpack with the slogan "it works on my machine." It's amusing, but it's also a cop-out. All too often, we force users to prove bugs before we're willing to investigate them. We need to understand and chase the issue wherever it takes us. Notice that this assumes the bug is consistent. The approach to solving bugs of this type is a two-pronged approach:

- Try to replicate the environment of the other machine

- Try to use the other machine for debugging

Both approaches have their trade-offs: remote debugging and developer observability[1] can help with the latter. Replicating the environment might include obvious aspects (e.g., OS differences), but often there are minor differences that are hard to isolate.

Story   A few years ago, I was working on replicating a bug reported by a user. The bug wasn't reproducing at all despite all my attempts to replicate (JVM version, OS, network connectivity, etc.). Eventually, that user sent a video demonstrating the bug, and I noticed he clicked in a different location in the

---

[1] Discussed in Chapter 11.

UI. Armed with that knowledge, I was able to reproduce and fix the issue. Communication issues with the user are at the root of many redundant debugging sessions.

Understanding the subtle differences in the replication environment is crucial. For this, we must have an open and clear communication channel with the person who can reproduce the problem. Some tools discussed in Chapter 3, such as `strace`, `dtrace`, etc., provide deep insight into a running application. Using these tools, we can notice the differences and misbehaviors when running the application. For example, the version on the client machine might access a configuration file you weren't aware of in the user's home directory.

The rise of container technology (e.g., Docker) removed most of these subtle differences as it normalized and simplified uniform environments. But this is often not enough. Networking differences, data source differences, and scale can significantly impact the environment even if everything else remains the same. Often, these are the hardest issues to debug. How do you reproduce an issue that only appears when you have 1000 requests per second in a large cluster?

Story   I was debugging a system that only failed at the customer's location. It turns out that their network connection was so fast; the round trip to the management server was completed before our local setup code finished its execution. I tracked it down by logging in remotely to their on-site machine and reproducing the issue there.

Bug That's Inconsistent

Logging is an important feature of most applications; it's the exact tool we need to debug these sorts of edge cases. We will discuss logging in Chapter 4 and the best practices related to that.

Inconsistent bugs are often a symptom of an issue in concurrent code. Here, the debugger can be a very useful tool in reproducing the issue:

- Use single thread breakpoints to pause only one specific thread and check if there's a race condition to a specific method.

- Use tracepoints where possible instead of breakpoints while debugging – blocking hides or changes concurrency-related bugs, which are often the reason for inconsistency.

- Review all threads and try to give each one an "edge" by making the other threads sleep. A concurrency issue might only occur if some conditions are met. We can stumble onto a unique condition using such a technique.

Try to automate the process to get a reproduction. When running into issues like this, we often create a loop that runs a test case hundreds or even thousands of times. We do that with logging and try to find the problem within the logs.

Story   At many companies, we have "long-run" tests designed to run all night and stress the system to the max. They help discover concurrency issues before they even occur in the wild. Failures were often due to lack of storage (filled up everything with logs), but often when we got a failure, it was hard to reproduce. Using a loop to rerun the code that failed many times was often a perfect solution. Another valuable tool was the "force throw" feature discussed in Chapter 1. This allowed us to fail gracefully and pass stumbling blocks in the long run.

Notice that if the problem is indeed an issue in concurrent code, the extra logging might impact the result significantly. In one case, I stored lists of strings in memory instead of writing them to the log. Then I dumped the complete list after execution finished. Using memory logging for debugging isn't ideal, but it lets us avoid the overhead of the logger or even direct console output.

Give Up

Well, don't "really" give up. Only give up on the ability to reproduce the issue consistently on your machine. We might end up spending all our time chasing the ideal case of reproducing them, like the great white whale. There's a point where we need to cut our losses and move to the next step in the debugging process. This isn't ideal, but it's the only thing we can do.

We need to make assumptions about the potential causes and create test cases that reproduce the potential assumptions. Some bugs are resistant to reproducing but can be simulated using such means, and that might be enough. It's important to add logging and assertions into the code, so if we don't resolve the bug, we'd have more to go on next time around.

Before you decide to go with this route, I suggest looking at the "Tips and Tricks" section at the end of this chapter. Sometimes, a cliché, trivial advice is what we need to get the job done.

Story   My startup was using App Engine when overnight our billing jumped from a few dollars to many hundreds of dollars daily. At this rate, our bootstrapped startup would have gone bankrupt by the end of the month. Unfortunately, App Engine had no usable production debugging capabilities at the time. Adding logging would have made billing even higher. We made educated guesses and fixed everything we could. To this day, we don't know the specific bug or if this was our fault. We solved the billing problem by brute force.

Isolating Assumptions

Debugging is the process of constantly narrowing the problem space until we find the root cause. We circle the bug by defining its quadrants, then use the process of elimination and carefully crafted experiments to circle the bug – much like a hunter and its prey.

This process is dangerous, since we need to make assumptions about the code. In most cases where debugging fails and takes longer than expected, it is due to wrong assumptions. A mistake in this stage can drag the debugging session much longer than a mistake in any other stage.

Story   I was working on a C++-based scheduling tool. It was common knowledge among our team that the Borland collection framework was buggy and didn't work as expected. It turns out that the library assumed that the less than ("<") and equals ("==") operators will behave consistently for sorted collections. We discovered this only when debugging into the native library. We had assumed that only the equals operator would be invoked when removing an element. Placing a breakpoint in the operator code to verify this would have revealed the problem instantly even without looking at the library code.

Everybody Lies

I love the show Dr. House. It's a Sherlock Holmes version of a medical drama with a grumpy misanthrope as the lead. Perfect. Medicine isn't like software debugging in most ways. We can replicate problems without hurting people. We can be very invasive without representations, and we can conduct our own tests and get results instantly.

But there's still a lot to learn, and one of the core tenants of the show is that everybody lies. People tell partial stories and miss crucial information for various reasons. This is a very common problem for debugging. The hardest bugs are often the ones where we spend most of our time on a wild goose chase. The reason for that is usually a lie or a misdirection because of a faulty assumption.

I often joke during my talks that the most common gesture developers do when we finish debugging is the face-palm. This is because of the nature of the most difficult bugs. In most such cases, we find that we got the assumption stage wrong and made a "stupid" mistake in this stage.

Double Verification

The solution to wrong assumptions is double verification. For every assumption, no matter how basic, find another approach for proof. Let's say we have a bug in code that depends on a result from a remote service. We assume the service works correctly, and we verified that by using the *cURL* program. To double verify, we also need to add a tracepoint in the code that shows we received the response.

As we slowly narrow our assumptions, we don't need to double verify every assumption. But if we feel the process is stuck, we need to go back and make sure that we verified every stage along the way. It's often the case that we miss something silly or simple. Make sure you verify the "low-hanging fruit" first.

Sometimes, double verification means stepping outside the debugger. In Chapter 3, I discuss some external tools such as `strace`, `dtrace`, `wireshark`, etc. These tools let us verify that the application is accessing the resources we expect on the operating system level.

Story   A company contracted me to help improve their process performance. In the morning meeting, everyone spun up theories about the system, which I didn't know at all. Every single assumption was wrong. Profiling revealed the truth. Assumptions are guesswork; thankfully, we have tools that can instantly point at the facts.

Defining the Assumptions

We can look at debugging as a process of hypothesis, prediction, and forming an experiment to prove the hypothesis. Assumptions fit into the hypothesis stage where we form the boundaries around the bug. Another approach is one of hunting.

Imagine setting up a fence to trap a predator within the fence. The biggest mistake you can make is a fence that's too small. Such a fence could leave the predator outside. You will be on the inside of the fence wasting time searching within the confines of an empty fence. The inverse is just as bad, when fencing off a large area, it will take a great deal of time to narrow down on the predator.

The same is true for our assumptions. We need to make basic assumptions, but we don't need to verify every little thing. It's hard to quantify the right amount, and this is where experience makes a difference. Awareness and methodology help boost that experience.

In Figure 2-2, I review the two initial layouts of my assumptions. Notice that this figure brings up an interesting situation. Our symptom, bug, and root cause might be in three completely different locations in the code. In those cases, our initial assumption circle might need to grow to fit in the bug.

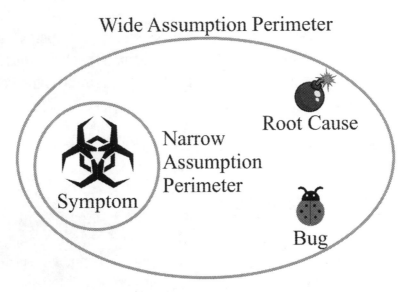

Figure 2-2. Two variations of the initial assumption perimeter

Increasing the circle of assumptions isn't necessarily a problem, but we need to be prepared for such an increase. There were many cases where I reviewed (and authored) bad fixes that addressed the symptom and not the root cause. Locating the bug and even fixing it aren't our goals when debugging. Understanding why the program behaves the way it does and the root cause for that is the ultimate goal. That isn't always an attainable goal as the track might run dry, but we can leave traps for next time and lay the long-term groundwork. I have more to say about defensive coding (fail-safe vs. fail-fast) in Chapter 4.

Story   Our crash reporting solution would periodically send us null pointer exceptions that "shouldn't happen." They happened in production on cases we never physically saw and had no access to. We tried multiple workarounds for the symptoms, but they just made the problem worse. By placing elaborate logging on code we assumed worked correctly, we were able to find an edge case race condition when dealing with native code.

The Right Direction

When we see a symptom, we need to prioritize the assumptions we make to find the root cause. Normally, we use our intuition and experience to guide us toward that root cause. But is there a better way?

We often make a shortcut, trying to get from the system to the root cause. That's often misleading. Our focus should be on the next stage, which is the bug itself, once we understand that the journey to the root cause is hard, but we have better tools for that.

When working with a wide assumption perimeter, intuition is the only guide. However, when circling the symptom, initial assumptions often become obvious. If a value is incorrect on the screen, we can start by verifying that the source returns the right value and work our way from there.

Corruption bugs are the type of bugs where a major portion of the information is incorrect or broken. These are often an indication of a symptom that's very much removed from the root cause. There are two major reasons for such issues:

- Corruption of memory/data due to overflow or similar bug

- Concurrency problem

We will get into the nuts and bolts of addressing both of these in this chapter.

Assumption Jump

Sometimes, we're left with a value that "shouldn't be here." This can be a variable value, a UI element, or any other artifact. It's a value that doesn't make any sense, and we don't understand how that value is returned from this method. At this point, we might not have an immediate "move." We know something is "clearly wrong," but we don't know how it got to that point or where the data came from.

If this is something you can reproduce and the data is in a field, then a well-placed conditional field watchpoint (from Chapter 1) can be illuminating. This helped me solve many such issues in the past. But sometimes it just isn't enough. The issue might not be easily reproducible, and in this case, we might have a problematic state that's hard to investigate. This is one of the best scenarios for time travel debugging (discussed in Chapter 5) which lets us traverse the state of the application after execution completed.

If you're using a safe language (a.k.a. managed languages) that's guarded against memory or stack corruption, then you have one option: add a tracepoint to every caller and slowly expand the assumption scope in that direction. For unsafe languages, you will need to check the debugger capability of memory guarding or use a memory guarded allocator.[2]

Figure Working Code

A common mistake we make is rushing to the line of code that contains the bug, since we already know where the problem is. We then get settled into a specific area around the bug and waste a great deal of time looking at that code. We're trapped by the lure of a quick fix, which we incorrectly assume we know. Due to a distance between the symptom and the root cause, we might be misled by the lure of familiar code.

We should first create a wider circle than we would expect by debugging the code we assume works correctly. When we do that, there are two eventualities:

- The assumption isn't working as expected – At this point, we can widen our search and might be closer to the solution.

- The assumption is working as expected – At this point, we can deepen our recollection of the code and understanding of the current application state. We have a solid base to proceed deeper.

The scope should typically start at the next logical abstraction level. If the symptom seems to be related to a private method, start verifying the public methods. If a specific class is misbehaving, verify the classes that provide it with input. I usually give the analogy of a mechanic checking all the nearby screws are tight before dealing with the actual problem.

A great example here is the invalid value of a field. Our initial assumption would usually be that we need better validation controls to stop the invalid value. This is probably bad input from the user that propagates all the way into the variable. Before we leap to that assumption, we need to verify that our code didn't propagate a bug onward.

Common Problems and Solutions

Through decades of programming, the bugs that we deal with remain similar regardless of the operating system, language, through mobile, desktop, and server. There are

---

[2] https://en.wikipedia.org/wiki/Guard_byte

some issues that aren't as common or changed significantly. Memory leaks are vastly different thanks to garbage collectors; memory corruption is rarely an issue in managed languages.

Concurrency issues are a mixed bag. Managed languages made threading issues more predictable for most parts. Asynchronous tools such as promises shifted some of the burden, but with these APIs, process scale became a big issue. When we have multiple concurrent containers working on the same data, concurrency problems are often harder to debug than localized threading issues.

The vast majority of bugs we deal with on a daily basis are related to the wrong application state. Second to that are exceptions and faults which we discuss in the next section. Concurrency-related issues are often the hardest to reproduce and fix, but for most systems, they're relatively rare.

Exceptions or Faults

Exception-related failures are relatively easy to detect. You usually get a stack trace directly to the error together with a description. We can place a breakpoint on all exceptions and verify that nothing "fishy" is happening behind the scenes in one of the methods (see Chapter 1). Exceptions are "loud" and "obvious," so unless someone silently catches an exception (which happens), we can track the root issue relatively easily.

I would also strongly recommend a linter rule that checks against swallowed or unlogged exceptions. Linters are tools that review your application code for common bugs and pitfalls. I highly recommend adding one to your CI/CD (Continuous Integration/Continuous Delivery) process. For example, Checkstyle, which is a common cross-language linter, supports a check[3] that blocks empty catch blocks. It still can't block stupid code that does "nothing" in that block, but it's a start.

Faults are standard in some languages but can also occur in a managed language where the VM crashes. They are usually coupled with a core dump that we can open in the debugger to investigate. Platforms like Java also include the full state of all threads in case of a fault; this can point us to a VM bug or an issue in a native library. It's very important to collect this information and analyze these crashes. Sometimes, a small change, such as a minor JVM version upgrade, can resolve such crashes.

---

[3] https://checkstyle.sourceforge.io/config_blocks.html

If you're facing a crash, you need to get a core dump to analyze. This is disabled by default, and we can enable it with a command such as

```
ulimit -c unlimited
```

Unfortunately, this is often not enough. Getting core dumps working on all OSs is tedious, so I would recommend checking out Oracle's documentation on the subject;[4] notice that this is specific to the JVM, but many of the concepts apply universally. Once we have a core file, we can open it with most native OS debuggers and inspect the stack traces of the crash.

Runtimes such as the JVM also include tools such as *jhsdb* which we can use from the command line or using a GUI. We can launch the GUI tool using a command similar to this. Replace the text in brackets with the core file and the path to the JDK, respectively:

```
jhsdb hsdb --core [path-to-file.core] --exe [path-to-java-home]/bin/java
```

Once we do this, you should see a simple GUI that will let you investigate the causes of the crash. Chapter 3 discusses jhsdb in more detail as it's a useful tool for debugging running VMs as well.

Bad Application State

Threads are a source of difficult bugs, yet most bugs result from bad application state. To track state-related issues, try separating the state elements that are modified concurrently and the state that's read by the problematic block of code.

Assuming you can, try overriding the variable value within your breakpoint by setting it during debugging. You can set variable values in the watch area or via the expression option in the debugger. This is a great capability that most developers don't utilize often enough. If you're able to narrow down the value of a specific variable as the cause of the problem, you're already well on your way to solving the problem.

If this isn't helping, try identifying specific fields that might be problematic. You can use a field watchpoint (discussed in Chapter 1) to track changes to state and even value reads.

---

[4]https://docs.oracle.com/en/java/javase/17/troubleshoot/submit-bug-report.html

If the problem persists, a powerful approach is returning a hardcoded state or a state from a working case. I'm normally not a fan of techniques that require code changes for debugging since I consider the two distinct tasks. However, if you're out of all options, this might be your only recourse.

The memory debugging capabilities and object inspection capabilities we discussed in Chapter 1 are also very helpful for these cases. A very common bug is a case where a copy of an object is made with slight modifications. Both objects appear identical to the casual observer, and as we debug, we might get subtle failures as a result.

Story   Back in the days JPA (Java Persistence Architecture) was new. I used to do quite a lot of consulting there, and a common bug was caused because developers implemented equals and hashcode correctly, at least in terms of Java coding conventions. The problem is that JPA has some problematic edge cases. This created a situation where the object identity changed between its unsaved and saved state, causing some issues. Specifically, the object ID will be null in the unsaved state and will have a value once the database returns the identity. As a result, we sometimes had two entity instances in RAM, and it was very hard to track such issues.

Concurrency, Timing, and Races

Thread problems have the reputation of issues that are hard to solve. We'll discuss these in greater detail in Chapter 14. Right now, we'll only focus on finding and understanding the bug, and that's a more manageable task.

The easiest way to check for threading issues is, as I mentioned before, logging your current thread and/or stack. Do that in the block of code that's causing the issue. Then add a similar tracepoint on fields used by the block of code. Thread violations should be pretty clear in the logs. Using marker objects to keep track of the various threads is also a powerful tool!

With threading issues, the key challenge is reproducing them consistently. Creating a massively threaded unit test is often the most powerful debugging tool you can have in your corner. Notice that you should probably avoid Java's "virtual threads" as they might skew the results.

If the problem is a deadlock, then you're probably in luck, as those are usually pretty clear once reproduced. The app gets stuck; you press pause, and the debugger shows you which thread is stuck waiting for which monitor. Monitors are the OS-level primitives that block a thread from entering a code block, roughly mapping to Java's synchronized keyword. You can then review the other threads and see who's holding the monitor. Fixing this might be tricky, but the debugger "tells us" what's going on.

With a livelock, we hold one monitor and need another. Another thread is holding the other monitor and needs the monitor we're holding as shown in Figure 2-3. A livelock can result in a deadlock; unlike a deadlock, a livelock can occur while threads are still functioning. It can seem that both threads are working correctly and aren't stuck. Because livelocks can occur with live threads, the code might appear fine on the surface without a clear monitor in the stack traces.

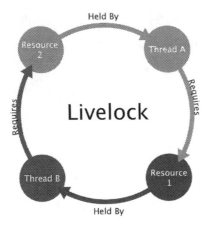

Figure 2-3. *In a livelock, two threads are waiting on each other's monitors*

Debugging this requires stepping over the threads one at a time in the thread view and reviewing each one to see if it's waiting for a potentially contested resource. It isn't hard on a technical level, but it's very tedious. That's why I recommended enabling thread groups in the thread view. A typical application has *many* threads which can make this hard to follow. This produces a lot of noise which we can reduce by grouping the threads and focusing on the important parts. Again, logging using tracepoints can be very helpful in these situations.

This is one of those elusive bugs, such as race conditions, which are often classified as thread problems (which they are), but during a debugging session, it's often easier to see them as a separate task.

Timing issues and race conditions often occur when your code has some unintentional reliance on performance or timing. The way I approach race conditions in threading code is this: "It's a state bug." It's always a state bug. When we have a race condition, it means we either read from the state when it wasn't ready or wrote to the state too late/early. Field watchpoints are your friends in this case and can really help you get the full picture of what's going on. You can also simulate bad state situations by changing variable values.

I suggest creating field watchpoints with conditions related to the current thread. This way, they will trigger if the wrong thread tries to access a field that it shouldn't.

Performance and Resource Starvation

Performance problems caused by monitor contention are harder to track with a debugger. I normally recommend randomly pausing the code and reviewing the running threads in your application. Is thread X constantly holding the monitor? Maybe there's a problem there. There are some system tools such as *strace* and *dtrace* which we can use to track overuse of monitors. We'll discuss these and many other tools in Chapter 3.

We can derive assumptions and prove them by logging the entry/exit point for a lock/synchronized block. Notice you can use a profiler and it sometimes helps, but it might lead you on the wrong path sometimes.

Resource starvation is an offshoot of performance issues. Often, you would see it as an extreme performance issue that usually only happens when you try to scale. In this case, a resource needed by a thread is always busy, and we just can't get to it. For example, we have too many threads and too few database connections – or too few threads and too many incoming web requests. This problem often doesn't need a debugger at all. Your environment usually indicates immediately that it ran out of resources. The problem is almost always plain and obvious.

The solution isn't always as clear. For example, you don't want to add too many threads or DB connections to work around the short-term problem. You need to understand why starvation occurred. This can happen because of two different reasons:

- Not releasing resources fast enough

- Not releasing resources in all cases

The first case is trivial. You can benchmark and see if something is holding you back, for example, if IO is slow or a query takes too long. The second is the more common:

a resource leak. We can miss this entirely when running in a GC (garbage collection) environment. But in a high throughput environment, the GC might be too slow for our needs. For example, a common mistake developers make is opening a file stream which they never close. The GC will do that for us, but it will take longer to do that, and the file lock might remain in place, blocking further progress.

This is where encapsulation comes in handy. We must encapsulate all of our resource usage (allocation/release). If we do that properly, adding logging for allocation and freeing should expose such problems quickly. This is harder to detect with DI frameworks like Spring where connections, etc., are injected for you. You can still use some tricks for injected data and resource tracking as well.[5]

Elimination

The process of elimination is one of the oldest and most powerful debugging techniques. The core principle is simple: slowly remove parts that aren't the cause of the problem until the problem reveals itself. We can accomplish this by commenting out code or by using debugger tricks such as force return (discussed in Chapter 1) to disable a specific code flow.

We can also use external tools. When experiencing a frontend issue, we often try to reproduce the issue in curl/postman to verify whether the issue is related to the frontend code. By eliminating large swaths of code from our bug search grid, we can find the issue faster. This is an especially powerful tool because it usually helps us narrow down on the bug and root cause – not just the symptom!

Unit Testing and Mocking

Unit tests are a great way to debug, as they can often isolate the problem to its core elements. We will discuss unit testing in more depth in Chapter 4. The biggest benefit of debugging through a unit test is that we can leverage mocking frameworks, such as Mokito. These frameworks let us remove large swaths of code and narrow the problem space considerably. The benefits of avoiding regression and simplifying our test cases are a bonus.

---

[5] https://stackoverflow.com/questions/50770462/springboot-2-monitor-db-connection

Notice that there are various "best practices" that cover the "right amount" of mocking per test. When building a test case to debug a specific issue, these practices don't apply as much. Mock everything you need to reduce the problem to its bare essence.

Eliminating in Flaky Environments

The process of elimination works great when we have a problem that's easily reproducible. Flaky issues, or issues that turn out to be flaky as we eliminate code, are a major problem. The solution for this is to only work on negatives and never on positives when performing elimination. This can be confusing, but it's an important rule.

If you eliminate a block and the problem doesn't reproduce, this doesn't mean that the problem is related to that block. It could be flakiness. However, if you eliminate a block and the problem reproduces, then this block is probably not at fault. So only rely on cases where the problem reproduces… I would also run checks repeatedly if you suspect flakiness to verify that the problem doesn't occur on multiple runs.

Story   We were chasing a complex threading issue and were commenting out code left and right. We made the incorrect assumption that a specific piece of code was the cause, since when we commented it out the problem stopped happening. We spent a lot of time looking at that code instead of continuing the investigation. That code just impacted performance and exposed a race condition located in a different location altogether.

Understand the Tongs Process

We use tongs to grab hold of an item on both sides. This same concept can apply to almost any piece of software, as pretty much all software has two or more directions of input/output. Let's give you some examples:

- Typical enterprise apps – One side is the web UI; the other side is the database.

- Operating system kernel – One side is a user space app; the other side is the computer hardware.

- Game – One side is the joystick and screen API; the other side is the game database.

- Web app – One side is the browser; the other side is the backend server release.

The tong motion is a crucial concept that we need to keep in mind when we're debugging. Think of debugging as tongs that go through the buggy software to try and grab the bug. We need to position the tongs so they match the sides and then squeeze to get the bug we're trying to grab. Figure 2-4 shows a sample process for slowly narrowing the surface area of a typical Java web application.

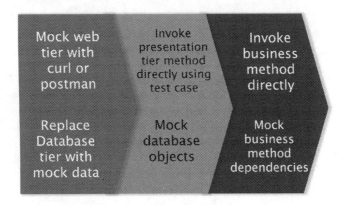

Figure 2-4. *Stages of debugging a multitiered web application*

A common mistake is to move only one prong of the tongs or not position the other tong. If you don't position the tongs, your investigation might impact the other side and you wouldn't know what's going on. You don't have to move both tongs for all cases, but if you're stuck, then you can always flip the direction of motion and investigate from the other side. Then flip back when convenient.

Story   We were debugging a performance issue in a server deployment. I replaced the web calls with a curl request, which moved the tongs toward the problematic area. On the DB side, I placed heavy DB logging to see the output as I reproduced bad SQL via curl. By leveraging both sides and moving deeper into the DB layer from both sides, I was able to locate a bug in the ORM (Object Relational Mapping) layer.

Process

We often debug ad hoc when building small or hobbyist projects. This works but can be problematic for larger problems where developers keep stepping on each other's toes as they work on the same/similar issues. Oftentimes, it's hard to understand that the root cause of an issue is because of a feature from another developer. It's hard to tell if two bug symptoms result from a single root cause. As a result, we can assign two developers to fix the same bug in parallel.

Issue

Don't work on a bug without an issue in your issue tracking system. Make sure they assign the issue to you and that it's marked as active. This way, the project manager and teammates can keep track. Keep up to date on other issues to avoid conflicts. Even if you and a teammate are working on two separate issues, if the investigation leads to the same area, your fixes might collide.

Issues are often easier to locate than pull requests or specific commits. When reviewing a regression, the ability to connect a pull request to the source issue is essential. We need to keep the discussion within the issue tracker and not in volatile environments like group chats.

Daily Meetings

Teamwork and a daily meeting are essential for projects with multiple active developers who work on similar things. Don't be a wallflower in such meetings. Update the team about your current theories and direction. If a colleague is describing something that sounds familiar, engage!

This is the reason to have these meetings, and if there's a chance of mid-air collision while working on a bug, you should work as a team and not as individuals. At this point, the project manager can help guide you on aligning your work.

Test

Many developers want to start the debugging process by creating a unit test that reproduces the issue. This isn't easy or even possible before you understand the problem. You should create a test before fixing the issue, and it should be a part of the pull request that fixes the issue. I would highly recommend requiring a 60% or higher coverage ratio per pull request, so changes that aren't covered by tests will be rejected by default.

The alternative is constant regressions, where an issue that was fixed comes back to bite us repeatedly. We'll discuss unit tests in depth in Chapter 4.

Notice that unit tests are usually ideal since they run fast, produce instant feedback, and can pinpoint the issue with razor sharp precision. Integration tests are wonderful and arguably even more important than unit tests. In some cases, they're the only way to reproduce an issue and that's OK.

Tips and Tricks

Up until now, we discussed general strategies when dealing with issues. In this section, I want to focus on some useful tips for debugging. These are several core techniques that will help us improve our productivity while debugging.

Rubber Ducking

The term rubber ducking originates with a developer who supposedly brought with him a rubber duck to talk to when facing an issue. This illustrates a common developer observation: when we consult a colleague, we often find the problem before the person we're talking to says a word...

Verbalizing the problem often forces us to pay attention to nuance that we sometimes gloss over. This works even when talking to an inanimate object and works even when running this exercise in your head (although not as effective for some). The script for a duck conversation should usually follow the line of

- Here's the problem.

- This is the area that might be the source of the problem...

- These areas can't be the cause because of...

- Here's what I'm trying to test...

During conversations, we often find that we've missed something in one of these stages.

Redefine the Bug

"Moving the goalposts" is awful when someone does that to you. It's a great way to attack a bug, though. Bugs usually start with a "user-level" description, which is usually very symptomatic, for example, wrong value for a UI element. As we work on the bug, we might find that this results from the backend that's wrong.

We can change the bug and redefine it (ideally on the issue tracker too), so our goal and scope of code are narrower. This is an iterative process of honing in on the bug, which we normally do intuitively. But we rarely go to the trouble of redefining the bug. This is an important mental exercise and also an important team communication tool. When you mention this in the dailies, it might trigger recognition in a team member and help lead to the correct fix.

Change the Angle

Every system has at least two directions. I discussed this in the tongs section earlier, but it bears repeating. If you're stuck, flip the direction and try from a different angle. There are many angles to approach any bug and many techniques. I'm a big fan of "pair debugging," whereas in a team we can share different ways and ideas to debug something unique.

Unlike pair programming, which can be a lengthy process, just five minutes with a teammate can help change your outlook on an issue and expose you to a completely different thought process.

Disrupt Your Environment

Hard-to-reproduce bugs are terribly frustrating. When you're faced with such a situation, try using external limiting factors that "break your environment" that might trigger the bug more readily. Good examples for such disruptions would be systems like network throttling, slow motion modes, etc.

I often debug client code when connected to a tethered phone. This removes me from the company's internal network, which is a major disruption. A common bug is inadvertently relying on company network topology. It also slows my connection significantly, which might impact the application. This can produce different error messages, reproduce an issue more consistently, fail to reproduce it entirely, or some other behavior. All of which are crucial clues in the bug hunting process.

Switch Environments

Similarly to the previous point, switching the OS entirely can sometimes expose interesting information about a hard-to-track bug. At Sun, we used to have Spark and Windows machines connected to a KVM (Keyboard Video Mouse switcher). We'd constantly toggle between the two and often found "weird" issues when moving code back and forth.

Switching the OS, browser, JVM, compiler, etc., can have a significant impact. The tooling of a specific environment might also provide a different angle. I prefer working with Firefox and its developer tooling when debugging frontend issues. Occasionally, I'll look at a problem in Chrome DevTools to get a different perspective where I might notice something I missed in Firefox.

Use Developer Extension Tooling

All development environments have special debugging extensions and tools we can use to get more information and insight and also perform disruptive investigations. Web development tools in the browser include deep inspection capabilities, and phones have developer mode that you can activate to leverage some amazing tooling. Server APIs like Spring include aspects for logging automatically on every method entry/exit, actuator, and so many other tools.

I will discuss some of the low-level tools like JMX (Java Management eXtensions) in the next chapter. We can use these tools either as an investigative prong or as a tool to impact the application as a disrupting mechanism. But in order to do that, we need to be deeply familiar with the environment we're running in and with the vendor tools for it. I was working deep into JetBrains plugin development before finding out about the developer mode of the IDE. That's on me. I was running too quickly and didn't spend the time to read a proper plugin development book before getting started.

Walk Away/Sleep

For many developers, sleep is the best debugging tool, as they wake up with the solution. I agree with one personal caveat: I'm a terrible sleeper. When I have a bug, I can't sleep. I need to "try everything" first; otherwise, I'll lie in bed frustrated. But I can get up and walk away from the computer and drink a cup of coffee. Have a conversation with someone about something else…

Disconnecting and then coming back to the problem puts us in a fresh mindset to tackle the problem. It's important not to jump right back into the place you were before when doing that. Try to forget everything and approach the problem "fresh" to notice the things you missed the first time around. I find that most frustrating problems result from something small I missed when I rushed when working on this problem initially.

At our offices, we have a gaming room where the R&D team spends time playing console games after lunch. This helps team bonding and helps them disconnect for a while from whatever they're working on.

It's like a Game

Debugging should be fun/challenging, and if it isn't, you should find a way to enjoy this puzzle/treasure hunt. I'm very competitive. As a result, I'm not a fan of most puzzles/ games because (like many) I don't enjoy losing. Debugging is a game I love because I'm good at it. I still enjoy it when I'm terrible at it (we all are sometimes) because like in any game, we have our good and bad days.

If you can't find the pleasure in debugging, try debugging code that isn't yours. Try debugging things that aren't a part of your job. Do you enjoy doing those?

We often conflate stress about having a bug or work stress related to the project. Since the debugging process is so amorphous, it can drag on. This makes us feel stupid and incompetent and can promote impostor syndrome. These are universal feelings that are shared by experienced and fresh developers alike.

I would suggest isolating whether these are job-related tensions that are causing this frustration or if they're related to personal embarrassment. If the latter, I suggest sitting down with the most senior developer you know and tell that person about your dumbest bug. I'm confident that they'll share a similar story. If not, feel free to send me your dumbest bugs. I spent a couple of days tracking a less than operator facing the wrong way.

A NASA engineer confused metric and imperial measurements costing them 327 million dollars because of that mistake.[6] I'm sure the engineers or the code reviewers are some of the smartest people out there. If they can have such a terrible outcome, then nothing you can do can rival it.

---

[6] https://everydayastronaut.com/mars-climate-orbiter/

If you feel that this is all due to work-related stress, I suggest taking time to talk to your manager about the stress. It's often counterproductive and could slow you down as you rush to debug, which is something that should be a more creative process. I suggest talking to a senior mentor and seeking help in such cases. Some developers have an issue with confrontation; a senior friend can help in such situations.

The Checklist

A checklist is one of the most important tools for process automation. As part of my debugging process, I follow the rules illustrated here and narrow them down based on the list. The big-ticket items on the list are as follows:

- Make the simplest assumption you can.

- Validate the assumption.

- While the bug isn't found, narrow the assumption and validate it.

By following this process and acknowledging the assumptions I've made, I can slowly hunt down a bug. The important part of this is keeping track of the assumptions made and implied. That's where we often fail when a bug gets out of hand. We assume things that might not always be true.

Story   A developer I worked with assumed a value in the stack couldn't change. But because of a bug in a different area of the code, this is exactly what happened in a C++ application. The result was a long debugging session that lasted all night. I'm not sure if this is something I would have noticed sooner these days. It was a tough issue.

List your assumptions. Some developers find that using pen and paper helps them visualize this. Then review them over and over as you slowly narrow down on the problematic area.

Summary

In this chapter, we learned the theory underlying the debugging process. We discussed the stages and how we can hone in on the source of the bug. If you follow through on your assumptions and catalog the bugs into one of the common pitfalls we discussed, then you're 90% of the way to understanding the root cause. Once you have that, fixing the problem becomes much easier.

We also briefly discussed the process of fixing, creating an issue, working with the team, and building a test case. We'll get more into the individual tools when we discuss this in Chapter 4.

Finally, I would suggest reviewing the checklist and tips discussed at the end of this chapter. Most of the advice is universal and applies regardless of programming language, platform, methodology, etc. While this chapter is highly theoretical, I tried to make it as actionable as possible and applicable to our day-to-day lives.

CHAPTER 3

The Auxiliary Tools

Debugging is like being the detective in a crime movie where you are also the murderer.

—Filipe Fortes

The debugger is the central piece of the debugging experience, but it's only one part of it. We sometimes need to step outside of the comforting embrace of the IDE to reproduce or track an issue. In this chapter, we'll review some tools you might find useful for these cases. I'm focusing on tools that are 100% debugging tools and not those that are useful for development testing.

For example, tools like *cURL* or *jq* are remarkably useful. You can/should use them while debugging. But you probably used them while building and testing the feature. So you would already be familiar with them and should have some sense of what they do. This chapter focuses on tools that you would mostly reach for when debugging.

The tools we cover in this chapter encompass the following categories:

- System monitoring tools – As is the case with *strace* and *DTrace*

- Network monitors – Also fit in the preceding bracket but warrant a category of their own

- VM/runtime monitoring – For example, tools that let us inspect the JVM, etc.

- Profilers and memory monitors

Notice I'm avoiding a big category of load monitoring tools (e.g., *JMeter*, etc.); these are very important tools, but the scope and complexity are so big we can't possibly cover them here, and they warrant their own book. The same is true for the field of performance tuning which has a symbiotic relationship to the field of debugging, but is a distinct subject with its own set of tools.

© Shai Almog 2023
S. Almog, *Practical Debugging at Scale*, https://doi.org/10.1007/978-1-4842-9042-2_3

DTrace

Back in 2004, I first heard about *DTrace* while working at Sun Microsystems. It became all the rage in the hallways as it was an innovation that Sun was promoting. *DTrace* was later ported into MacOS X (it originated on Solaris). Today, there are ports on Windows and Linux as well.

DTrace is a powerful low-level dynamic tracing framework. But that's just another superlative, and if you never used such a tool and don't have a background in systems programming, you might be feeling a bit confused: What the hell does it do?

Here are some common things developers use it for:

- Want to know which files a process has opened?

- Want to know who invokes a kernel API and get a stack trace to the caller?

- Want to know why a process dies?

- Want to know how much CPU time is spent on an operation?

You might think that dtrace is one of those tools that will destroy your CPU completely. But here's the killer feature: it's fast enough to run in production with minimal to no performance impact. It was revolutionary when it was launched almost two decades ago, and it's still the case to this day!

Running DTrace

DTrace is a risky "low-level" system service and should be treated as such.

Caution   Save your data! This tool can easily crash your machine, and enabling it requires disabling important security facilities on MacOS.

On a Mac, *DTrace* conflicts with "System Integrity Protection" which is a security feature that blocks some interactions between processes (among other things). Under normal circumstances, this would be great. But if you want to run *DTrace*, this would be a problem.

The solution is booting to recovery mode on Intel Macs; this means holding the Command-R keys on boot. On an ARM Mac, just long press the power button. Then, in a recovery mode terminal, issue the command: *csrutil disable.*

Upon reboot, *DTrace* should work as expected. If you wish to reenable integrity protection, follow the same instructions, but instead of `csrutil disable`, use `csrutil enable`.

Note   You can optionally use `csrutil enable --without dtrace`; however, this might not work reliably for commands that rely on `dtrace`.

Basic Usage

As mentioned before, dtrace is a very powerful tool. There are whole books written about it. It has its own programming language based on C syntax that you can use to build elaborate logic. For example, the following command will log some information from the given callbacks:

```
sudo dtrace -qn 'syscall::write:entry, syscall::sendto:entry /pid ==
$target/ { printf("(%d) %s %s", pid, probefunc, copyinstr(arg1));
}' -p 9999
```

The code snippet passed to the dtrace command listens to the sendto callback on the target process ID (9999 in this case). Then it prints out the information to the console, for example, *9999 text*.

If this seems like a bit too much and too hard to get started with, you're 100% right. It's a powerful tool when you need it. But for most of our day-to-day usage, it's just too powerful. What we want is to know a bit of basic stuff, and this is just too much.

Simple Usage

As luck would have it, we have a simple solution to the inherent complexity of `dtrace`. Man pages aren't always helpful, but in this case, they are very useful:

```
man -k dtrace
```

This prints out a list of tools that's worth reading just to get a sense of how extensive this thing is. Here are a few interesting lines of output from that command:

```
bitesize.d(1m)          - analyse disk I/O size by process. Uses DTrace
dapptrace(1m)           - trace user and library function usage. Uses DTrace
errinfo(1m)             - print errno for syscall fails. Uses DTrace
iotop(1m)               - display top disk I/O events by process. Uses DTrace
plockstat(1)            - front-end to DTrace to print statistics about
                          POSIX mutexes and read/write locks
```

It's worth your time going over this list to realize what you can do here. The full list is very long, and this tool alone warrants its own book. Let's say you're facing elevated disk write issues that are causing the performance of your application to degrade... But is it your app at fault or some other app?

```
sudo rwbypid.d
```

It will print out the reads/writes to the disk:

```
PID CMD                 DIR    COUNT
2957 wordexp-helper      W        1
2959 wc                  W        1
2961 grep                W        1
```

... snipped for clarity ...

```
637 firefox             R      6937
637 firefox             W     15325
343 sentineld           W    100287
```

In this case, we can see that the security software (Sentinel) is holding performance down. You can also use *bitesize.d* to get more specific results on the number of bytes written and their distribution. That's pretty high level though. What if you want specifics: file name, process name, etc.?

```
sudo iosnoop -a
```

It prints out an output that includes pretty much everything you would need:

```
STRTIME                  DEVICE  MAJ MIN   UID   PID D     BLOCK
SIZE                     PATHNAME ARGS
2022 Jun 30 12:16:56 ??        1  17    501   1111 W  150777072
4096 ??/idb/3166453069wcaw.sqlite-wal firefox\0
2022 Jun 30 12:16:56 ??        1  17    501    661 W  150777175
487424  ??/index-dir/the-real-index Slack Helper\0
2022 Jun 30 12:16:57 ??        1  17    499    342 W  150777294
4096 ??/persistent/.dat.nosync0156.ztvXap sentineld\0
```

Now we can see the process ID and how many bytes it wrote to the specific file. Let's say your program spans processes and you want to see what's going on. For example, I run a source code build in a server I built:

```
sudo errinfo
```

Lets us detect the error returned from system calls and the command that originally triggered that:

EXEC	SYSCALL	ERR	DESC
WindowServer	workq_kernreturn	-2	
WindowServer	workq_kernreturn	-2	
SentinelAgent	workq_kernreturn	-2	
SentinelAgent	workq_kernreturn	-2	
Signal	Helper	0	
Google	Chrome	0	
Brave	Browser	0	
Google	Chrome	0	

These are just the tip of the iceberg. I suggest checking out this old dtrace tutorial[1] from Oracle or the book.[2] Disclaimer: I didn't read the book...

---

[1] www.oracle.com/solaris/technologies/dtrace-tutorial.html

[2] www.bookdepository.com/DTrace-Brendan-Gregg/9780132091510?ref=grid-view&qid=1656581174175&sr=1-1

strace

The *strace* tool also originated at Sun Microsystems in this case in the 1990s. This isn't surprising though as the list of technologies originating from Sun Microsystems is absolutely mind numbing.

strace is much simpler than dtrace in both usage and capabilities – for better and for worse. Since *DTrace* requires deep OS support, it never became an official feature of common Linux distributions, and as a result, on Linux people use *strace* instead of *DTrace*. They aren't interchangeable and are wildly different tools despite the name similarity and similar domains.

strace is enabled thanks to the kernel feature known as *ptrace*. Since *ptrace* is already in Linux, we don't need to add additional kernel code or modules. Typically, *DTrace* requires deeper kernel support; to get around licensing issues on Linux, it's in a separate loadable module, but that still presents some challenges.

Working with *strace* is akin to printing a log entry every time we make a kernel call. This creates very verbose logging for every command you execute. As a result, you can follow what's really going on under the hood of a running process.

Running Strace

Nowadays, *strace* is commonly used in Linux; it's my favorite system diagnostic tool on that platform. It's remarkably convenient to work with since we can run it with no special privileges. Notice that unlike *DTrace*, you should keep *strace* away from production environments (unless the code is segregated). It carries a significant performance overhead and would bring a production system down.

The most basic usage of *strace* is just passing the command line to it:

```
strace java -classpath. PrimeMain
```

The output of *strace* for this is pretty long; let's go over a few of the lines:

```
execve("/home/ec2-user/jdk1.8.0_45/bin/java", ["java", "-classpath.",
"PrimeMain"], 0x7fffd689ec20 /* 23 vars */) = 0
brk(NULL)                                = 0xb85000
mmap(NULL, 4096, PROT_READ|PROT_WRITE, MAP_PRIVATE|MAP_ANONYMOUS, -1, 0) =
0x7f0294272000
```

```
readlink("/proc/self/exe", "/home/ec2-user/jdk1.8.0_45/bin/j"...,
4096) = 35
access("/etc/ld.so.preload", R_OK)      = -1 ENOENT (No such file or
directory)
open("/home/ec2-user/jdk1.8.0_45/bin/../lib/amd64/jli/tls/x86_64/
libpthread.so.0", O_RDONLY|O_CLOEXEC) = -1 ENOENT (No such file or
directory)
stat("/home/ec2-user/jdk1.8.0_45/bin/../lib/amd64/jli/tls/x86_64",
0x7fff37af09a0) = -1 ENOENT (No such file or directory)
open("/home/ec2-user/jdk1.8.0_45/bin/../lib/amd64/jli/tls/libpthread.so.0",
O_RDONLY|O_CLOEXEC) = -1 ENOENT (No such file or directory)
stat("/home/ec2-user/jdk1.8.0_45/bin/../lib/amd64/jli/tls", 0x7fff37af09a0)
= -1 ENOENT (No such file or directory)
```

Every one of these lines is a Linux system call. We can google each one of them to get a sense of what's going on. Here's a simple example:

```
open("/home/ec2-user/jdk1.8.0_45/bin/../lib/amd64/jli/tls/x86_64/
libpthread.so.0", O_RDONLY|O_CLOEXEC) = -1 ENOENT (No such file or
directory)
```

Java tries to load the *pthread* library from the *tls* directory using a system call open to load the file. The exit code of the system call is *-1*, which means that the file isn't there. Under normal circumstances, we should get back a file descriptor value from this API (positive nonzero integer). Looking in the directory, it seems the *tls* directory is missing. I'm guessing that this is because of a missing *JCE* (Java Cryptography Extensions) installation. This is probably OK but might have been interesting in some cases.

Obviously, the amount of output is overwhelming sometimes. We usually just want to see things like "which file was opened" and "what's going on with our network calls." We can easily accomplish that by only looking at specific system calls using the *-e* argument:

```
strace -e open java -classpath . PrimeMain
```

This will only show the open system calls:

```
open("/home/ec2-user/jdk1.8.0_45/bin/../lib/amd64/jli/tls/x86_64/
libpthread.so.0", O_RDONLY|O_CLOEXEC) = -1 ENOENT (No such file or
directory)
open("/home/ec2-user/jdk1.8.0_45/bin/../lib/amd64/jli/tls/libpthread.so.0",
O_RDONLY|O_CLOEXEC) = -1 ENOENT (No such file or directory)
open("/home/ec2-user/jdk1.8.0_45/bin/../lib/amd64/jli/x86_64/libpthread.
so.0", O_RDONLY|O_CLOEXEC) = -1 ENOENT (No such file or directory)
open("/home/ec2-user/jdk1.8.0_45/bin/../lib/amd64/jli/libpthread.so.0",
O_RDONLY|O_CLOEXEC) = -1 ENOENT (No such file or directory)
open("/home/ec2-user/jdk1.8.0_45/bin/../lib/amd64/tls/x86_64/libpthread.
so.0", O_RDONLY|O_CLOEXEC) = -1 ENOENT (No such file or directory)
open("/home/ec2-user/jdk1.8.0_45/bin/../lib/amd64/tls/libpthread.so.0",
O_RDONLY|O_CLOEXEC) = -1 ENOENT (No such file or directory)
open("/home/ec2-user/jdk1.8.0_45/bin/../lib/amd64/x86_64/libpthread.so.0",
O_RDONLY|O_CLOEXEC) = -1 ENOENT (No such file or directory)
open("/home/ec2-user/jdk1.8.0_45/bin/../lib/amd64/libpthread.so.0", O_
RDONLY|O_CLOEXEC) = -1 ENOENT (No such file or directory)
open("/etc/ld.so.cache", O_RDONLY|O_CLOEXEC) = 3
open("/lib64/libpthread.so.0", O_RDONLY|O_CLOEXEC) = 3
open("/home/ec2-user/jdk1.8.0_45/bin/../lib/amd64/jli/libjli.so", O_
RDONLY|O_CLOEXEC) = 3
open("/home/ec2-user/jdk1.8.0_45/bin/../lib/amd64/jli/libdl.so.2", O_
RDONLY|O_CLOEXEC) = -1 ENOENT (No such file or directory)
```

There are many system calls you can learn and use to track many behaviors such as these: connect, write, etc. This is only the tip of the iceberg of what you can do using *strace*. Julia Evans wrote some of the most exhaustive and entertaining posts on *strace*.[3] If you want to learn more about it, there's probably no better place (also check out her other stuff... Amazing resources!).

---

[3] https://jvns.ca/categories/strace/

Strace and Java

As you saw before, *strace* works great with the JVM. Since *strace* predates Java and is a very low-level tool, it has no awareness of the JVM. The JVM works like most other platforms and invokes system calls which you can use to debug its behavior. However, because of its unique approach to some problems, some aspects might not be as visible with *strace*.

A good example is allocations. System tools use *malloc*, which maps to kernel allocation logic, but Java takes a different route. It manages its own memory for efficiency and easier garbage collection logic. As a result, some aspects of memory allocation will be hidden from *strace* output. This can be a blessing in disguise, as the output can be overwhelming sometimes.

At the time of this writing, threading works well with *strace*. But this might not be the case moving forward as project Loom might change the one-to-one mapping between Java threads and system threads.[4] This might make *strace* output harder to pinpoint in heavily threaded applications.

Track Regressions with Git Bisect

We don't typically think about git as a debugging tool. Sure, it's a great tool to study the history of a file and narrow down causes. But as a debugging tool? It can be used for one special case of debugging: regression tracing.

In this chapter, I cover a lot of magical tools, and git bisect is one of the best examples of such magic. The hardest part in debugging is knowing the general area of the bug; bisect literally shines a light on the specific commit that caused it if it's a regression!

Before we begin, let's make one thing clear: bisect is a tool for finding regressions. It does nothing for regular bugs. When we have a regression, we typically know that the issue used to work in a specific release; we would typically have a specific revision where the code worked. We would typically know that it doesn't work in the current version, but which commit along the way causes the failure?

---

[4] By introducing virtual threads to the JVM specification which is, at the time of this writing, a preview feature of Java 19.

In the Old Days

Back in the old days of SVN (or CVS, SourceSafe, etc.), we used to check out an older version of the repository and test on it. If it failed, we'd go further back, and if it succeeded, we'd go forward to hone in on the specific commit that failed. Those among us who were lucky enough to work with competent QA departments could often pass this task to them. Ultimately, the work was manual.

When zeroing in on the issue, we'd follow the sensible search strategy of dividing the number of revisions in half and going to the middle of the set instead of going one step at a time. This significantly shortened the time spent looking for the problematic revision. However, there are still many revisions to search through. At this point, you might wonder, why didn't you automate these things?

We sometimes did, but since no versioning system was as dominant as git, these automations didn't last, and I'm not aware of such an automation that made it into any version control system. But git bisect made it in and is the automation of this heuristic.

Find the Bug. Automatically!

Git bisect does exactly that. The simplest use of git bisect starts with the command:

```
git bisect start
```

This switches us into bisect mode. We can now define the "good" version where things used to work properly. For example, for *github.com/codenameone/CodenameOne* I can use the revision *79a8e37adb7dd48093779bd3657142e607bdd2d9* as the good revision. We can thus mark it using the command:

```
git bisect good 79a8e37adb7dd48093779bd3657142e607bdd2d9
```

Once we do, we can activate bisect traversal by marking the bad revision. For most cases, this means the current head revision which is the default, but we can also specify a revision as an argument to this command just like we did in the good command. Normally, we don't need to specify a revision in the bad command, and I didn't in this case:

```
git bisect bad
```

This command marked the revision as bad. Once this is done, we can move between revisions by redefining the good or bad revisions. I ran these commands on the Codename One repo and got this output:

```
$ git bisect start
$(master|BISECTING)> git bisect good
79a837adb7dd48093779bd3657142e607bdd2d9
$ (master|BISECTING)> git bisect bad
Bisecting: 8 revisions left to test after this (roughly 3 steps)
[68dabb4f70c8295887d2da5c466dbe89fc910408] Update AsyncMediaSample.java(#3595)
```

Notice the value *68dabb4f70c8295887d2da5c466dbe89fc910408* at the bottom. This is the current revision we "jumped" to. We can now mark this revision as good or bad based on our manual testing. I marked it as bad. I could have marked it as "good" and that would have worked fine. This moved bisect to the next revision we need to test:

```
$ ((7.0.74) |BISECTING)> git bisect bad
68dabb4f70c8295887d2da5c466dbe89fc910408
Bisecting:
4 revisions left to test after this (roughlv 2 steps)
[53f0e7d106dbe1888bb76f936d27c9a39d06e58] Fixed error dialog when loading
designer through maven cn1: designer goal.
https://github.com/codenameone/CodenameOne/issues/3586
```

Notice there were eight revisions to test, and suddenly there are only four. We don't need to test all eight revisions since we take the divide and conquer approach of splitting the revisions in the middle. Notice that in this example, I only tested three revisions to find the bug.

Can We Automate This?

Going through every revision manually is a major pain! It's better than randomly looking through revision logs and jumping through revisions while keeping our place in our head – but just barely better. Luckily, there's a better way: run.

Bisect can run an arbitrary command for us on every revision it encounters. If the command returns zero (as a process exit code), the revision is good. If it returns something else, it's bad. This way, the broken revision will be identified automatically for us with no human interaction.

Normally, this works great for a shell command, but as a Java developer, this is a bit of a pain. Typically, I would have a unit test that shows the failure. Unfortunately, that unit test doesn't exist in the older version of the project. Then I also need to compile the project for this to work. So while git bisect seems cool with the run command, how do we use it for a compiled language like Java?

This is actually pretty easy. We can create a complex command line, but personally I prefer something like

```
git bisect run testMyJavaProject.sh
```

Then I implement the shell script with the commands that build/test. But before that, I need to create a unit test that fails for that specific bug. I assume this is something most of us can accomplish easily. Now that we have a unit test, creating the shell script is trivial. The following code assumes you use maven for building:

```
#!/bin/sh

mvn clean
mvn package -DskipTests
mvn test -Dtest=MyTestClass
```

That's it. Notice that if compilation will fail because of dependencies within the test class, you might end up with the wrong revision. So keep the test simple!

When you're done with git bisect or wish to stop for any reason, just issue the command:

```
git bisect reset
```

Git bisect is probably the simplest tool I will cover in this chapter. But it's also one of the most important tools. Learning to use it effectively can save you days of tedious work and hunting around for an issue. Despite these huge benefits, it's a relatively obscure feature. The reason for this is that for 98% of the time, we don't need it. But in that 2%, we **really** need it. Hopefully, the next time you run into a regression you'll remember that it's there and use this post to hunt down the issue.

JMXTerm

When tracking a bug, we need to take a two-pronged approach. It is similar to tongs that wrap the buggy module from both sides and squeeze it to find the problematic part. Up until now, we discussed tools that are very low level. Some can be used to debug system-level services. Today, we'll discuss the other side of the stack but still a very advanced management tool. To understand this, you need to understand the field we're in.

As developers, we deal with code and applications. Deployment is for OPS/DevOps, and the tooling they use is often alien to us. It's not that they have bad tools. On the contrary, they have amazing tools. But they're usually designed for massive scale. When you need to manage thousands of servers, you need a way to control things in all of them. For that, we need a different set of tools.

Management tools let us traverse through clouds of machines and manage the applications running on them. We don't always need the scale that these tools provide, but the management capabilities are a powerful tool that's very useful for developers. There are some standards that implement application management. Java introduced JMX (Java Management eXtensions) to encapsulate their differences. JMX lets applications, and the JDK itself, expose information and functionality for manipulation by external tools.

This is a remarkable feature that exposes information and tuning levers, for dynamic manipulation in runtime environments. Activating JMX is outside the scope of this tutorial, so I won't go too much into detail, but you can check some of the basics in this Oracle article.[5] Once we have this running, we can use visual tools to debug, but I'll focus on command-line tooling. This is important since I can use some of this tooling directly on the production servers right from the console.

Note   There are many management standards exposed through tools such as Prometheus, etc. I would strongly recommend taking time to learn more about these tools.

---

[5] `https://docs.oracle.com/javadb/10.10.1.2/adminguide/radminjmxenabledisable.html`

How Does JMX Work?

JMX exposes management "beans" (MBeans); these are objects that represent control points in the application. Your application can publish its own beans which lets you expose functionality for runtime monitoring and configuration. This is very cool as you can export information that an administrator can wire directly to a dashboard (APM, Prometheus, Grafana, etc.) and use that for decision making.

If your server has multiple users connected concurrently, you can expose that number in JMX, and it can appear in the company dashboard thanks to some wiring from DevOps. On your side, most of the work would be exposing a getter for the value of interest. You can also expose operations such as "purge users," etc. An operation is a method you can invoke on a JMX bean.

Spring also supports exposing a lot of server details as management beans via actuator.[6] It exposes very deep metrics about the application and helps you jump right into "production ready" status!

JMXTerm Basics

Usually, one controls and reads JMX via web interface tools or dedicated administration tooling. If you have access to any of them, I suggest you pick one of them up and use them as it would work pretty well. Some developers like `JConsole`; I didn't use it much. I've used some of other tools, and I prefer them in some cases. I also enjoy using IntelliJ/IDEA Ultimate's support for actuator which is a pretty powerful visualization tool that you can see in Figure 3-1.

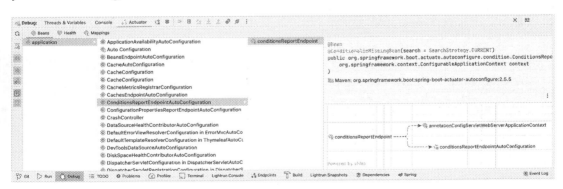

Figure 3-1. *IntelliJ/IDEA Ultimate actuator support*

---

[6] Read more about it here: `www.baeldung.com/spring-boot-actuators`

JMXTerm is just as powerful but doesn't include the visualization aspect; in that sense, it's exceptionally convenient when we need to understand something quickly on a server that might be alien. It's also pretty useful for getting high-level insights from the server internals. We can get started by downloading JMXTerm from `https://docs.cyclopsgroup.org/jmxterm`.

Once downloaded, we can use it to connect to a server using this code:

```
java -jar ~/Downloads/jmxterm-1.0.2-uber.jar --url localhost:30002
```

Notice that JMX needs to be explicitly enabled on that JVM. When dealing with a production or containerized server, there will probably be some "ready-made" configuration. However, a vanilla JVM doesn't have JMX enabled by default.[7]

Once JMX is enabled, you should update the hostname/port based on your connection. Once connected, we can list the JMX domains using the prompt:

```
$>domains
#following domains are available
JMImplementation
com.sun.management
java.lang
java.nio
java.util.logging
javax.cache
jdk.management.jfr
```

We can then pick a specific domain to explore; a domain can be any string, but it usually corresponds to package names. Domains help us identify the group of beans in much of the same way as packages group classes together. This is where the visual tool is usually beneficial as it can provide you with faster navigation through the hierarchy and quick assessment of the information. In this case, I just want to set the logging level:

```
$>domain java.util.logging
#domain is set to java.util.logging
```

We can follow this by listing the beans within the domain. Then pick the bean that we wish to use since there's only one bean in this specific domain:

---

[7] You can read about enabling JMX here: `https://docs.oracle.com/javadb/10.10.1.2/adminguide/radminjmxenabledisable.html`

```
$>beans
#domain = java.util.logging:
java.util.logging:type=Logging
$>bean java.util.logging:type=Logging
#bean is set to java.util.logging:type=Logging
```

What can I do with this bean? For that, we have the info command that lists the operations and attributes of the bean:

```
$>info
#mbean = java.util.logging:type=Logging
#class name = sun.management.ManagementFactoryHelper$PlatformLoggingImpl
# attributes
   %0    - LoggerNames ([Ljava.lang.String;, r)
   %1    - ObjectName (javax.management.ObjectName, r)
# operations
   %0    - java.lang.String getLoggerLevel(java.lang.String p0)
   %1    - java.lang.String getParentLoggerName(java.lang.String p0)
   %2    - void setLoggerLevel(java.lang.String p0,java.lang.String p1)
#there's no notifications
```

Once I have these, I can check the current logger level; it isn't set since we didn't set it explicitly and the global default is used. The following code is equivalent to invoking the getLoggerLevel method:

```
$>run getLoggerLevel "org.apache.tomcat.websocket.WsWebSocketContainer"
#calling operation getLoggerLevel of mbean java.util.logging:type=Logging
with params [org.apache.tomcat.websocket.WsWebSocketContainer]
#operation returns:
```

I can explicitly set it to INFO and then get it again to verify that the operation worked as expected using this code. Here, we invoke the setLoggerLevel operation (method), with two parameters. The first parameter is the name of the class where the log level should be changed. The second parameter is the INFO logging level:

```
$>run setLoggerLevel org.apache.tomcat.websocket.WsWebSocketContainer INFO
#calling operation setLoggerLevel of mbean java.util.logging:type=Logging
with params [org.apache.tomcat.websocket.WsWebSocketContainer, INFO]
```

```
#operation returns:
null
$>run getLoggerLevel "org.apache.tomcat.websocket.WsWebSocketContainer"
#calling operation getLoggerLevel of mbean java.util.logging:type=Logging
with params [org.apache.tomcat.websocket.WsWebSocketContainer]
#operation returns:
INFO
```

This is just the tip of the iceberg. We can get many things such as spring settings, internal VM information, etc. In this example, I can query VM information directly from the console:

```
$>domain com.sun.management
#domain is set to com.sun.management
$>beans
#domain = com.sun.management:
com.sun.management:type=DiagnosticCommand
com.sun.management:type=HotSpotDiagnostic
$>bean com.sun.management:type=HotSpotDiagnostic
#bean is set to com.sun.management:type=HotSpotDiagnostic
$>info
#mbean = com.sun.management:type=HotSpotDiagnostic
#class name = com.sun.management.internal.HotSpotDiagnostic
# attributes
  %0  - DiagnosticOptions ([Ljavax.management.openmbean.CompositeData;, r)
  %1  - ObjectName (javax.management.ObjectName, r)
# operations
  %0  - void dumpHeap(java.lang.String p0,boolean p1)
  %1  - javax.management.openmbean.CompositeData getVMOption(java.lang.
        String p0)
  %2  - void setVMOption(java.lang.String p0,java.lang.String p1)
#there's no notifications
```

JMX is a remarkable tool that we mostly use to wire management consoles. It's remarkable for that, and you should very much export JMX settings for your projects. Having said that, you can take it to the next level by leveraging JMX as part of your debugging process.

Server applications run without a UI or with deep UI separation. JMX can often work as a form of user interface or even as a command-line interface as is the case in JMXTerm. In these cases, we can trigger situations for debugging or observe the results of a debugging session right within the management UI.

jhsdb

Java 9 was all about modules. It was the big change and also the most problematic change. It sucked the air out of every other feature that shipped as part of that release. Unfortunately, one victim of this vacuum was *jhsdb* which is a complex tool to begin with. This left this amazingly powerful tool in relative obscurity. That's a shame.

So what is *jhsdb*? Oracle documentation defines it as follows:[8]

> *jhsdb is a Serviceability Agent (SA) tool. Serviceability Agent (SA) is a JDK component used to provide snapshot debugging, performance analysis and to get an in-depth understanding of the Hotspot JVM and the Java application executed by the Hotspot JVM.*

This doesn't really say much about what it is and what it can do. Here's my simplified take: it's a tool to debug the JVM itself and understand core dumps. It unifies multiple simpler tools to get deep insight into the native JVM internals. You can debug JVM failures and native library failures with it.

Basics of jhsdb

To get started, we can run

```
jhsdb --help
```

This produces the following output:

```
clhsdb          command line debugger
hsdb            ui debugger
debugd -help    to get more information
jstack -help    to get more information
```

---

[8] https://docs.oracle.com/en/java/javase/11/tools/jhsdb.html

```
jmap    --help    to get more information
jinfo   --help    to get more information
jsnap   --help    to get more information
```

The gist of this is that *jhsdb* is really six different tools:

- *debugd* – Acts as a remote debug server we can connect to.

- *jstack* – Stack and lock information.

- *jmap* – Heap memory information.

- *jinfo* – Basic JVM information.

- *jsnap* – Performance information.

- Command-line debugger – I won't discuss that since I prefer the GUI.

- GUI debugging tool.

debugd

The debugd command isn't as useful for most cases as you probably don't want to run debugd in production. However, if you're debugging a container locally and need to get information from within the container, it might make sense to use debugd. Unfortunately, because of a bug in the UI, you can't currently connect to a remote server via the GUI debugger. I could only use this with command-line tools such as *jstack* (discussed later).

With the command:

```
jhsdb debugd --pid 72640
```

I can connect to a process ID and expose it externally; you can get the PIDs of JVMs using the jps command. I can then use the command:

```
jhsdb jstack --connect localhost
```

to connect to the server with the *jstack* operation. Notice that the --connect argument applies globally and should work for all commands.

---

[9] https://stackoverflow.com/questions/73201268/jhsdb-cant-attach-the-java-process-in-macos-monterey

> **Note**   Some developers experienced issues with the debugd command.[9] I couldn't reproduce the issue when pointing at the right PID. Notice that you don't need to use sudo for this command. I would also suggest using the jps command to verify the process ID. I also suggest verifying that jhsdb and the JVM are the same version. It's possible this will work well in a docker environment with the additional --cap-add=SYS_PTRACE command-line argument.

jstack

Normally, we would run the command directly with the process ID instead of going through a server connection. This command produces a thread dump that you might find very familiar and yet helpful. If you're looking at a stack process in a user machine or production environment, this is an invaluable tool. Just run:

```
jhsdb jstack --pid 72640
```

> **Note**   Some Mac developers experience an "Operation not permitted" error when running these commands. Make sure that the Terminal application you use has full disk access. Also try following my previous instruction in the chapter to disable integrity protection with csrutil disable.

Then review the status of the JVM... Here are a few lines of the output:

```
Attaching to process ID 72640, please wait...
Debugger attached successfully.
Server compiler detected.
JVM version is 11.0.13+8-LTS
Deadlock Detection:

No deadlocks found.

"Keep-Alive-Timer" #189 daemon prio=8 tid=0x000000011d81f000 nid=0x881f
waiting on condition [0x0000000172442000]
   java.lang.Thread.State: TIMED_WAITING (sleeping)
```

```
   JavaThread state: _thread_blocked
 - java.lang.Thread.sleep(long) @bci=0 (Interpreted frame)
 - sun.net.www.http.KeepAliveCache.run() @bci=3, line=168
(Interpreted frame)
 - java.lang.Thread.run() @bci=11, line=829 (Interpreted frame)
 - jdk.internal.misc.InnocuousThread.run() @bci=20, line=134
(Interpreted frame)

"DestroyJavaVM" #171 prio=5 tid=0x000000011f809000 nid=0x2703 waiting on
condition [0x0000000000000000]
   java.lang.Thread.State: RUNNABLE
   JavaThread state: _thread_blocked
```

Notice a few things of interest:

- We get information about the JVM running.

- It detects deadlocks automatically for us!

- All threads are printed with fullstack and compilation status.

This snapshot can help us infer many details about how the application acts in production. Is our code compiled? Is it waiting on a monitor? What other threads are running and what are they doing?

jmap

If you want to understand what's happening under the hood in RAM, then this is the command you need to use. It prints everything you need to know about the heap, memory, etc. Here's a simple use case:

```
jhsdb jmap --pid 72640 --heap
```

It starts with this output, and it goes a lot further!

```
Attaching to process ID 72640, please wait...
Debugger attached successfully.
Server compiler detected.
JVM version is 11.0.13+8-LTS
```

```
using thread-local object allocation.
Garbage-First (G1) GC with 9 thread(s)

Heap Configuration:
   MinHeapFreeRatio         = 40
   MaxHeapFreeRatio         = 70
   MaxHeapSize              = 17179869184 (16384.0MB)
   NewSize                  = 1363144 (1.2999954223632812MB)
   MaxNewSize               = 10305404928 (9828.0MB)
   OldSize                  = 5452592 (5.1999969482421875MB)
...
```

When you tune GC flags to get better performance and reduce GC thrashing (especially when collecting very large heaps). The values you see here can give you the right hints on whether something is used. The true benefit is the ability to do this on a "real process" without running in a debug environment. This way, you can tune your GC in production based on real environment conditions.

If you could reproduce a memory leak but you don't have a debugger attached, you can use

```
jhsdb jmap --pid 72640 --histo
```

This prints a histogram of the RAM, snipped as follows for clarity. You can find the object that might be the trigger of this leak:

```
Attaching to process ID 72640, please wait...
Debugger attached successfully.
Server compiler detected.
JVM version is 11.0.13+8-LTS
Iterating over heap. This may take a while...
Object Histogram:

num       #instances      #bytes        Class description
--------------------------------------------------------------------
1:        225689          204096416     int[]
2:        485992          59393024      byte[]
3:        17221           23558328      sun.security.ssl.CipherSuite[]
```

4:	341376	10924032	java.util.HashMap$Node
5:	117706	9549752	java.util.HashMap$Node[]
6:	306720	7361280	java.lang.String
7:	12718	6713944	char[]
8:	113884	5466432	java.util.HashMap
9:	64683	4657176	java.util.regex.Matcher

There are a few other capabilities in the jmap command, but they aren't as useful as those two for day-to-day work.

jinfo

This prints the system properties and the JVM flags. This isn't as useful as the other commands since we probably know those already. However, if you're debugging on a machine that isn't yours, this can be a helpful starting point:

```
jhsdb jinfo --pid 72640
```

jsnap

jsnap prints a lot of internal metrics and statistics including the number of threads started since JVM launch, peak number of threads, etc. These are very useful if you want to tune elements such as thread pool sizes, etc.

```
jhsdb jsnap --pid 72640
```

This is the snipped version of the output for such a command:

```
Attaching to process ID 72640, please wait...
Debugger attached successfully.
Server compiler detected.
JVM version is 11.0.13+8-LTS
java.threads.started=418 event(s)
java.threads.live=12
java.threads.livePeak=30
java.threads.daemon=8
java.cls.loadedClasses=16108 event(s)
java.cls.unloadedClasses=0 event(s)
java.cls.sharedLoadedClasses=0 event(s)
```

```
java.cls.sharedUnloadedClasses=0 event(s)
java.ci.totalTime=23090159603 tick(s)
...
```

GUI Debugger

I'll skip the CLI debugger. You can launch the GUI debugger with no argument and use the file menu to connect to a core file, server, or process ID. Or you can use the standard command line that works for every other command. For the command-line case, we can just use

```
jhsdb hsdb --pid 72640
```

This launches the debug UI that you can see in Figure 3-2.

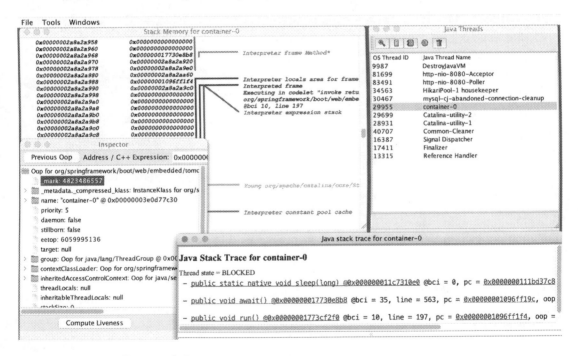

Figure 3-2. hsdb GUI debugger

The amount of capabilities and information exposed in this tool is absolutely fantastic. A lot of it might be too low level if we're debugging from the Java side. But if you're working with JNI native code, you can see the addresses matching the JVM thread/methods in the stack. This can put in context some native code debugging where the symbols might not be exposed coherently.

You can get the stack information for a specific thread (similar to *jstack*). The inspector tool contains deep internal JVM state information per thread that can provide internal status. Most of that information isn't as useful for debugging typical application-level bugs, but if you're trying to understand the root cause of a JVM crash, it might come in handy, especially if you're somewhat familiar with VM internal monikers.

There are many other features in the "Tools" menu such as Class Browser, Code Viewer, Memory Viewer, etc. All of those are very low-level access tools that might come in handy for tracking crashes or niche edge case issues.

jhsdb is a remarkably powerful and useful tool that I hope you will add into your toolbox. Its biggest fault is that it's too powerful and too low level. As a result, most Java developers might find it intimidating. This is fair when dealing with some of its more esoteric features that only make sense when interacting with native code.

However, *jhsdb* also includes many high-level capabilities from deadlock detection to JVM information. Those are easily accessible and easy to use. They're performant enough for production environments, and since they're a part of the JDK, they should be available out of the box and in the command line. When you need to explore a JVM crash, often after the fact where all you have is a core file, this is the best tool for the job. It's also a pretty great tool if you need to tune your GC, thread pools, or JVM configurations. If you're debugging JNI code and misbehavior, this can be the tool that makes a difference.

Wireshark

Wireshark is a free open source packet sniffer and network protocol analyzer originally developed by Eric Rescorla and Gerald Combs. It supports capturing packets on practically any network interface/protocol you can imagine and is an invaluable tool in our debugging arsenal. Wireshark displays packets in a tree structure called a "proto view"; this allows easy identification of protocols and ports used in the current session. It is very similar in basic functionality to tcpdump, but the graphical frontend makes it much easier to work with.

Capturing raw network traffic from interfaces requires elevated privileges on some operating systems. This caused security issues in the past and could be a serious risk. A more secure approach is using a tool like tcpdump to capture packets into a file. We can then open the file with Wireshark in user space with no special permissions. Both tools are highly synergetic and useful together.

Many users of this tool do very low-level networking work, security, browser development, etc. As a result, most of the tutorials and documentation are geared toward developers doing system-level development. This is a shame since this tool is remarkably helpful even to a high-level application developer tracking web requests and web service dependencies. To be fair, the network monitoring tool built into the browsers would probably satisfy most application developers. Both Chrome and Firefox have amazing tools that show the flow of a network request; these should be your first recourse when possible. Wireshark makes more sense when you can't resolve issues with the existing tools or are building an application that isn't a standard web interface (e.g., native mobile app). In the past, I used it to discover a case where a native application was failing when the server returned chunked HTTP responses; this required inspecting successful and failed requests to understand the differences.

Getting Started with Wireshark

You can download and install Wireshark from their website; it's open source and free for use.[10] Notice that there are separate steps to install command-line tools, etc., so I suggest reviewing the instructions. Once you install and launch the application, you would face the UI in Figure 3-3.

---

[10] `www.wireshark.org/download.html`

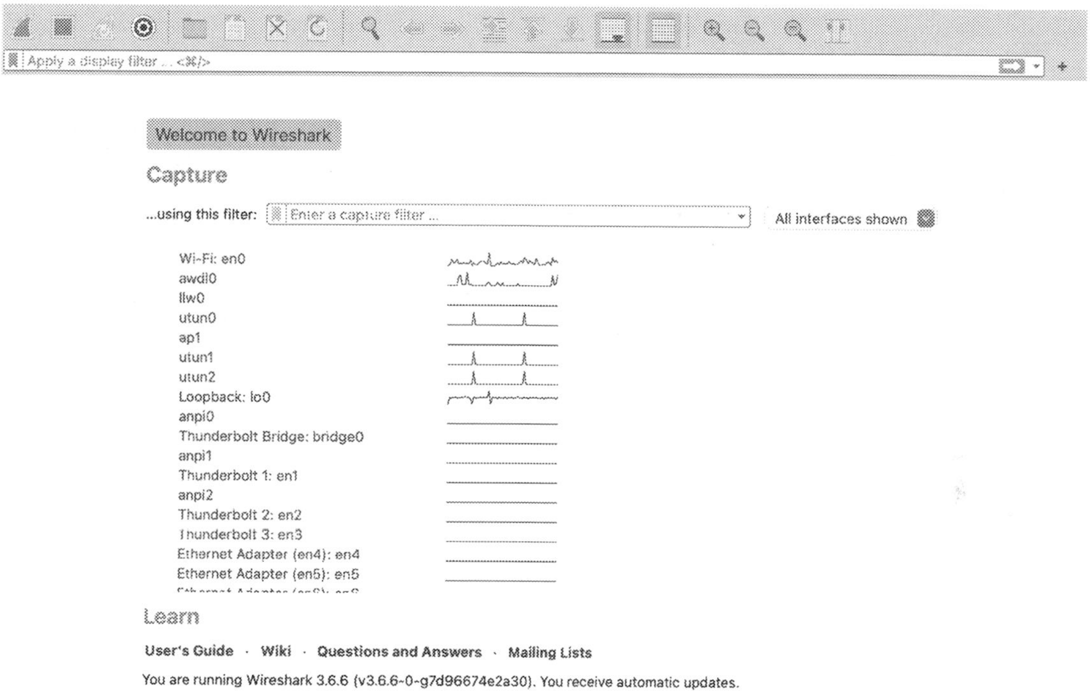

Figure 3-3. *Wireshark initial UI*

Here, we need to decide which network interface we wish to capture. This can be confusing if you don't come from a networking background. You might debug a local server and assume that you need to debug the en0 interface. This isn't the case. If the server is running locally, you should debug the Loopback.

Look at the activity graph on the right-hand side. This shows you instantly which interface is active and which one isn't. You probably only care about active network interfaces, so it has to be one of those. But even when we pick the right interface, the challenges are still severe. Wireshark is a packet capture solution. It doesn't distinguish between apps; we get a lot of noise when connecting to an interface, as you can see in Figure 3-4, which only shows a small portion of a constantly updating screen!

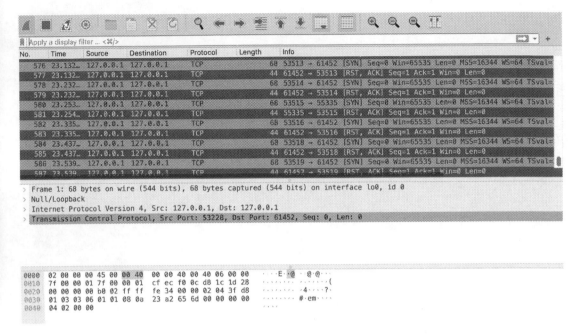

Figure 3-4. *Wireshark monitoring all networking on an idle machine is noisy*

The volume of TCP traffic is pretty big, and I'm not doing anything yet... All of that is just background noise that's interesting to dive into in our spare time. But probably not what we want to look at when we're trying to narrow down a damn bug...

Luckily, we have display filters that let us remove the noise by focusing only on the specific port which we're interested in with the condition *tcp.port == 8080*. Notice that my server is running on that port which makes it pretty easy to filter everything else. This brings down the noise considerably as you can see in Figure 3-5.

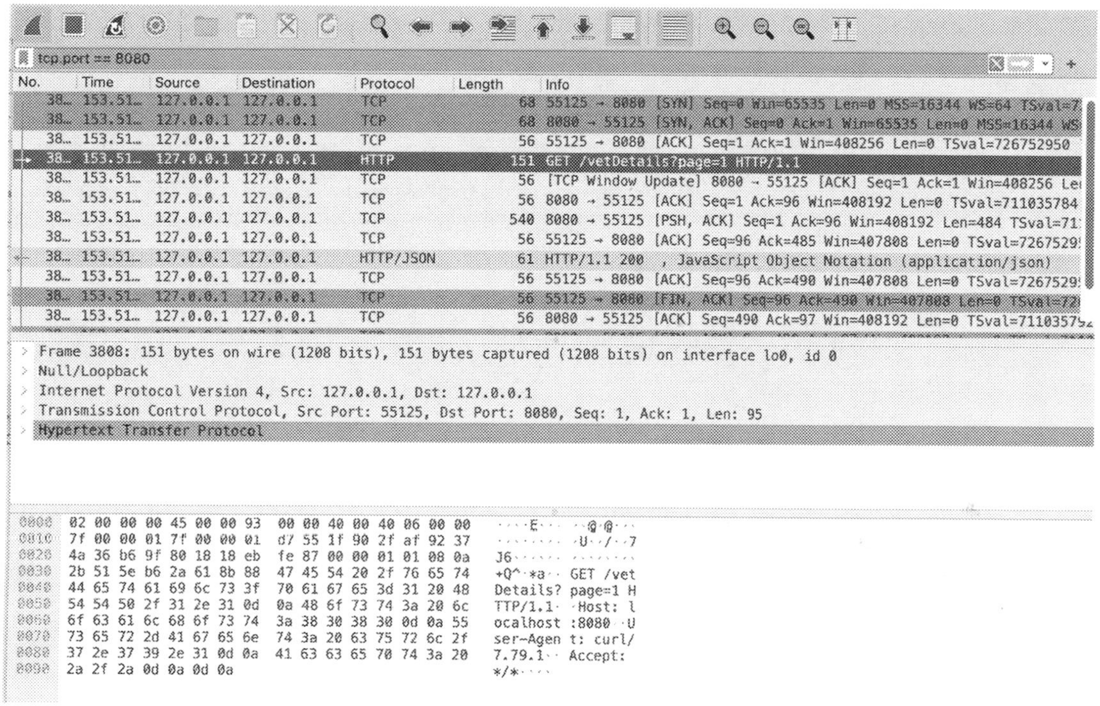

Figure 3-5. *Applying a basic display filter to reduce the noise*

Still there's a lot of noise because of the protocol. Notice that Wireshark is smart enough to recognize and even highlight the HTTP request I made to the server. Assuming I don't care about the nuances of TCP, I can further reduce the noise by adding an HTTP condition as *tcp.port == 8080 && http*. This will limit everything to only HTTP requests and responses – again very useful stuff that can have a big impact if you're dealing with many HTTP requests and connections. We can see the result in Figure 3-6.

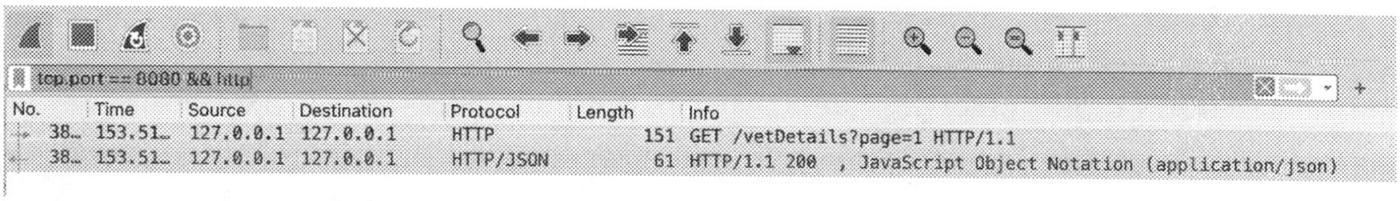

Figure 3-6. *Including HTTP in the display filters reduces the noise even further*

---

[11]www.wireshark.org/docs/dfref/

The display filter syntax is pretty powerful and supported by auto-completion within the filter bar; you can read about it in the user guide.[11] You can filter by IP address (not as useful for Loopback), source port, hostname, protocol, content, and so much more. This is just the start though. You'll notice the second entry is the response from the HTTP server, and it's marked as JSON. Wireshark detects the response type and displays it conveniently as shown in Figure 3-7.

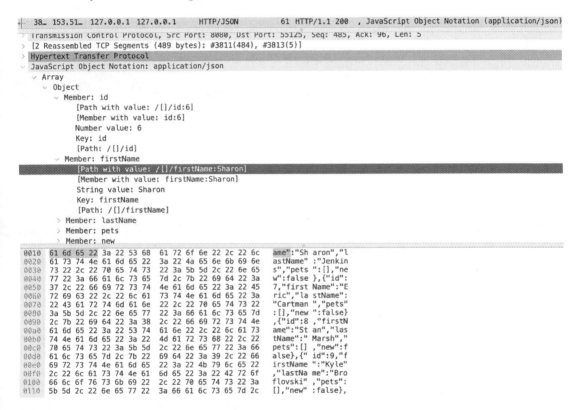

Figure 3-7. *JSON rendered as a tree with hex and packet view below*

On the bottom portion of the screen, we can see the raw packet display, which is typical for sniffer tools. In the bottom-left corner, you can see the hexadecimal values returned from the server. On the right, you can see the matching ASCII (or UTF-8) characters matching the hex. This is readable but might be a bit "unpleasant" for developers that aren't accustomed to debugging network traffic. If you look one level up, you will see a tree marked as "Array"; this is the JSON array from the response.

---

[12] Debugging over SSL is covered well by this post: www.trickster.dev/post/ decrypting-your-own-https-traffic-with-wireshark/

Wireshark detected the HTTP protocol. Then it detected that the response type was JSON. It then parses the JSON and displays it as a tree for you to read conveniently even if the packet is minimized and obtuse. When I make a selection within the tree, it highlights the place in the packet so we can inspect the surroundings and see that everything is in order. This lets us instantly see what went on when conncccting to a server/client and act accordingly.

I'd love to go into more details about Ethernet networks, decrypting HTTPS, debugging devices, and other complexities, but this is mostly the pain of configuring OS-specific settings, browsers, and a whole mess of things to look into the SSL traffic.[12] Personally, I try to disable security for debugging; it makes this much simpler. But sometimes there's just no choice.

Using Wireshark As a Debugging Tool

When we debug, we need to verify our assumptions, and in many cases, that assumption relates to something that happens outside of our control area. A common issue I experienced more times than I care to admit is an invocation of a web service that failed because of something internal. This means the web server rejected my request even before my code was reached.

One way to debug this is to go into the server implementation code and look at what's happening over there. This is something I did more than once. But often this isn't trivial as the code is hard to read and overly general. Debuggers are sometimes out of sync with the code, and it's a painful experience overall. Using Wireshark to review the request/response and understand why something failed is very helpful, especially for the cases where one client works and another fails.

I've had several cases where a new client implementation failed to connect to the same server which wasn't under my control so no access to sources. Using Wireshark, we discovered that this relates to HTTP chunked mode that is initialized implicitly in the Java SE URL API. By changing the way we invoked the API, we could get the new client to work in the same way as the old client. I can't imagine finding or fixing this bug without Wireshark.

I don't reach for Wireshark often in my day-to-day work. There are usually simpler ways to solve these issues than inspecting network packets. But when I need Wireshark, it's a fundamental change. The capture process is trivial when compared to far more complex tools. The capture filters are powerful and fast. As a general-purpose network protocol analyzer, it's absolutely fantastic and has so many deep use cases I can't even begin to get into (e.g., mobile devices).

tcpdump

There are three cases where I might not want to use Wireshark directly to observe traffic:

- Security restricted environment

- Remote server

- Customer machine

In these scenarios, running a command-line tool to just grab all the data and then working over it later would be more convenient. Luckily, this is pretty easy thanks to tcpdump which lets you capture network connection traffic and save it to a file. We can then open this file in Wireshark and follow through. This is one line in the console:

```
$ sudo tcpdump -i <interface> -w <file>
```

There are two things you need to pass as an argument. The network interface which in my case is *en0* indicating my wireless connection and the output file name. This can be any name. Once you do that, the process is running. You will get no indication; do the things you'd like captured, then press *ctrl-c* to stop the process. This was how I ran it on my machine (notice the ^c where I chose to stop and the packet size):

```
sudo tcpdump -i en0 -w output
Password:
tcpdump: listening on en0, link-type EN10MB (Ethernet), capture size
262144 bytes
^C3845 packets captured
4189 packets received by filter
0 packets dropped by kernel
```

Once you have the file, you can open it in Wireshark using *File* ➤ *Open* and use it as usual. There are two unique challenges you need to pay attention to. If this is an old version of tcpdump, you might need to add the *-s 65536* flag to indicate that you want to store larger packet sizes. The default in old versions was pretty small.

The second challenge is knowing the interface you need to support. If you're running on a remote machine, you might not be familiar with the options. You can use the ifconfig command to list the network interfaces on a machine. It's a bit much but would at least narrow down the search area.

Combining Wireshark with tcpdump solves the few remaining use cases and makes for a combination that's both relatively easy to use and powerful. I'm using the word relatively because it isn't a simple tool by any stretch of the imagination. Both of these tools have a great deal of power under the hood that I barely touched on and that doesn't make for an easy tool.

Summary

There's an alphabet soup of "*trace" utilities in various forms that keep borrowing ideas from one another. It's a significant challenge to keep up with all of that noise. There are just too many great tools to cover, and I skipped a couple that I would have covered if I had more time/space (btrace comes to mind).

The tools I discussed in this chapter take many different approaches to solve similar problems: How do we understand what a binary application "really" does? Security researchers and hackers use these tools to understand your program. They don't need the code and don't need a disassembly to see what you're actually doing. You can use them to understand your own application and the impact of third-party libraries/tools.

You can also use these tools to understand the impact of your own actions. We often invoke an API and let things end there. But the devil is in the details, and those details can carry a heavy toll. As a Java developer, I rarely think about signal delivery, process management, or such low-level staples. But I do spend time looking at these things since they ultimately impact the stability and performance of my application.

CHAPTER 4

Logging, Testing, and Fail-Fast

Pain that has not yet come is avoidable.

—Patanjali

This is a chapter about preventing future pain. We can significantly impact our future debugging experience by writing code that's easier to debug. Many best practices such as KISS,[1] DRY,[2] etc., will significantly improve your debugging experience. While this isn't a book about best practices, I will focus on a few that make debugging easier and failures manageable. One such best practice is fail-fast; it lets us detect a bug when it's closer to the symptom.

Logging is precognitive debugging. It's the process of laying out the breadcrumb clues for a future debugging session. Developers often take this to the extreme and overlog. This is a major problem as it makes it harder to find and follow the relevant information, but it can also make logging prohibitively expensive.

Testing is the subject of many books; I don't want to get into the nuances of this huge field. In this chapter, we'll focus on the basics and the aspects related to debugging. How do we create a unit test as part of the debugging process? How do we generate tests from a bug as observed in the debugger, etc.?

---

[1] Keep It Simple Stupid – don't complicate things.

[2] Don't Repeat Yourself – reuse code instead of writing the same logic over again.

© Shai Almog 2023
S. Almog, *Practical Debugging at Scale*, https://doi.org/10.1007/978-1-4842-9042-2_4

Logging

The joke about logging is that it's the "oldest debugging in the world." It lets us document the execution process of the application so we can review it in case of a failure. There's a great deal of confusion regarding the difference between logging and printing (to console). In Table 4-1, I highlight some of the big differences between printing and logging.

Table 4-1. Logging vs. Printing

	Printing	Logging
Filtering	Partially. Only on strings and assuming data isn't lost	Filters based on log level, logger name, etc.
Output Medium	Console (can be redirected or piped)	Console, file, cloud. Can be different logs to each destination
Metadata	No	Sophisticated including MDC[3]
Purpose	Ad hoc short term	Long-term record of events
Storage Management	Can exhaust storage when redirected to disk	Logger policy can be configured to purge, cycle, remove, or zip old logs
Output Format	Text	Text, structured (XML or JSON)
PII Reduction[4]	No	Some implementations

There's a lot going on in Table 4-1. The gist of it is that logs are sophisticated long-term systems designed for scale and processing. Printing is a trivial tool that provides no nuance other than a short-term hack. Usually, one should prefer tracepoints (see Chapter 1) over simple print statements. Tracepoints have several core advantages over print statements, specifically:

- You can't accidentally commit a tracepoint into the project.

- Tracepoints can be modified without recompiling or restarting the application.

---

[3] MDC – Mapped Diagnostic Context

[4] PII – Personally Identifiable Information. PII reduction will hide sensitive information logged accidentally, e.g., SSN numbers, credit card numbers, etc.

- Tracepoints can be conditional.

- Tracepoints can connect to filters and other IDE capabilities; they can be applied at scale.

Modern loggers support machine-readable formats, MDC, get ingested, etc. We can search through logs that originated from multiple machines in the cluster using common ingestion tools. Subtle details decided during development time can have a significant impact when we analyze a problem of scale.

Logging is one of the pillars of observability, which we'll discuss in Chapter 9. In this chapter, the focus is on coding, before we reach production. When we discuss the observability aspect of logging, we'll do so from a different context – that of analysis, maintenance, and system integration.

Before we proceed, I have one important tip: **don't roll out your own logger.** Some developers still choose to roll out their own logging frameworks or wrappers around the existing logging libraries. It makes sense to have abstractions, but abstracting the abstraction imposes its own set of problems. The main reason for an abstraction is the ability to add features in the abstraction layer. If we do that for the logger and a third-party library uses that same logger, we will end up with uneven functionality.

Rolling your own is redundant. There are many complexities involved. Anything you fix or save will probably come back to bite you. As we saw with the Log4J security vulnerability,[5] it can also introduce nuanced performance pitfalls and might miss complex custom output expected by ingestion.

Too Much of a "Good Thing"

When our applications fail in production, we usually reach for the application log. It's our first "line of defense." If it isn't enough, we will need to reproduce the problem in some way, and that isn't trivial. While logging does receive a lot of tooling attention and appreciation, the practice and standardization around it is lacking. Most companies don't have a "best practices" guide or any significant standardization around it.

---

[5] `www.cisa.gov/uscert/apache-log4j-vulnerability-guidance`

Logging is the very definition of debugging ahead of time. We write the log before there's a bug and then rely on it to point us in the right direction. If we could, we'd log everything. Unfortunately, that's a disaster waiting to happen.

Story   A recent Reddit thread[6] described a situation where a new project spent 100k USD on Azure logging ingestion costs over the span of a few days (notice that this would have probably affected AWS or GCP just the same).

Overlogging is a major problem. The cost of logging in production environments is often estimated as roughly one-third of the total cloud costs. That's a tremendous amount to spend on a problem that might not happen. This doesn't account for the performance overhead incurred due to logging. That can cascade into significant additional costs overall.

Cutting down on logging is a double-edged sword. If we run into a production issue and a log is missing, then we have no way of tracking down the issue. There were multiple attempts at working around this issue, such as log levels. These are good ideas, but the standardization around them is too general. To make matters worse, developers don't apply standardization uniformly, even within the same project.

The common solution to this problem is a "Logging Best Practices" document, similar to the ones we have for coding standards.[7] Such a document should be a part of onboarding in companies and should be referred to by developers during peer reviews.

Use MDC (Mapped Diagnostic Context)

I'm not religious about loggers. I will use the one we have in a project without complaining about implementation nuances or small performance differences. If your logger doesn't support MDC, switch to a different logger. MDC isn't a feature you should compromise about or glaze over. Still, for such an important feature, you'd expect to get some name recognition for MDC, but it's still a feature that's relatively unknown.

---

[6] www.reddit.com/r/devops/comments/udgohy/comment/i6i3oyo/?utm_source=share&utm_medium=web2x&context=3

[7] Here's one I created as a sample: https://talktotheduck.dev/logging-best-practices-mdc-ingestion-and-scale

MDC provides a way to associate a process with context information. Let's say you have a process that implements a REST API response. The REST endpoint that received that request would be interesting contextual information, right?

MDC associates arbitrary information with a process (thread, callback chain, etc.). The logger includes that information for every line printed by the logger. This is especially important in production where you can easily narrow down requests. A common MDC entry is the user ID which lets us filter requests from a specific user and resolve user-specific issues faster. We can add information to MDC using code like this (in Java):

```
MDC.put("userId",userId);
```

But there is a "catch." If we add such information to the MDC, we must remove it as well. If we don't, the information can pollute future operations, for example, the user ID can become associated with an unauthenticated user since threads in Java are pooled and other platforms reuse threads. The solution is to remove the MDC value when we're done with it:

```
MDC.remove("userId");
```

This is problematic because we might have a failure before the remove call is made. An exception might be thrown in the thread, and as a result, the MDC code might be missed. We need to guard against that and make sure that threads are clean. The strategies for that are too varied to include here, but there are usually best practices covered in the MDC documentation from your logging vendor.

Should I Log?

The biggest question in logging is this: What should I put into the log and where? This is a difficult question to answer in a general enough way, but I will try. For most cases, I recommend having one log per method before the return statement. This means we can log the return value, which is usually the most important aspect of the method.

To make this strategy tenable, we need to avoid multiple return statements and ideally break down methods into smaller pieces. Both are good strategies to begin with. But these aren't rules; they're guides. Developers sometimes have an issue with changing the return statement from

```
return methodCall(value);
```

to

```
ObjectType result = methodCall(value);
logger.log("Method X returned {}", result);
return result;
```

This policy is valuable in the case of logging, but also makes debugging much easier in the debugger itself. We can inspect the result more easily and efficiently in the debugger. I advocate the second form even though it feels "inelegant" by comparison. The value outweighs the cost, and the result is still very readable. Arguably, it is even more readable than the terse alternative.

I suggest picking a random bug; as you step over the code, look at the log statements along the way. Do they include the variables you inspect in the watch area? Can you deduce the rest? After running through this exercise a few times, you should develop a sense for the "right amount of logging."

The most important tip I can offer after this is to read the resulting logs regularly. This is an obvious task that most of us don't undertake. Go through the logs in depth and familiarize yourself with them just as you would with the code. You should develop a feel for what makes up a "healthy log." When you're debugging an on-call issue at 2am, this training will pay off. It will also pay off when you find small issues before they turn into major issues. This should be a part of a weekly "health" task that everyone on the team should have scheduled to their calendars (ideally at different times). This task should also include a review process of other observability monitors.

Testing

Debugging and testing are two vastly different subjects. There are many books on testing, and this shouldn't be considered one of them. Yet they both have a few convergence points of interest which we need to cover within this section. Before we get into those points, it's probably a good place to discuss some basic testing terminology that's thrown around.

Mocking replaces an object with a "fake" object that masquerades as a specific type while returning preprogrammed results.

The clean definition of *unit tests* is one where they test a specific method or function in complete isolation. They only test the method itself and nothing else. The inverse of that are *integration tests*, which test a more realistic scenario where multiple layers of the application are running. In modern usage, these lines are blurrier than one would expect. Using too much mocking is considered problematic since it reduces the quality of the tests. Integration tests can include mocking. Unit tests have two major advantages over integration tests:

- They're fast, which means we can run them all the time – sometimes even as we type within the IDE!

- They fail in a way that's very readable. It's often easier to understand a failure in a unit test since there are fewer "moving parts."

Integration tests tend to have greater test fidelity. You cover more "ground" with a single test and can run into unpredictable bugs with such a test. Table 4-2 illustrates the key tradeoffs between unit and integration tests.

Table 4-2. *Unit Tests vs. Integration Tests*

	Unit Tests	Integration Tests
Speed	Fast	Slow
Consistency	High	Moderate
Coverage	Minimal	Wide
Error	Pinpoint	General
Execution	Easy	Can be challenging

Coverage is the metric by which we check if we have enough tests. It instruments the code and verifies that every line and statement is reached when running the tests. It produces a report which comes down to a percentage of the lines and statements covered by tests. While quality shouldn't be measured by a simplistic numeric value, this number is often standardized by organizations. Some require 100% test coverage, which means every line and statement must be reached. This often follows a law of diminishing returns as coverage grows.

Role of Tests in the Debug – Fix Cycle

We discussed this briefly in Chapter 2. When we find the cause of the bug, the best practice is to write a test (preferably a unity test) that reproduces the failure. Then focus on passing the test before verifying the bug itself was fixed. This has a couple of advantages:

- By adding a test, we can verify the bug won't return.

- Running a test is usually faster than running the entire application and restoring the buggy state.

The bug fixing cycle is illustrated in Figure 4-1 and includes the following stages:

- Find bug – This book is about this stage in the cycle. This stage is the debugging process itself. The debugging process through which we understand why the bug occurs.

- Create test – We must create a test that reproduces the problem we encounter. A unit test is often ideal for these situations since it's faster and easier to debug.

- Fix bug – Notice that this should come after the creation of the test. You need to create a test that fails and verify the failure. This provides two important benefits. We now have double verification for the fix of the bug, the unit test, and the code. The second benefit is an automated test that will prevent the bug from recurring.

- Run test – Verifying the fix against the test is usually easier and faster than doing so against the entire application.

- Run code – This is the final goal. We need to verify that the fix works with the actual application code. If it doesn't, we need to restart the cycle all over again.

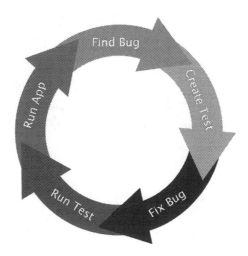

Figure 4-1. *The bug fixing cycle*

In the interest of brevity, I omitted some stages from this cycle. Specifically, I chose to omit version control and issue tracker processes. These are important aspects, but they're better served by a book dedicated to software quality.

Using the Debugger to Compose Unit Tests

Typically, unit tests are easy to write. We invoke a method using various parameters and define the success criteria. The devil is in the details though; tuning coverage numbers to higher values is challenging and very difficult. Testing a specific bug or behavior and mocking appropriately are all challenging too.

Luckily, the debugger can help with the task of composing effective tests with good coverage. We can compose good tests without a debugger, but it would mean stopping execution, recompiling the test, and running again. The basis for all of these is "jump to line" which we discussed in Chapter 1. We can move the current execution to a point before the method was executed and rerun the test over and over until we get the desired result. Think of it as a reset button that doesn't require recompilation and rerunning and lets you create any imaginary state. We can traverse the testable method repeatedly while verifying coverage with "step-over" and tuning variables to suit our needs. Once we understand the set of variable values that produce the desired test constraints, we can code a unit test with those parameters.

A typical test coverage report will highlight a line or a condition that isn't reached by a test. In Figure 4-2, we can see a highlighted `if` statement whose body is always skipped in unit tests, thus resulting in a test without full coverage. By using the set value capability of the debugger, we can verify that the code is reached. In this case, you will notice that the next line in the body is a `rejectValue` call which will throw an exception. I don't want an exception thrown as I still want to test all the permutations of the method. I can drag the execution pointer (arrow on the left) and place it back at the start of the method.

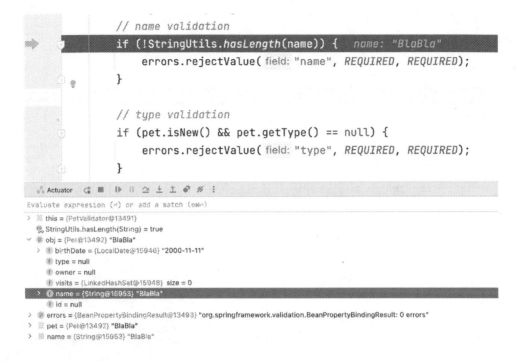

Figure 4-2. *Increasing unit test coverage dynamically*

This example is relatively trivial, but when we're faced with complex conditions within a method, we need all the tools we can get. We can detect the right objects that need mocking for an invocation by stepping over and inspecting. Using a debugger to review the implementation would make things easier.

Note   This approach has one theoretical drawback. It couples the implementation and the tests. I'm from a school of thought that accepts this situation in the case of unit tests, but some would disagree.[8]

---

[8] https://vimeo.com/68375232

Writing Good Tests

There's a school of thought among TDD (test-driven developers) that somehow debugging is a bug. If you write the right tests, you will never need debugging. Typically, in a project with high test coverage, I find that the test code is at least as big as the project source code. When I double the source code, I introduce more bugs. Most of the bugs I have in such projects originate in the tests. Most of the time I spend debugging in these projects is spent debugging the test cases.

It's often that test cases are hard to debug. This is due to the following factors:

- Bad bootstrapping – Some developers build tests badly so they can only run from the command line and can't be run from the IDE. This makes the debugging experience painful.

- Nonstandard test frameworks – This is something we need to avoid at all costs. The ecosystem surrounding the test framework is big, tooling, coverage, static analysis, etc. If you do pick a nonstandard framework, make sure it's debuggable.

- Problematic dependencies – Tests that have interdependencies or environment dependencies.

- Flakiness – Tests fail only when run in the CI/CD environment and only occasionally. When run locally or in the debugger, they pass.

- Container tests – In recent years, tests are often executed in a container environment that makes them harder to debug properly. We will discuss containers in Chapter 6.

Tests must be written so they can be run in isolation using standard test harnesses. This lets us run them in the IDE and debug them under all conditions. The main problem is that even when we follow those guidelines, we still run into flakiness in tests. Good testing practices typically correlate with easy debugging and easier tracking of flaky tests.

Remove external dependencies from unit tests. If you rely on a web service, it must not be a part of the test. It will make debugging harder and can make the test flaky. Instead, mock the service. Arguably, this should be done for **some** integration tests as well (not all of them).

Clean up the environment completely when running tests. Some developers disable that intentionally so they can review test failures after the fact. This triggers hard-to-catch failures and perpetuates problems. Most test environments support executing in a clean container environment, which I would recommend.

Increase logging for flaky tests. This is an obvious tip. Still, it bears repeating. Flakiness often goes away when adding logging, which is typically a sign of a race condition. This can be verified by adding a short sleep period to the start of the test to check if this relates to the environment setup (or in some cases, a teardown of the previous test environment). These are remarkably hard to reproduce since they relate to edge case behavior of the underlying APIs. With logging, we can narrow the failure or state corruption area that can help us point at a specific dependency that might not be ready.

Running the test in a loop, possibly with random test ordering, can help reproduce such flaky tests repeatedly. This is helpful when we're trying to narrow down flakiness and isolate the problem.

I highly recommend running the test in isolation with a tool such as `strace` (which we will discuss in Chapter 5). `strace` provides insights into the true environmental requirements of the test. We can review them to understand what's happening under the hood and adapt our thought process accordingly.

Writing Debuggable Code

I love cooking and use my Thermomix a lot. Thermomix is a magical kitchen robot... When the team at Vorwerk designed the Thermomix, they took the approach of fail-safe instead of fail-fast. This is a smart choice in this case, but it has its drawbacks.

For example, my machine tried to recover from a failure which sent it into an infinite recovery loop. I literally couldn't pull out the food from the lid that was sealed shut. But normally, it's one of the most reliable devices I own. It kept working even though I accidentally burned it in an open flame. Kitchen environments are hazardous. Which approach should we take and how does that impact our long-term reliability?

Fail-Fast vs. Fail-Safe

In case you aren't familiar with the terms, fail-fast means a system that would quickly fail in an unexpected condition. A fail-safe system will try to recover and proceed even with bad input. Historically, Java tries to take the fail-fast approach, whereas JavaScript leans a bit more toward the fail-safe approach. Note that this is a broad rule of thumb, and both approaches are taken within the respective ecosystems.

A good example of fail-fast behavior would be the respective approaches to null handling. In Java, a null produces a `NullPointerException` which fails instantly and clearly. JavaScript uses `"undefined"` which can propagate through the system.

Which One Should We Pick?

This is hard to tell. There's very little research, and I can't think of a way to apply the scientific method objectively to measure this sort of methodology. It has both technical aspects and relates to core business decisions. Fail-fast is typically easier to debug; a failure is immediate and usually obvious. A fail-safe implementation will be more robust and will survive in a hostile production environment (like my kitchen).

Companies using microservices are committed to some form of fail-safe. Resiliency is a common trait of microservices, and that is the definition of fail-safe. Modern approaches to fail-safe try to avoid some pitfalls of the approach by using thresholds to limit failure. A good example of this is a circuit breaker, both the physical one and software based. A circuit breaker disconnects functionality that fails so it doesn't produce a cascading failure.

Companies who pick the fail-fast approach take some risks but reap some big rewards. When you pick that approach, failure can be painful if a bug reaches production, but there are two significant advantages:

- It's easier to catch bugs in fail-fast systems during the development/ debugging cycle.

- These bugs are usually easier to fix.

The fail-fast approach handles such bugs better since there's a lower risk of cascading effect. A fail-safe environment can try to recover from an error and postpone it. As a result, the developer will see an error at a much later stage and might miss the root cause of the error.

My bias is toward fail-fast; I believe it makes systems more stable when we reach production. But this is anecdotal and very hard to prove empirically. I think a fail-fast system requires some appetite for risk, both from engineering and from the executives – possibly more so from the executives.

Notice that despite that opinion, I said that the Thermomix was smart to pick fail-safe. Thermomix is hardware running in an unknown and volatile environment. This means a fix in production would be nearly impossible and very expensive to deploy. Systems like that must survive the worst scenarios. Imagine a failure in mission-critical systems of an airplane or a landing module. We need to learn from previous failure. Successful companies use both approaches, so it's very hard to pick the best approach.

Hybrid Environment in the Cloud

A more common "strategy" for handling failure is to combine the best of both worlds:

- Fail-fast when invoking local code or services, for example, DB. Notice that a DB might be in a separate container, but it's often "near" our actual service.

- Fail-safe when depending on remote resource, for example, remote web service. A remote web service can be in the same container, but it can be completely detached in a separate datacenter or managed by a different company altogether.

The core assumption behind this direction is that we can control our local environment and test it well. Businesses can't rely on a random service in the cloud. They can build fault-tolerant systems by avoiding external risks but taking the calculated risks of a fail-fast system.

For any such strategy to work, we need to clearly outline these decisions on all levels. These decisions need to be present in coding processes, code reviews, and project management decisions. They should be enforced in tooling and tests. But first, we need to redefine failure.

Defining Failure

The discussion of failure is often very binary. Code fails or succeeds; there's a crash or "it works." This is a very problematic state of mind. A crash or downtime is bad. But by no means is it the only type of failure or even the worst type of failure. A crash usually marks a problem we can fix and even work around by spinning up a new server instance automatically. This is a failure we can handle relatively elegantly. The whole industry of orchestration was designed to handle just this type of failure.

Data corruption is a far more sinister failure. A bug can result in bad data, making its way into the database and potentially causing long-term problems. Such a corruption can have widespread impact on security and reliability due to corrupted data. These types of problems are much harder to fix as it requires reworking the data which might be unrecoverable. A fail-fast system can sometimes nip such issues in the bud.

With cloud computing, we're seeing a rise in defensive programming such as circuit breakers, retries, etc. This is unavoidable, as the assumption behind these solutions is that everything in the cloud can fail. An important part of a good QA process is long-running tests that take hours to run and stress the system. When reviewing the logs of these tests, we can sometimes notice issues that didn't fail but conflict with our assumptions about the system. This can help find the insidious bugs that went through.

Don't Fix the Bug

Not right away. Well, unless it's in production, obviously. We should understand bugs before we fix them. Why didn't the testing process find it? Is it a cascading effect or is it missing test coverage? How did we miss that?

When developers resolve a bug, they should be able to answer that question on the issue tracker. Then comes the hard problem: finding the root cause of the failure and fixing the process so such issues won't happen again. This is obviously an extreme approach to take on every bug, so we need to apply some discretion when we pick the bugs to focus on. But this must always apply to a bug in production. We must investigate bugs in production thoroughly since failure in the cloud can be very problematic for the business, especially when experiencing exponential growth.

Debugging Failure

Now that we have a general sense of the subject, let's get into the more practical aspects of a book focused on debugging. There's no special innovation here. Debugging a fail-fast system is pretty darn easy. But there are some gotchas, tips, and tricks we can use to promote fail-fast. There are other strategies we can use to debug a fail-safe system.

To ensure a fail-fast system, use the following strategies:

- Throw exceptions – Define the contract of every API in the documentation and fail immediately if the API is invoked with out-of-bounds state, values, etc.

- Enforce this strategy with unit tests – Go over every statement made in the documentation for every API. Write a test that enforces that behavior.

- If you rely on external sources, create tests for unavailable situations, low performance, and sudden unavailability.

- Define low timeouts, never retry.

The core idea is to fail quickly. Let's say we need to invoke a web service; a networking issue can trigger a failure. A fail-fast system will expect a failure and present an error to the user.

For fail-safe, the core idea isn't so much to avoid failure as it's unavoidable. The core idea is to soften the blow of a failure. For example, if we take the web service example again, a fail-safe environment could cache responses from the service and would try to show an older response. We can build a test case to validate that behavior.

The problem here is that users might get out-of-date information, and this might cause a cascading effect. It might mean it will take us longer to find the problem and fix it, since the system might seem in order. The obvious tip here is to log and alert on every failure and mitigation so we can address them. But there's another hybrid approach that isn't as common but might be interesting to some.

Hybrid Fail-Safe

A hybrid fail-safe environment starts as a fail-fast environment. This is also true for the testing environment and staging. The core innovation is wrappers that enclose individual components and provide a fail-safe layer. When a system is nearing production, we need to review the fault points within the system, focusing on external dependencies but also on internal components.

A fail-safe wrapper can retry the operation and can implement recovery policies. There's some ready-made software tools that let us define fail-safe strategy after the fact, for example, Failsafe, Spring Retry, and many other such tools. Some of these tools are at the SaaS API levels and can mitigate availability or networking issues.

This has the downside of adding a production component that's mostly missing in development and QA. But it includes many of the advantages of fail-fast and keeps the code relatively clean.

This approach has some drawbacks when it comes to debugging; fail-safe behavior is encapsulated by libraries and can be hidden. When something fails and then retries, we can lose some context information. This is further compounded by the differences between production and development environments. While this isn't an ideal approach, I would pick it for a case where I need fail-safe support.

Summary

We covered three very different subjects in this chapter, but there's one surrounding theme: debugging starts when you write the code. The choices you make as you start will impact your debugging experience moving forward. Logging, testing, and architectural decisions such as the fail-fast policy all have long-term implications.

I hope this chapter will help you focus on the practices listed here and help you make more conscious decisions. If you don't have a logging best practices document, make sure to add one. If your unit tests aren't focused on enforcing policies such as fail-fast or fail-safe, they probably should. If your tests are flaky, you should take this seriously; that might be a bad omen.

In the next chapter, we'll talk about a unique approach to debugging that very few of us use, time travel debugging. It is uniquely suited for some types of exceptional bugs. It lets us dig into the execution of the application after it is finished. It's as if your log could talk.

CHAPTER 5

Time Travel Debugging

O brave new world That has such people in't!

—Aldous Huxley/William Shakespeare

I think there's no better quote for a chapter about time travel debuggers than this. A forgettable Shakespeare quote became significant as Huxley plucked it from relative obscurity with his groundbreaking book. This is the perfect analogy for time travel debuggers, a.k.a. back-in-time debuggers.

Time travel debuggers (TTDs) don't debug. They track everything we do when using an application. Once we're done with the application or experienced the failure, we can use the TTD to analyze the broken state and figure out what went wrong. This takes away some of the convenience we have in a regular debugger. We can't change something and see the impact within the debugger. We can't change the flow. In that sense, they're weaker than a regular debugger.

They make up for these weaknesses with exceptional power: the ability to go anywhere within the execution and see everything that happened in great detail. In this chapter, I'll explain how they work and what we can do with them. Notice that there are **many** tools in this field. There's a great deal of variance, so it's worth keeping up with specific tools. I'll try to avoid discussion of specific tools and focus on features, capabilities, and usage, with a few notable exceptions.

© Shai Almog 2023
S. Almog, *Practical Debugging at Scale*, https://doi.org/10.1007/978-1-4842-9042-2_5

Table 5-1. *Typical Debugger vs. TTD*

Typical Debugger	Time Travel Debugger
Interactive, disrupts user experience	Runs in the background, can be used by nontechnical people
Sees flow of execution	Sees flow of entire execution
Can impact flow of execution	Flow and values are fixed
Impacts flow inadvertently	Lesser chance of flow impact
Familiar experience	Different process
Can be low overhead	Impact is always noticeable
Used by developer	Can be used in CI process and by QA
General-purpose tool	Ideal for hard-to-reproduce bugs and bugs where the cause and effect are far between

Why Haven't They Won?

In late 2021, I was asked to write predictions for the future, and one of my big ones was this:[1]

> **Time Travel Time Debugging Will Make a Comeback**
>
> This is an old idea that never caught on with a wider audience back in the day. A lot of things changed since then, and we're seeing some companies such as Replay trying to bring this to the masses again. I think this time this will work. Developers today are already used to pretty sophisticated tools. The languages are managed, and thus implementing the debugger is easier/more consistent. We also have a more mature developer relations process that helps educate the market.

I don't know if this prediction will come true, but I do think a huge problem is in the awareness and education problem. Another problem is in the availability of mass market tools in this specific field.

A great incentive for using such tools is the rise of functional and asynchronous APIs. Such systems are challenging to debug with typical systems. The one thing

---

[1] https://vmblog.com/archive/2021/12/03/lightrun-2022-predictions-logging-debugging-and-observability-in-2022.aspx

working against this rise is that typical debuggers are taking pages off the time travelers' playbook. They stitch asynchronous stack traces and provide tools such as the stream debugger (see Chapter 2). I believe we'll see more innovations such as these as time travel debugging slowly inches into the mainstream.

Their Usage Is Awkward

This is probably the main reason such debuggers didn't pick up as much traction as they could. Our typical debugging process is very iterative. We make changes, step over, inspect, and repeat. TTDs expect you to use them for every execution, then review the results after the fact. This is similar to the process of inspecting logs.

For most of us, this requires breaking deeply seeded development habits. The benefit is pretty big. We can run our tests with the back-in-time debugger and then review a flaky execution after the fact. A QA engineer can run with the debugger turned on and let us debug a specific failure after the fact. We no longer need to reproduce the issue on our machine.

But these use cases require a different way of looking at the code. We're also faced with the risk of impacting execution due to the usage of the debugger. Running with it "all the time" is a different kind of risk.

No One Ruled Them All

As I mentioned before, there are many time travel debugging tools. This is a problem. Borland and Microsoft popularized the modern-day IDE by creating the market-leading IDEs of their time. No equivalent market leader rose in this field.

Microsoft did publish their own TTD, but it's a low-level tool designed by system developers. In that sense, its scope is relatively limited; it's still very impressive as you can see in Figure 5-1. I do believe that as mainstream vendors promote these capabilities more aggressively, we'll see a major shift in the market. I don't think such debuggers will become the norm. But I do believe they are an amazing tool we should all wield on occasion.

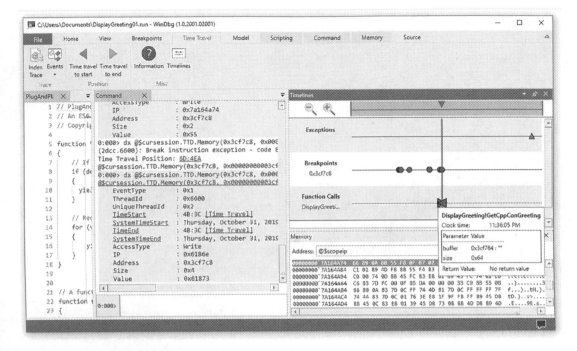

Figure 5-1. *Microsoft's time travel debugger*

The Different Types

The final problem is that we don't know what TTDs are. There are so many types of debuggers and many ways to use them. High-level languages such as JavaScript express very different problems and solutions within a TTD when compared to C or Rust. As a result, the surrounding tooling can be vastly different to the processes we're used to. Or it can be surprisingly familiar.

Some debuggers present the regular IDE debug interface combined with tools to go back and forth through "time" and threads. Others can express the data in charts and let you follow execution with sequence diagrams. The variety is significant.

Getting Started

The experience of getting started with most TTDs is a painful one. Unlike a regular debugger, we almost always perform the equivalent of remote debugging. As a result, we have at least two separate stages with a disconnect in between. Furthermore, most tools use low-level native calls and can pose issues when running on a different hardware or OS combination. I'm writing this on an M1 Mac (they use ARM instead of x86 chips), which is still relatively new at this time; quite a few tools don't work on my personal machine.

For example, the highly popular rr tool from Mozilla provides record and replay capabilities for native applications, but it's only available on Linux. The main reason for this is reliance on low-level system semantics and CPU architecture to capture state. To write this chapter, I went through over a dozen different tools that were mostly flaky or Linux only.

Frontend Debugging with Replay

In Figure 5-2, we see the Replay debugger view. This presents some of the very cool aspects of TTD, especially when dealing with UI bugs. At the bottom of the screen, you can see a timeline that you can drag to position execution at a specific point in time. On the top right, you can see the web UI at that time. This means we can scroll through the execution timeline to see everything that's going on – events, network requests, exception, etc. We can correlate all the operations with a full omnipotent view of the code and the application state.

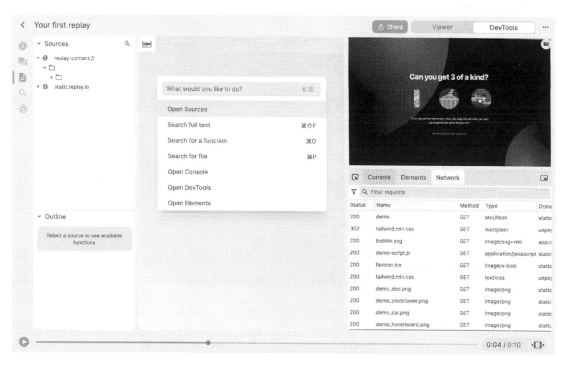

Figure 5-2. *Replay debugger view*

This illustrates a few of the benefits and problems of these tools. If a debugging session grows too long, the user experience quickly deteriorates. Finding the needle in the haystack becomes a far more challenging process. The benefit is obvious; we can never miss a thing.

It might seem that we're missing a staple of debugging: the venerable print statement. But this is not the case, as you can see in Figure 5-3. When we hover over a line in the source code, the tool indicates the number of times this line was reached in the execution (very useful information). We can then use a standard print statement that references variables, etc. This will get printed as we go back and forth in the timeline.

Figure 5-3. *Print debugging in Replay*

Notice those arrows next to the print entry. When a line was reached more than once, you can use them to toggle between the occurrences of this line. It will update the timeline and all the variables accordingly.

Low-Level Debugging with rr

The rr project was started by the Mozilla Foundation to support debugging tools like Firefox. It's a remarkably powerful tool for narrowing down hard-to-reproduce bugs. But it's a very low-level, spartan tool. We can install it on Linux by downloading a release from the git website[2] or building from source.

Once installed, we can record any binary application by prepending its execution with the `rr record` command. Notice that this will significantly impact the performance of your application. I recorded an execution of the spring boot pet clinic demo application using the following command:

```
rr record java -jar spring-petclinic-2.5.0-SNAPSHOT.jar
```

This in turn generated a recording which I could play back using the command `rr replay`. The replay process launches gdb, which isn't a time travel debugger. gdb is a low-level hacker-friendly debugger that works on the command line. Without a GUI, gdb is a very advanced debugger; personally, I don't feel productive in it because of its complexity. `rr` adds a few extra capabilities we don't normally have in gdb, specifically:

- Executing `run` again restarts the recording so you can cycle through the failure again and again. The breakpoints you set will remain and work as they did before.

- The `continue` command is standard in debuggers. It proceeds with execution as usual, until the next breakpoint is hit. With `rr`, we have `reverse-continue` which continues backward to the previous break-point hit.

- The `step` in gdb is equivalent to step into in most debuggers; next is like step over. With `rr`, we have the `reverse-step` and `reverse-next` commands.

There are a few other tricks available there, but my main point in this section is to give you a sense of `rr`. It's a relatively simple tool for a simple use case. You run into a bug in Firefox and don't know how to fix it? Just run it with `rr` and send the result as part of an issue attachment. The engineer at Mozilla would be able to debug it as if the debugger was running on your machine. This is spectacular, albeit somewhat spartan. There are some solutions for this such as Pernosco which lets you upload the recording directory and view the information using a convenient UI.

---

[2] https://github.com/rr-debugger/rr/

The main problem with `rr` is in virtualized environments. It can work in some virtualized environments but requires some control over the virtual machine. For example, this is a warning I got when running it on a virtual server:

```
rr: Warning: You appear to be running in a VMWare guest with a bug where
a conditional branch instruction between two CPUID instructions sometimes
fails to be counted by the conditional branch performance counter. Work
around this problem by adding monitor_control.disable_hvsim_clusters = true
to your .vmx file.
```

That's a problem for most cloud environments where we don't have access to the virtualization controls. This significantly limits the utility of this tool to Linux desktop machines. That's a shame, but it's understandable since inspection happens at a system level and requires deep access.

Summary

I wish I could write more about time travel debuggers. There are amazing tools out there such as Jive which shows UML (Unified Modeling Language) flow diagrams representing the execution of your Java application. Unfortunately, it's an academic tool whose utility is limited when running on real-world applications.

I left this chapter in because I think we should all know about these tools. As awareness of these amazing tools grows, we might see convergence and movement from the "big players." I also hope to see features of TTDs make their way into mainstream debuggers (similarly to the excellent IntelliJ/IDEA stream debugger discussed in Chapter 1). I think TTDs have a bright future ahead of them, and I hope this chapter will raise your curiosity enough to give them a chance.

With this, we conclude Part 1 of this book. In this part, we focused on the basic techniques and tools in local debugging. Part 2 is about scaling the problems of modern debugging. In Chapter 6, we'll jump ahead to debugging in Kubernetes and distributed systems. It's a huge and complex subject that's seeing more interest in the past few years thanks to the rise of cloud computing.

PART II

The Modern Production Environment

CHAPTER 6

Debugging Kubernetes

In programming, if someone tells you "you're overcomplicating it," they're either 10 steps behind you or 10 steps ahead of you.

—Andrew Clark

Despite the title of this chapter, a lot of the ideas explained here aren't unique to Kubernetes and can apply to all large-scale distributed systems. I have a popular talk on debugging Kubernetes applications. The talk assumes a lot of preexisting knowledge about Kubernetes basics, which is problematic. I don't want to force too much exposition into a 45-minute talk, but here I can cover some basic introduction and point you at some references you can use to build up from there. If you're familiar with Kubernetes, you might find the terminology I'm using is relatively basic and oversimplistic. The reason for that is that I don't want to explain tooling from the perspective of a DevOps engineer. I don't want to explain everything that is Kubernetes.

Most of the talks and articles I see on the subject are very DevOps oriented and assume the type of problems and approaches to solutions. While I think developers should learn DevOps processes, I don't think that should be a requirement. The focus of this chapter is on the angle of the programmer who wants to be effective in fixing application problems in production, without having to learn the tooling, concepts, and processes of DevOps. Notice the term "application problems" as opposed to configuration file problems, etc. These are problems we would typically face in the actual application source code.

Short Kubernetes Introduction

First, we need to make sure we're all on the same page regarding Kubernetes, its purpose, and roots.

© Shai Almog 2023
S. Almog, *Practical Debugging at Scale*, https://doi.org/10.1007/978-1-4842-9042-2_6

History

In the "old days" when we wanted to deploy a complex application in production, we had to put a machine somewhere. Developers would either physically set it up or telnet into it (this predated widespread use of SSH). We'd set everything up and it was all good, until we had to do that again on another site. For that, we built complex installation scripts that would often fail because of dependencies, versions, etc. It also made it very difficult to deal with elaborate settings and manage the resource.

Virtualization solved that by creating a virtual machine replicating the x86 OS environment. We could just boot up a ò"ake machine" and then set it up in the comfort of our office. Then we copy the image file to deploy it everywhere. Virtualization lets Amazon, Google, Microsoft, etc., sell space on their cloud servers. Thanks to virtualization, we have a guarantee that my app won't collide with one from a different developer. It's amazing, but it still has two drawbacks:

- The overhead of virtualization is significant.

- Each virtualization vendor had their own standard. If I built an image using one virtualization server, it might not work on another.

Containers solved both problems. They used some kernel capabilities to isolate the current running code. This meant it wasn't fully virtualized on the machine, but ò"elt" like a separate machine in most ways that matter (to learn more, check out namespaces and cgroups on Linux). A container can run on top of a virtual machine without adding much overhead. The second part was the standardization of a container format by Docker. It gained traction and made it very easy to move container images around.

This let developers package an entire application as an image, but it also raised a problem. Say I have an image of my application and it depends on an image of a database. That works perfectly well, but it isn't the end of it. We need a caching server and an authentication server, and we want to scale; so, we need monitoring, observability, etc. We might move to a microservice architecture where we have many servers. That's the beauty of containers; they make image creation trivial. Because of that, we create many images.

Containers enable massive scale. They have very little overhead,[1] but we can further reduce this by creating containers that don't include the full operating system (distroless,

---

[1] https://dominoweb.draco.res.ibm.com/reports/rc25482.pdf

bare). This sounds like nitpicking in the age of massive storage/RAM. But an OS image with everything can have a massive impact when scaled. By reducing this overhead, we can fit more containers on the same hardware and reduce our costs considerably.

There are a few things containers don't cover though: dynamic, failover, updates, scale, etc. These are solutions that sit above the container runtime. They make sure the service isn't down or overloaded and can dynamically provision additional resources.

Enter Kubernetes

How do we deal with these containers and the dynamic nature of deployment? The solution is orchestration; Kubernetes (a.k.a. k8s[2]) is an orchestration solution. Container orchestration essentially moves you from ò"ost-centric" to ò"ontainer-centric" infrastructure. It lets you define all the different parts of your deployment, including where you want it to scale, how you want it to scale, etc. Figure 6-1 shows the winding road to scaling with Kubernetes.

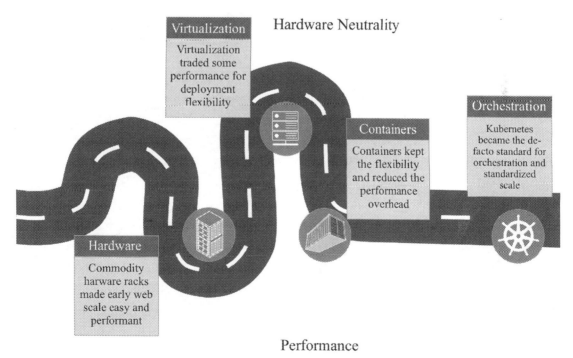

Figure 6-1. *The road to scale*

---

[2] Due to the eight letters between the K and the S in Kubernetes.

The problem is it isn't magic. For Kubernetes to work properly, everything needs to be set up correctly. Let's imagine I logged in to a container and changed its state while we're running. A good example would be adding a configuration option. If this fails and Kubernetes needs to replace the container (or scale it up), we might run into serious problems. As you might surmise, this makes debugging Kubernetes harder as we discuss as follows.

Check out Figure 6-2 to understand a small part of the responsibilities and positioning of Kubernetes. Kubernetes is massive! Developers only focus on the small area marked as ò"*your code*" within Figure 6-2. Consider that this is a deeply simplified view of the overall structure of a Kubernetes deployment.

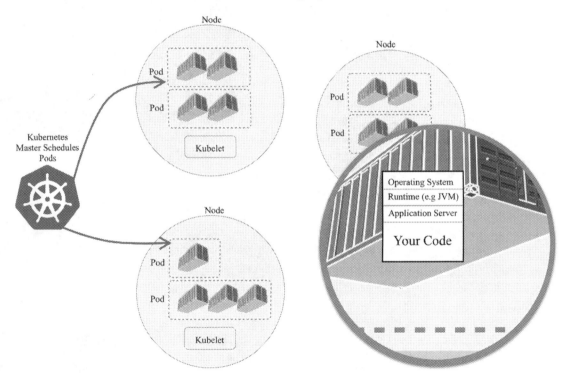

Figure 6-2. *Simplified view of Kubernetes deployment*

My goal isn't a ò"et started" tutorial. There are better resources[3] for that. There are also many tools with which we can use Kubernetes effectively. I won't discuss the process of setting up a Kubernetes cluster, minikube, etc. But I will discuss some

---

[3] For example, `https://blog.gruntwork.io/the-docker-kubernetes-terraform-and-aws-crash-course-series-dca343ba1274`

commands with the assumption that you already have things running. The first step would be listing the pods (pods are the Kubernetes units of work; we'll discuss them further soon).

```
$ kubectl get pods
NAME                      READY   STATUS    RESTARTS   AGE
  my-first-pod-id-xxxx    1/1     Running   0          13s
  my-second-pod-id-xxxx   1/1     Running   0          13s
```

We can use commands like `kubectl describe pod` to get information about the pod and general details. Sometimes, this would be enough to understand what's going on, but only if we've got a configuration problem.

An important command when working with Kubernetes locally is `kubectl logs`. It lets us list logs for a specific container and even for a crashed container with `--previous`. But why is it only important locally?

Typically, in production your logs would be ingested and piped to remote storage. In that case, the fact that you're using Kubernetes becomes irrelevant. You should be able to see the logs for all containers in the cloud. There are special cases, but for the most part container logs aren't as interesting in day-to-day production debugging. This assumes that you ingest logs (which you should) and that you are a developer. There is the case of the system logs which is important, but this book is aimed at developers who would typically be the second line of defense for these types of error messages. If a container crashes because of configuration or a system-level failure, then it requires a different skill set to track. I will cover some of those common things in this chapter, but very briefly.

It's Not Just About Scale

I want to stop for a second and revisit the core concept of "why we need Kubernetes." As one website[4] put it quite correctly, we probably don't. Most of us don't need the type of scale Kubernetes offers, and the overhead is often not worth the extra cost. Many problems can be solved with a single VPS (Virtual Private Server – typically built on top of a virtualization solution); Kubernetes makes simple solutions much harder.

This is true. There's no question that many Kubernetes adopters are suffering from RDD (Resume-Driven Development) and are picking it up to bolster their CVs – not

---

[4] https://doyouneedkubernetes.com/

due to business needs. But there are some advantages that go beyond scaling that make Kubernetes an attractive deployment option for many cases, even where scale isn't a problem.

The pod vs. container abstraction is powerful. It lets us focus on building our application in a container while ignoring the external elements. In a case where we need to provision a container with access to a caching API, we can ignore the caching requirement in the code and spin up a container. We need a remote database server, ignore that requirement too, and spin a pod containing the database server. The database server needs to scale too; that's a separate problem, and we can easily deal with it later without changing a single line of code. This is powerful stuff. It lets us treat applications and their surrounding requirements as if they were Lego bricks with which we can assemble a custom architecture to fit our deployment.

This means we can punt on multiple complexities and choose simplified, prepackaged solutions for all these things. Then update or replace them relatively easily because every piece is modular. Observability servers can be placed in the same pod as a separate container. This means they'll be physically near our application but will still have a strong separation. We don't need to concern ourselves with the needs of observability during the development process.

This value proposition is compounded by the massive third-party ecosystem that sprung around Kubernetes and the Cloud Native Computing Foundation (CNCF).[5] This ecosystem lets us integrate solutions and monitor and leverage infrastructure like never before.

In our industry, being "cloud neutral" is somewhat of an "inside joke." Vendors keep promising it but deliver only partial solutions. Companies that start completely neutral slowly bind themselves to a single vendor because costs such as egress are too steep. Kubernetes isn't vendor neutral, especially if you use vendor support for it. But it's a piece of the puzzle that lets you encapsulate individual problems. Those can be fixed individually and addressed moving forward.

The Problem with Kubernetes

Before we reach the debugger and go through the entire process, we need to understand the core problem. A core idea in Kubernetes is that one shouldn't modify container

---

[5] www.cncf.io/

instances. If you do that, you might cause issues as Kubernetes brings up new instances. You can log in to a container running in the given pod using kubectl exec, which gives us a prompt as if we're logged in to a physical machine, for example:

```
kubectl -- exec -ti pod-name
```

The first problem we run into with the kubectl exec command is that we're running without basic tools. No vim, no traceroute, no basic capabilities. If you're used to running Linux (or Unix) commands to understand what went wrong in the environment, you will be sorely disappointed. Worse, some container images have nothing installed, not even a shell (barebone, distroless images). We would have no way to work with such a container. If the container crashes, we can't log in to it, but we'd still want to examine the last state of the container. Exec doesn't solve these core problems.

When the container has apt or apk and when the pod isn't crashed, we could theoretically just invoke apt get install vim. But this violates the principle of keeping the containers unmodified. We don't want people in production installing packages left and right. Even if it's cleaned up, the risks are sometimes too high. Pods shouldn't be touched in production once deployed. We should describe all the information and state of a pod in its manifest. The problem might not seem too bad, but an installation might trigger dependencies which might cause application failures in unpredictable ways.

Ephemeral Containers

The solution to these problems is ephemeral[6] containers. Kubernetes has a higher abstraction on top of containers called pods. Pods group together related containers, and they have unique access to one another. Ephemeral containers are added to the same pod as the container you're trying to debug, but they are temporary and separate. What you do in them doesn't impact the overall application. You don't need to restart anything, and you can still get special access to the container.

There are many ways to create such a container, but the most powerful is probably with kubectl debug. Initially, it seems to work similarly to the exec command, but that's misleading. It creates a separate ephemeral container in the same namespace as the container you're trying to debug. As a result, we have a separate image which can run a completely separate version of the OS. It can reside in the same namespace, so we have

[6] Wikipedia defines Ephemerality as (from the Greek word ἐφήμερος, meaning "lasting only one day") the concept of things being transitory, existing only briefly.

access to the same processes. The container's root filesystem is mounted to the /root directory, and we have access to everything. When we run something like

```
kubectl debug myapp -it --image=ubuntu --share-processes --copy-
to=myapp-debug
```

we're not connecting to our container. We're creating a new container from the given ubuntu base image. This is an ephemeral container, and it will disappear when the pod is destroyed. In it, we can check things about the actual container of interest. We can use an arbitrary image for that container. This means that if the original container crashes, our ephemeral container will still work and can still inspect it. If it has no shell, we can still log in to our debug container where we have an entire OS. We can install arbitrary tools on the fly since they won't impact the debugged container, and we can use them to debug. It's very cool!

My team at Lightrun created an open source project called KoolKits,[7] which makes the process even smoother. It's a set of images for kubectl debug that are programming runtime specific, currently for Go, Java, Python, and Node. Most of us need roughly the same set of tools when we debug projects. KoolKits is the ò"itchen sink" containing the entire set of everything we all need. No need to seek out packages every time you want to check for a minor issue. I can improve the preceding command for Java developers by using

```
kubectl debug myapp -it --image=koolkits-jvm --share-processes --copy-
to=myapp-debug
```

After running that, I'll have access to a dizzying list of JVM-related tools and many other general-purpose tools right on the command line. I reviewed some of these tools when talking about external debugging tools in Chapter 3. I would recommend checking out KoolKits and submitting a PR[8] if your favorite tool is missing.

Source Debugging

Debugging using the tools we described up until now is great. We can solve many problems using these tools. But they are not debuggers; solving problems deep within

---

[7] https://github.com/lightrun-platform/koolkits/
[8] https://github.com/lightrun-platform/koolkits/

the code is hard without debuggers. The best approach is to reproduce the problem without Kubernetes and outside of production, but in some cases, this just isn't an option.

Using jdb

For these cases, we need a "proper" debugger. But since we're remote, this can be a challenge. With kubectl debug, we can connect to the container and run a regular command-line debugger. I've been a Java programmer since its first beta, and I never used jdb (Java Debugger). jdb is a command-line debug interface for Java; essentially, it's the equivalent of gdb. The process of doing this is simple. First, we need to kill the process and relaunch it with debugging turned on using a command like

```
java "-agenlib:jdwp=transport=dt_socket,server=y,suspend=y,address=*:5005"
-jar MyApplication.jar
```

The whole area in quotes is mostly boilerplate for keeping the process ready for a debugger connection. Once we run the project, we can use JDB to connect to it using the following commands (assuming the process is running as process ID 666):

```
$ jdb -connect com.sun.jdi.ProcessAttach:pid=666
> stop at MyClass:66
Set breakpoint MyClass:66
>
Breakpoint hit:  "thread=main", MyClass.myMethod(), line=66 bci=30
66                    field++;
main[1] step
>
Step completed: "thread=main", MyClass.myMethod(), line=65 bci=38
65                    for(int iter = 0 ; iter < calcSize() ; iter++) {
```

Let's go over what we did here. The jdb command launches the command-line debugger and attaches to the specific process ID. I'm then faced with a prompt, the > character. At the prompt, I issue the stop command and give it a class name followed by a line of code. This is equivalent to setting a line breakpoint.

The breakpoint is hit, at which point I can issue a step command. This isn't hard, but it's very tedious when compared to the experience in the IDE.

Remote Debugging

It might seem like we took too long to reach the obvious ò"unchline," but we didn't.
I needed to go through all of that to explain some of the core problems in remote
debugging. Remote debugging works very similarly to our `jdb` process from the previous
section.

Basics

Remote debugging is a feature of pretty much any programming language or platform,
but it's common in Java using the JDWP (Java Debug Wire Protocol), which I'll discuss
soon. It's a wire-agnostic protocol that defines the connection between the IDE and the
JVM when debugging.

Notice that the real value proposition of remote debugging is on local and not on
a remote machine. The value is in connecting to a running process that's outside of
our development environment. It's great for connecting to a container running on our
machine. I'll elaborate on this later in the chapter.

The `java` command we used to launch the preceding application will work almost
perfectly for remote debugging if you're running on a local machine without Kubernetes.
For Kubernetes, it will fail. Kubernetes masks the networking ports by default. This lets
us run servers that listen to network connections on the same port within the same
machine, and they won't collide with one another. In order to broadcast the port to
external connectors, we need to expose that port; this is done via the manifest.

Don't touch that manifest! We don't expose JDWP to the external world; this is
a huge security vulnerability (more on that later). The trick we used to do in the days
before Kubernetes is SSH tunneling using a command like this on your local machine:

```
ssh remoteUser@remoteHost -L 5005:127.0.0.1:5005 -N
```

This command links the port on the remote machine to the local machine. That
means that port 5005 on `localhost` will map to port 5005 on the remote host. I would be
able to debug the remote machine as if I'm working on a process running locally, and the
server won't expose any port. All traffic will be encrypted over SSH!

This won't work on Kubernetes, though. For that, we will need to port forward using
a slightly different command with the same impact:

```
kubectl port-forward podname 5005:5005
```

Once we have that, we can connect our IDE to the remote server as if the code was running on our local machine. In IntelliJ/IDEA, all I need to do is open the Run/Debug configuration and add a "Remote JVM Debug" entry. The defaults should work as expected since it will point to the `localhost` on port 5005 as you can see in Figure 6-3.

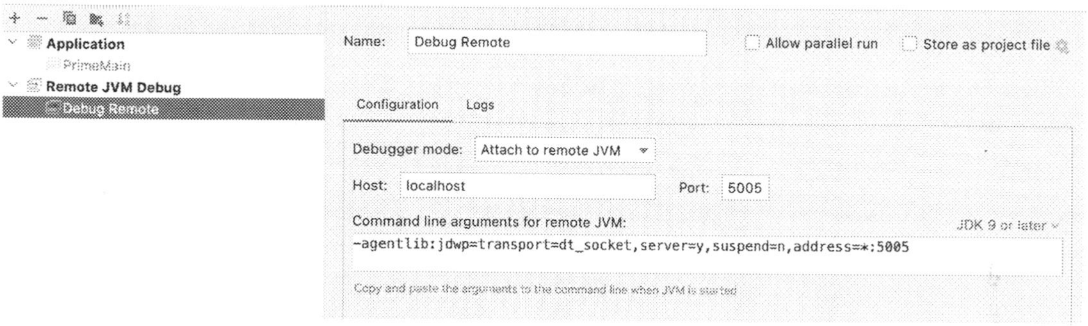

Figure 6-3. *Remote debugging run configuration in IntelliJ/IDEA*

VS Code uses a JSON-based configuration, which is slightly more manual, but the concept is the same. We need to add a remote debugging configuration and provide the port as follows:

```
{
    "type": "java",
    "name": "Debug (Attach)",
    "request": "launch",
    "mainClass": "MyClass",
    "projectName": "MyProjectName",
    "request": "attach",
    "hostName": "localhost",
    "port": 5005
}
```

Once set, we can run this configuration and start debugging as if the application is completely local to the IDE. Everything should work as if it's local. Breakpoints, tracepoints, exception filters, and most of the stuff we covered in Chapter 1 should work seamlessly. That sounds too good to be true, right? It is…

The Problems with JDWP

When I lecture and raise a point related to security, I often use the analogy of an onion. This is a common cliché, yet it's still a powerful analogy for people who are new to the concept. The equivalent analogy I would pick for remote debugging is like leaving your front door open with all your valuables piled in easy-to-spot and well-labeled boxes. Calling JDWP insecure doesn't make sense. It wasn't designed to be secure; it isn't. It's a wide-open door and an open invitation.

JDWP was designed for testing internally. Over the past few years, I've run into quite a few individuals that made the mistake of leaving it on even in production! Even internally, it's a major risk with 60% of breaches originating from inside the organization.[9] This isn't just a security risk that could essentially give every hacker the "keys" to your server and full access to your server code. It's also a serious stability hazard that could easily crash your production servers.

I write about JDWP since I'm deeply familiar with the protocol. But don't think that these problems are unique to JDWP. Remote debugging protocols weren't designed with security in mind and are inherently insecure as a rule. Most remote debugging protocols are a product of a different era – an era that gave us telnet and HTTP. Most aren't even encrypted by default. Just leaving JDWP enabled warrants a CVE[10] (Common Vulnerabilities and Exposures).

JDWP allows remote code execution. It lets you access all the bytecode of the server which is almost the same as giving access to your full server source code. It lets attackers do almost anything since it wasn't designed with security in mind. It enables man-in-the-middle attacks and so much more.

Third-party attacks can be mitigated with SSH tunneling or port forwarding. But the weaknesses are still there; they're just harder to reach. Vulnerabilities are still exposed to malicious users who have access. It's also possible to leverage a different exploit to reach a point where access to the wire protocol will be exposed.

Security isn't the only problem. JDWP isn't an atomic protocol and doesn't include protections. A small mistake by the developer, such as defining a watch that's CPU intensive, can bring down the system. Operations are often multipart, requiring client-server back and forth. Failure in the middle of these operations can leave the system hanging in an invalid state.

---

[9] www.idwatchdog.com/insider-threats-and-data-breaches/
[10] https://nvd.nist.gov/vuln/detail/CVE-2018-5486

Legal and Privacy Issues

Modern security is far more nuanced than mere "hacking." GDPR (General Data Protection Regulation) is an EU regulation that places restrictions on the type of data companies can collect and expose. Whether you agree with it or not, it's significant legislation that has had wide-ranging impact on the field. Additional laws and regulations went even further. The result is a significant motion of the security goalposts to encapsulate privacy.

Imagine stopping at a breakpoint in the login code of the application where you can inspect the username and password or adding a tracepoint to the code that saves credit card numbers. These don't matter when debugging on staging, but in production you can do serious damage. If another employee takes advantage of such an opening, the company and developers might be liable for negligence.

Breakpoints Break

Imagine a user stuck on a breakpoint waiting for a response while you're in the IDE over a slow network connection. IDEs weren't designed for that. You can use tracepoints which I discussed before, but then you lose out on all the richness the breakpoint delivers. Adding a tracepoint requires CTRL-clicking the IDE or picking a different mode. Adding a breakpoint by mistake is a very feasible mistake. Since breakpoints suspend all threads by default, this can be terrible.

Scale: Breadth and Depth

Debuggers were designed to work on a single process. Kubernetes was designed as the exact opposite of that, and the load balancer might send the request you're trying to grab to a completely different container. A debugger can help with depth; assuming you can stop at a breakpoint (which you can't), you can gain deep insight into the code.

But you can't follow through different servers. In theory, you can connect to more than one container from a debugger. But keeping track of multiple concurrent debuggers isn't tenable. The solution to all of these is developer observability, which we will discuss in Chapter 10.

Configuration Troubleshooting

I know I said I wanted to focus on the developer side rather than on the ops side. Still, we need to understand issues with target containers and what OPS are dealing with every day. If you're lucky enough to have a DevOps engineer on staff, then you probably don't need to know a lot of the problems we discuss here. I think it's still worthwhile to build some basic knowledge about the problems we can run into with Kubernetes configurations since there's a lot of overlap. The line where the roles end is blurry, and we need to venture into each other's realms to understand some issues.

Typically, we would see most configuration issues in the status column when issuing the `kubectl get pods` command. Here are some common errors you might run into and a brief explanation on how you can resolve them.

CrashLoopBackOff

This is a general-purpose issue with several causes. You will need to get further details by using `kubectl describe pod pod-name` and inspecting the output. A common failure is insufficient resources, which might mean you need to scale up the cluster to fit additional nodes. Volume mounting can fail if the storage is defined incorrectly for the pod.

Image Error

Errors that mention the word image such as `ErrImagePull` or `ImagePullBackOff` typically mean a container fetch failed. One container in the configuration file can't be fetched. Check that docker pull works with the image name to make sure we typed it correctly and that there aren't any ò"nvalid characters" somewhere. Some failures in docker pull (and here) can occur because of problematic credentials, secrets, or authorization.

Node Not Ready

This often means there was a physical issue with a node host. You can see this issue by invoking the `kubectl get nodes` command and inspecting the nodes. A reboot of the problematic machine or VM might solve the issue in some cases, and Kubernetes should ò"elf-heal" within five minutes.

CreateContainerConfigError

We get this error due to missing configuration keys or secrets. Kubernetes supports a config map which lets us define values such as a database host. A secret is an API key or similar value which we don't want to place in version control or expose. It's important to separate that information outside the YAML or IaC files so we can change it later and for security purposes (in the case of secrets).

The problem is that because of that separation we can end up with missing information since the actual configuration process requires a config map. You should use `kubectl describe pod pod-name` to get further information about the problem.

Debugging the Dockerfile

A relatively new addition to the configuration troubleshooting process is *buildg*.[11] Buildg is an interactive debugger for docker configuration that lets us run a configuration file while stepping over the stages. We can set breakpoints like we can with any debugger. It integrates nicely with *VS Code* and other IDEs through the Debug Adapter Protocol (DAP).

While stepping over, we can inspect the state of the container to see the impact of the previous line. As of this writing, this is a very new tool.

Summary

The problems we face when debugging Kubernetes are the same ones we faced when debugging most large-scale systems. The success of Kubernetes is both a blessing and a curse. It made scaling remarkably easy, and as a result, we scale a lot faster than we used to. We run into scale-related problems earlier when we might not be prepared for them and might not have the infrastructure to deal with such complexities.

Tools haven't caught up to this scale as fast as they should. The developer observability tooling is the only realistic contender for production debugging in this scenario. With the complexity of debugging as illustrated earlier, I would also use it for staging. `kubectl debug` and KoolKits go a long way to making the process of diagnosis easy. In that regard, Kubernetes made a huge leap forward as it lets us review a crashed

---

[11] https://github.com/ktock/buildg

or even distroless container. This is a tremendous achievement. But it mostly applies to those of us with greater DevOps inclinations. Remote debugging is a tremendous tool for digging into source-related issues, but it has many pitfalls and limitations.

In the next chapter, we'll discuss serverless debugging and dealing with that unique environment. Both chapters discuss the problem of heterogeneous polyglot distributed systems at scale. With Kubernetes, we maintain some control at the expense of more administrative overhead. With serverless we give up control for lower administration complexity. One of the costs is fewer tools for debugging such deployments.

CHAPTER 7

Serverless Debugging

Only when the tide goes out do you discover who's been swimming naked.

—Warren Buffett

Like many things in software, the benefits of serverless (or Platform as a Service) are great. We can ignore infrastructure complexities and focus on code. Scaling becomes seamless and, when compared to some alternatives, affordable. Performance is also great under the right conditions. Here's where engineers expect the other shoe; what's the downside?

The downsides are many. Costs are hard to control and can unexpectedly run amok. Performance is sometimes hard to navigate in a decoupled architecture. But to me the worst offender is the process of debugging. It facilitated a culture of debugging in production using logs. Serverless deployments are so complex and nuanced; they grow to a point where local debugging becomes untenable. Best practices such as a dev or staging environment become completely disconnected from production. This chapter doesn't provide a magic bullet; this inherent problem of debugging in serverless isn't easy to solve. I recommend developers use serverless as we use duct tape. Serverless is great at solving things but not at serving as an architecture on which to build your software, at least not at the moment.

Basics

Serverless isn't a single standard – far from it. There are many competing vendor-specific tools and various levels of abstractions. Every tool has a very different process, and despite multiple attempts, we don't have successful standardization. The upside is that most frameworks are similar.

© Shai Almog 2023
S. Almog, *Practical Debugging at Scale*, https://doi.org/10.1007/978-1-4842-9042-2_7

In this chapter, I will focus on AWS Lambda, which is popular and supports multiple languages, including Java. Most of the concepts that apply here would apply to other serverless frameworks as well.

Serverless debugging could be viewed as an oxymoron. It's a managed, deeply controlled, and disconnected environment. We don't have most of the typical debugging tools at our disposal. The distributed and controlled nature of the environment essentially blocks any chance of remote debugging. The external tools we discussed in Chapter 3 are out of the question. The problems of concurrency and scale can be very extreme in the world of serverless. To make matters worse, subtle changes in the underlying platform can cause sudden failures.

Serverless deployments tend to be fail-safe, for the most part. This approach can create cascading failures that balloon into serious cost issues. This can be financially hazardous. In this chapter, we'll discuss the following debugging strategies when dealing with a serverless problem:

- Local debugging

- Feature flags

- Staged rollouts and Canaries

Eagle-eyed readers will notice I skipped a couple of things. Logging is one of the most common tools when debugging serverless deployments, for example, with tools such as CloudWatch. Since we covered logging in Chapter 4, I omitted it from the list. The same is true for tracing and observability, both of which I will cover in Chapter 9. I will also cover developer observability in Chapter 10, which is one of the most powerful tools for serverless debugging.

Because of these complexities, testing is a remarkably important feature of serverless code. I suggest reviewing the discussion in Chapter 4 about unit testing and working on test coverage. For serverless, this is often the best option.

Logging is pretty much the only option advocated by most serverless users. Logging has many benefits and many faults. To me, the biggest fault is the storage and CPU. With serverless deployments, we pay for CPU time, and logging slows down execution and brings up the price we ultimately pay. The problem of overlogging that I discussed before is compounded when running in a serverless environment. Still, there's not much else we can do!

Idempotency

One of the ways serverless providers have evolved over PaaS is through the adoption of functional programming concepts. An important one is idempotency, which is a concept rooted in mathematics, meaning a function will have the same results if we pass in the same values.

This seems obvious. If we have a function called add to which we pass the values 2 and 3, the result should always be 5. At first, when you hear about this concept, it seems that this is the way our code works. But it isn't always the case. If your function relies on an external web service, the result might change; at that point, it will no longer be idempotent. A good example would be if the add function would handle currencies and then would return a different currency (e.g., adds Euro and returns USD). In that case, the result would fluctuate with currency conversion changes. But there's a simple solution: accept a timestamp. By requiring a timestamp for the currency value, we can force consistency in the results.

This is functional programming 101, but it's also good programming practice in general. It makes debugging and testing serverless functions easier. We can rely on consistent, verifiable results. A log that will include the input should (in theory) match the output. Then once we have the logs, we should be able to reproduce any problem.

Staging and Dev

A common best practice in development is using a separate environment; this is useful for testing. We would usually have a dev environment into which nightly builds are uploaded and staging, which is a step before production. These environments let us test that our application is working correctly in a pseudo-production environment without the risk.

These environments are one of the chief advantages of using Kubernetes. Setting up mirrors of the production environment becomes trivial, especially when using IaC (Infrastructure as Code) such as Terraform. With serverless deployments, this isn't as trivial, and because of the nuances involved, it's very hard to get these environments in sync.

The main challenge is maintaining consistent environments. A typical deployment is complex; it can include multiple dependencies and endpoints. IaC can help with this process as well. Unfortunately, this raises the complexity level which reduces some of the benefits in adopting a serverless architecture.

Local Debugging

Simpler web services can be debugged locally. It's still unpleasant and not nearly as helpful. To get started, we need the following tools and accounts:

- Docker desktop/Docker[1]

- AWS account[2]

- AWS SAM CLI[3]

I'll skip the process of creating and deploying a hello world application.[4] To follow through with this process, you can see the AWS Hello World tutorial.[5] We can run the hello world application using the `sam` command line:

```
sam local start-api
```

Once we do that, we can trigger the endpoint using a `curl` command:

```
$ curl http://127.0.0.1:3000/hello
{ "message": "hello world", "location": "212.143.164.185" }
```

This is already a valuable outcome. We can run tests locally and perform basic trial and error experiments. But this isn't debugging. To debug, we need to run the application using this command:

```
sam local start-api -d 5005 --debug
```

Once launched in this way, the application is paused. We can invoke `curl`, but it won't do anything. The debug mode waits for a debugger to connect before proceeding. To do that, we need to connect using remote debugging to the local host as explained in the previous chapter. We can add the run configuration in the IDE matching remote

---

[1] See this for instructions: https://docs.docker.com/get-docker/

[2] See http://aws.amazon.com/premiumsupport/knowledge-center/create-and-activate-aws-account/

[3] See https://docs.aws.amazon.com/serverless-application-model/latest/developerguide/serverless-sam-cli-install.html

[4] You can see the full project here: https://github.com/shai-almog/HelloLambda

[5] https://docs.aws.amazon.com/serverless-application-model/latest/developerguide/serverless-getting-started-hello-world.html

debugging to the localhost as seen in Figure 7-1. We can then debug in the IDE as shown in Figure 7-2.

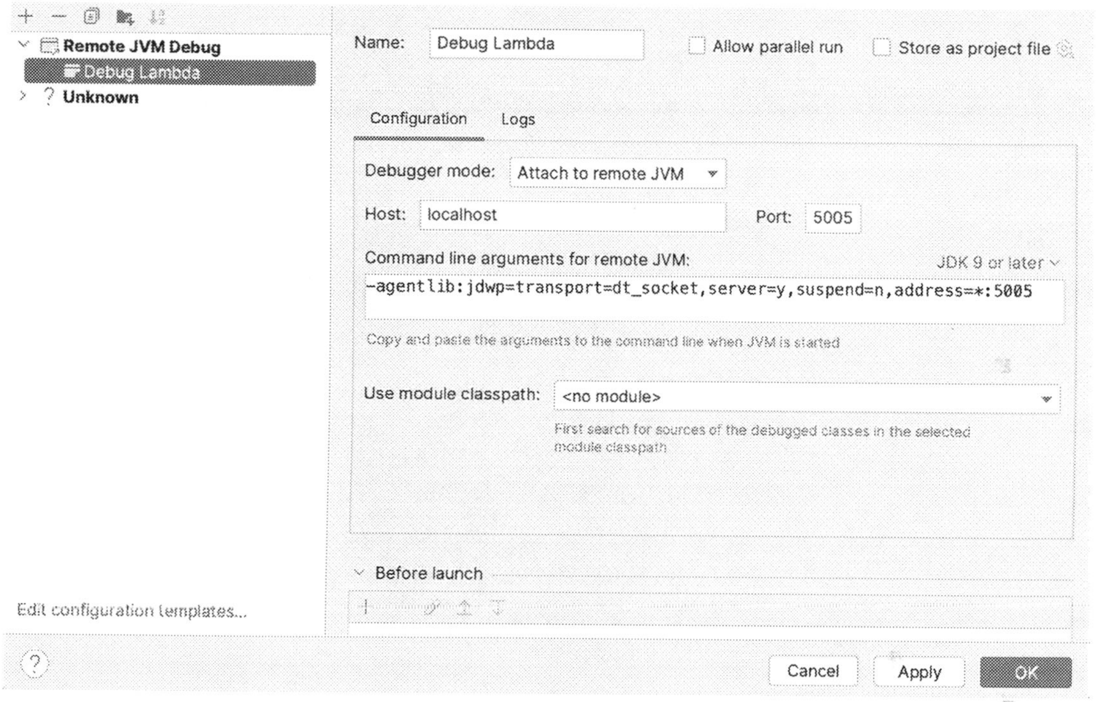

Figure 7-1. *IntelliJ/IDEA run configuration remote debug settings*

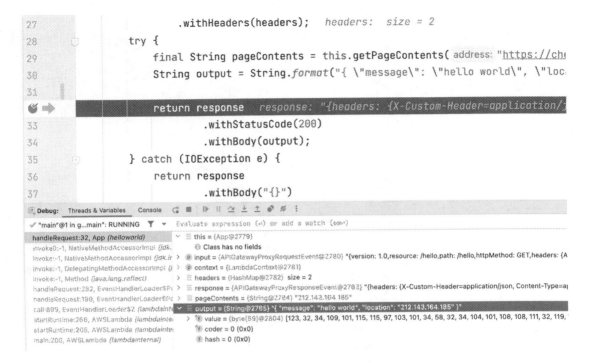

Figure 7-2. *Debugging a serverless Lambda function in IntelliJ/IDEA*

Once connected, the `curl` command will execute, and the debugger will exit. If you have a breakpoint set before running the debugger, it will stop at the breakpoint and will let you step over it. But there's a serious caveat. The debugger times out very quickly. This is a terrible user experience because a Lambda is designed to run quickly and succeed or fail. If it takes too long, the cost will be prohibitive. That's why Lambdas have a very short timeout; you can configure this in the `template.yaml` file. Notice the `Timeout` property, which is a value in seconds. For this to take effect, you will need to re-issue the `sam build` command:

```
Resources:
  HelloWorldFunction:
    Type: AWS::Serverless::Function # More info about Function Resource:
https://github.com/awslabs/serverless-application-model/blob/master/
versions/2016-10-31.md#awsserverlessfunction
    Properties:
      Timeout: 10
      CodeUri: HelloWorldFunction
```

This might still not be enough, and we might need to simulate running on the actual AWS stack. For this, we will need a solution such as SST[6] or MerLoc.[7] Since those are specific to AWS and relatively niche, I won't cover them here.

Feature Flags

Feature flags aren't specifically related to serverless debugging. I would recommend picking them up for a monolith too, perhaps even more so. I'm discussing them here since they are a great tool for lowering the risk of testing in production. In a serverless environment, these are one of the chief mitigating capabilities.

With feature flags, we can dynamically enable or disable a feature. We can include it for a specific subset of our users or only for testing. This lets the general population work with code that was previously working. When adding a new feature, we can wrap the risky code in a check:

```
if(featureFlags.isActive(FeatureList.FEATURE)) {
    // invoke feature-related code
}
```

Thanks to checks like this, we can dynamically check functionality in production and instantly revert a feature if it causes a regression. The core functionality of a feature flag is trivial; it can be something as simple as a lookup file or a database table. But that might not scale in a serverless or microservice environment where constraints might be more complex.

Some feature flag tools support segmentation of users, which you can use to enable a feature only for beta testers and not the general population. This gets very complicated, especially when a feature crosses tiers. A great example is a feature that requires changes in multiple serverless environments and in client-side code. All the pieces might take a while to deploy separately; a feature flag can keep the feature hidden until all the pieces are deployed. Once deployed, we can enable the feature for testers, and it will activate on the client-side code as well as all the server logic.

---

[6]https://sst.dev/examples/how-to-debug-lambda-functions-with-visual-studio-code.html

[7]https://github.com/thundra-io/merloc

A less naïve version of the preceding feature flag code would pass more details to the API so we can segment appropriately. This is what the LaunchDarkly SaaS feature flag platform does:

```
LDUser user = new LDUser.Builder(userId)
  .name(user.getDisplayName())
  .build();
if (client.boolVariation(FEATURE_FLAG_KEY, user, false)) {
  // feature is on
}
```

We can pass additional metadata to decide on the feature. Notice that data is cached locally, but it's also invalidated in case of changes from the server.

Staged Rollouts and Canaries

When releasing a serverless feature to production, we can stage the rollout so a failure would be detectable. We can determine the percentage of requests that will receive the new code in Lambda. We can also use a Canary – a segment that will receive the new code, for example, a specific country only. This isn't ideal; we don't want an entire country to receive a failure. But it's better than a failure for all the users of the application.

Sophisticated deployments such as these can be accomplished via an API gateway or via the serverless platform itself.

Summary

Debugging serverless is a painful experience. Thankfully, there's a better way, which I didn't discuss here. It's through developer observability tools that I will cover in depth in Chapter 10. Chapter 9 covering observability tools should be interesting as well.

Even with these solutions in place, the process of debugging serverless deployments is painful. It's a regression and a serious throwback. It's the main reason I'm not a big fan of serverless deployments. When something fails, it can fail badly. A company can lose a significant amount of money due to a resource hogging bug. In fact, such a thing happened to me in the days of PaaS, and I was stuck in a situation where I had no way to debug the problem. To this day, I don't know which of my workarounds succeeded. I couldn't log properly since this would have increased our costs even further. It was a problematic environment, and I was debugging in the dark.

Serverless improved on PaaS by focusing on small pieces that can vanish instantly. This works well as duct tape for bringing together separate services. I think that's a good analogy to stretch for debugging. We love working with duct tape to solve things, but it isn't something we can fix or inspect.

In the next chapter, we will talk about the deeper side of debugging, going fullstack from the client side to the backend. We will review client-side bugs and the process of following them through, whether they're a symptom or the full expression of the bug.

CHAPTER 8

Fullstack Debugging

The most fundamental problem in software development is complexity.
There is only one basic way of dealing with complexity: divide and conquer.

—Bjarne Stroustrup

The definition of fullstack is shifting like quicksand to match whatever the observer considers to be the stack. I've seen some definitions that include OPS aspects into the mix. A more common definition follows the process of writing both the frontend and the backend.

I define fullstack as a process of submitting a pull request that covers all the parts required to implement a feature, backend, database, frontend, and configuration. It doesn't make us an expert in all of these, far from it. It means we work on a vertical feature and enter domains where our knowledge is cursory. This is good when we have a reviewer who is a domain expert and can guide us through the pitfalls of the domain.

Fullstack debugging works in a similar way. A symptom would usually display in the frontend in some way, and we would need to track it through the layers. Ideally, we would want to isolate it as quickly as possible. Isolating the issue isn't a simple task. In this chapter, we'll talk about debugging tricks for the web frontend, how to track an issue through the layers, and the type of issues we often run into.

Fullstack debugging is also about debugging the surrounding environment. A few years ago, we were experiencing production problems where a WebSocket connection would disconnect frequently. This only happened in production, and we couldn't find the reason. Eventually, my colleague Steve Hannah found out that our CDN (Cloudflare) was timing out the WebSocket after two minutes. It's hard to discover an issue like that without debugging a complete system.

© Shai Almog 2023
S. Almog, *Practical Debugging at Scale*, https://doi.org/10.1007/978-1-4842-9042-2_8

Frontend Debugging

Frontend developers have an aversion to debugging tools. A common meme among frontend developers is that `console.log` is the only debugging tool they need. CSS developers have similar memes covering setting the background of elements to red. This is understandable; the frontend is normally very localized. The frontend debugging tools are different and complex. In the past, the frontend was much simpler, and its complexity didn't justify tooling. Obfuscation made tools hard to use, and dependencies made debugging challenging.

As the complexity of the frontend grew, this is no longer true. We need tooling, but old habits die hard, and JavaScript developers have a hard time picking up these tools. Pretty much everyone uses the web developer tools, but a lot of the advanced capabilities hidden within these tools aren't used. There are multiple ways to launch the developer tools. The simplest is from the menus, as we can see for Firefox in Figure 8-1 and for Chrome in Figure 8-2.

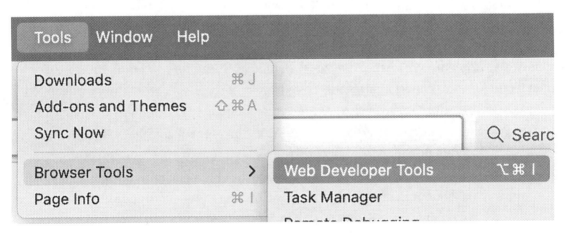

Figure 8-1. *Launching the Firefox web developer tools*

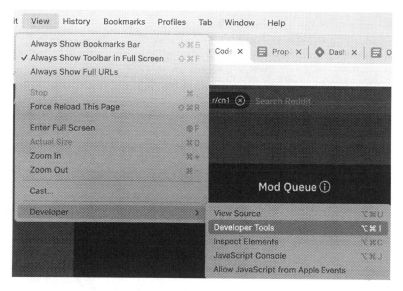

Figure 8-2. *Launching the Firefox web developer tools*

Once launched, we're faced with many capabilities for debugging browser-related issues. One of the most powerful and unfortunately least useful is the debugger capability, which you can see in Figure 8-3 for Firefox and in Figure 8-4 for Chrome.

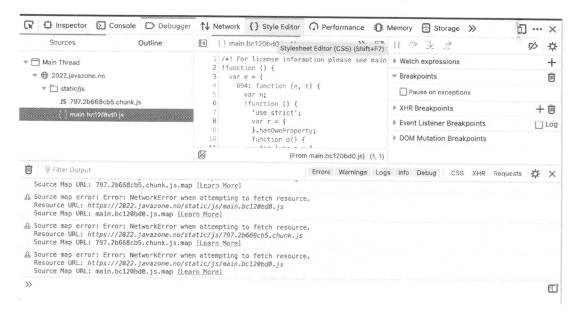

Figure 8-3. *Firefox JavaScript debugger and console*

Figure 8-4. *Chrome JavaScript debugger and console*

Tip   Notice the Chrome tools are docked to the right by default and the Firefox tools docked to the bottom. You can move both to either side or to the bottom. This is especially important when debugging issues related to responsiveness.

Obfuscation

Code obfuscation is very common in frontend code and for good reason. We're publishing our source code. That code might contain proprietary information; obfuscation will make it harder to read. The second benefit is reducing code size, which will improve performance by reducing download size, RAM overhead, etc.

Obfuscation is great, but it makes debugging very difficult. That's why we have the {} button in the bottom toolbar area in both debuggers. When you click it, a single line obfuscated file will become a "well-formed" debuggable file. Both Figures 8-3 and 8-4 were initially obfuscated. This is an important capability as during debugging we might want to step into obfuscated framework code.

A source map might be generated when you process the JavaScript file or compile it from a different language. If such a file is generated, you can use it to completely de-obfuscate the file including comments. At the bottom of the obfuscated JS file, add a source mapping comment:

```
//@ sourceMappingURL=myfile.js.map
```

For this to work in Chrome, you need to make sure "Enable JavaScript source maps" is enabled in the developer tools settings as shown in Figure 8-5.

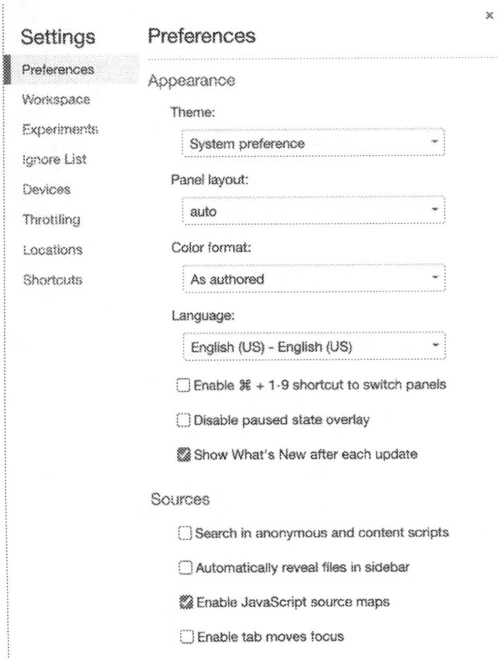

Figure 8-5. Enabled JavaScript source maps in settings

Launch Debugger

Instead of printing the stack trace, one of the neat tricks in JavaScript is instant debugging. Just use the debugger keyword to launch the debugger on that line. If you have an error handling method, it would be an ideal place for that call.

This is probably not something we'd like to leave in a production environment. But it can be very useful in a debug version of your site, assuming you have a preprocessor that can remove that call for production.

We can trigger the debugging of a function directly from the console. For example, this code in the console would trigger the debugger when the last line is invoked:

```
function hello(name) { console.log("Hello " + name) }
debug(hello)
hello("Hi World")
```

The debug(hello) statement adds a breakpoint into the hello function. When we invoke the function in the last line, we're sent directly into the debugger.

DOM Breakpoints

Think of them as the field watchpoints of the browser. We can place a breakpoint that will be hit when a specific area of the DOM is mutated. This only works for Chrome and Firebug (which is a Firefox plugin), but this is easy to use. Just right-click the DOM and select "Break On" followed by the behavior that you're interested in.

Figure 8-6 shows the DOM breakpoint context menu on the Chrome web browser. Notice that this is in addition to conditional breakpoint and line breakpoint capabilities. Both capabilities are supported by all major browser development tools.

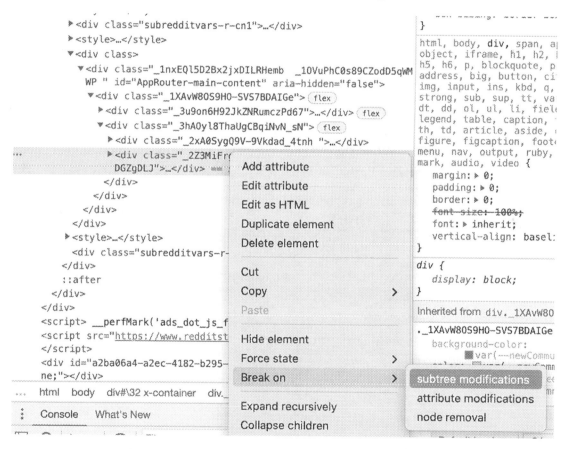

Figure 8-6. *DOM breakpoint context menu in Chrome*

XHR Breakpoints

Browsers have some amazing HTTP traffic monitoring capabilities that let us inspect all the outgoing requests and responses in detail. These are fantastic capabilities that I use often. They show every request as a set of bars indicating the time, size, and all the technical information (body, headers, etc.).

They're missing one crucial piece: the culprit. Who made the specific request? This is often trivial to find; we can search for the URI. But in some cases, the URI might be assembled dynamically or might arrive from multiple sources, and the flow is unclear. For these cases, we have the XHR breakpoint which we can set in Chrome or Firebug by defining a substring of the URI that we wish to break on. When a request arrives to fetch that URI, Chrome will hit that breakpoint and stop the execution of the script.

Figure 8-7 shows the XHR breakpoint area in Chrome. It's located in the sources tab under the call stack. Notice that if we don't fill in the URL filter, an XHR breakpoint is set for any XHR request which might get noisy.

Figure 8-7. *XHR breakpoint menu in Chrome*

Faking Browser Settings

When debugging hard-to-reproduce issues, a common technique is to spoof or simulate the problematic environment. These are some techniques we can use to simulate such an environment. Since debugging on a mobile device is a bit more challenging, it's often easier to simulate some behaviors that are more common there in our desktop browser.

The override section within Chrome settings lets you spoof functionality within the browser. There are several elements we can spoof:

- User agent

- Location services

- Touch operations

- Device orientation

Simulating a different user agent can help us isolate browser- or OS-specific issues that might be triggered because of server-side platform-specific content. This can be customized in Chrome in the settings section. For Firefox, you will need to install an extension to accomplish the same.[1]

You can use a database to find the user agent you wish to spoof, but I find it simpler to look at the user agent submitted from the browser where the code is working. You can inspect headers received in a failed server request and then try using that same user agent in another browser.

Touch gestures might produce different behaviors when compared to typical events. You can select "Emulate Touch Events" in the override options. In Firefox, if you're in the responsive design view, you could emulate a touch event.

Frontend Logging

We discussed logging in Chapter 4, but frontend logging is different in many regards. The first big difference is the quality of debugging via printing. As you may recall, I'm a big advocate of using tracepoints (see Chapter 1) instead of logging. Tracepoints (a.k.a. logpoints) are still superior to print statements in most regards, but in frontend programming, the difference isn't as pronounced.

In a frontend flow, we constantly reload, refresh, and switch browsers, and as a result, the development is very fluid. A tracepoint can become a hassle as we test extensively. Features such as ingestion, logging to a file, etc., aren't useful in the frontend, and thus we don't have the same level of need for a logger. It's still a "best practice" to use a logger rather than invoking `console.log` directly, but it isn't as much of a problem as print could cause on the backend.

One of the big advantages `console` has over simple print statements is its support for log levels. There are five supported levels: log, debug, info, warn, and error. Log and debug are indistinguishable from one another, and info is sometimes rendered in the same way. Figure 8-8 demonstrates the output of each level. The browser lets us filter the output so we can focus on a specific logging level similarly to typical server-side logs.

[1] https://addons.mozilla.org/en-US/firefox/addon/user-agent-platform-spoofer/

```
>> console.log("Hello Log")
   Hello Log
<- undefined
>> console.info("Hello Info")
(i) Hello Info
<- undefined
>> console.warn("Hello Warn")
⚠ Hello Warn
<- undefined
>> console.error("Hello Error")
🛑 ▸ Hello Error
<- undefined
```

Figure 8-8. *Log levels in the console*

We can create completely custom versions of logging with CSS thanks to the way JavaScript works. We can add an additional logger method into the console and use CSS to customize the output. For example, the following code prints out "Dazzle" with a pink background as seen inFigure 8-9. Notice we're using %c which indicates substitution with CSS. After the comma, we see the CSS that's applied. Notice we can use more than one substitution block to mix CSS styles; this can let an API print out text with multiple distinct styles.

```
console.customLog = function(msg) {
    console.log("%c" + msg,"color:black;background:pink;font-family:system-
    ui;font-size:4rem;-webkit-text-stroke: 1px black;font-weight:bold")
}
console.customLog("Dazzle")
```

```
>> console.customLog = function(msg) {
   console.log("%c" + msg,"color:black;background:pink;font-family:system-ui;font-size:4rem;-webkit-text-stroke: 1px
   black;font-weight:bold")
   }
<- ▸ function customLog(msg)
>> console.customLog("Dazzle")
```

debugger eval code:2:9

Dazzle

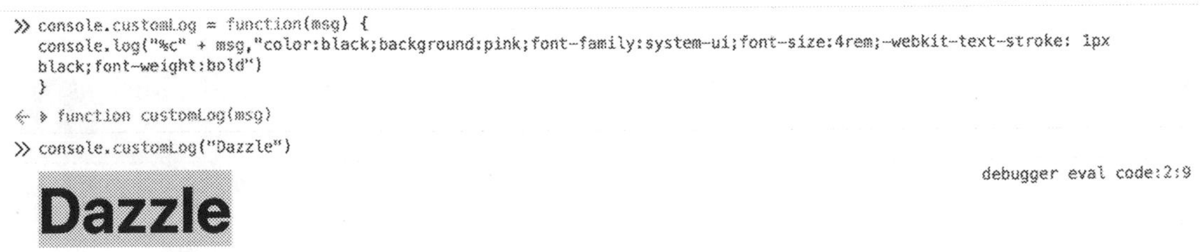

Figure 8-9. *Custom logging with CSS*

The `console.trace` method can print the stack trace to the current location. This isn't as useful due to the asynchronous nature of JavaScript code. But in some circumstances, that might prove useful.

Besides logging, we can use assertions in the code to implement "design by contract." Assertions let us determine an assumption we make while coding. Assert is used to verify a statement that **must** be true. If it isn't, our application will fail with a clear error. In the browser, this isn't as dramatic and is closer to the effect of `console.error` as seen in Figure 8-10.

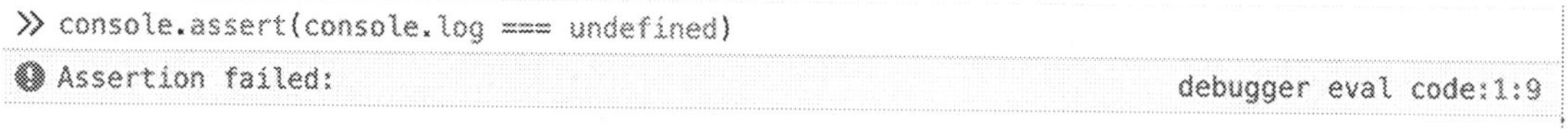

```
>> console.assert(console.log === undefined)
● Assertion failed:                                       debugger eval code:1:9
```

Figure 8-10. *Assertions*

One of the most powerful features of asserts is the ability to strip them out in a production build. We can remove the performance overhead of testing everything while promoting a "fail-fast" (see Chapter 4) mindset. Some minifiers support the ability to remove asserts in production.[2]

We can apply deep formatting to printed information; one common example is printing a table of data. For example, code like `console.table(["Simple Array", "With a few elements", "in line"])` can print a table with the array of items. We can create more sophisticated examples by printing an object as a table; the elements of the object become the columns and rows of the table. We can see samples of both approaches in Figure 8-11.

---

[2] `https://github.com/Couto/grunt-groundskeeper` supports removing assertions in the minified file

Figure 8-11. *Printing a table*

Printing the content of an object to the console is possible in various ways. We can use the `copy(object)` method to copy the content of an object into the clipboard so we can paste it anywhere. The `console.dir(object)` API provides a far more powerful option of inspecting an object as we do in a debugger. This is an amazing way to explore an API and the state of the environment as we see in Figure 8-12. Similarly, we can use `dirxml(object)` to view an object as xml or use the `inspect(object)` method to open the inspect panel with the given element or object.

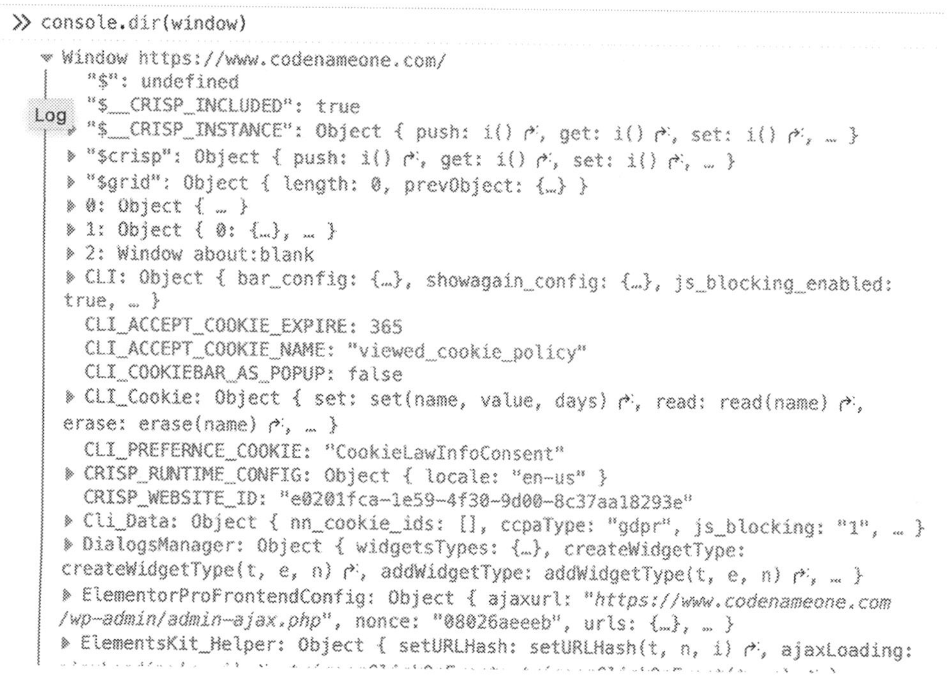

```
>> console.dir(window)
    ▼ Window https://www.codenameone.com/
        "$": undefined
        "$__CRISP_INCLUDED": true
Log  "$__CRISP_INSTANCE": Object { push: i() ↱, get: i() ↱, set: i() ↱, … }
      ▶ "$crisp": Object { push: i() ↱, get: i() ↱, set: i() ↱, … }
      ▶ "$grid": Object { length: 0, prevObject: {…} }
      ▶ 0: Object { … }
      ▶ 1: Object { 0: {…}, … }
      ▶ 2: Window about:blank
      ▶ CLI: Object { bar_config: {…}, showagain_config: {…}, js_blocking_enabled:
      true, … }
        CLI_ACCEPT_COOKIE_EXPIRE: 365
        CLI_ACCEPT_COOKIE_NAME: "viewed_cookie_policy"
        CLI_COOKIEBAR_AS_POPUP: false
      ▶ CLI_Cookie: Object { set: set(name, value, days) ↱, read: read(name) ↱,
      erase: erase(name) ↱, … }
        CLI_PREFERNCE_COOKIE: "CookieLawInfoConsent"
      ▶ CRISP_RUNTIME_CONFIG: Object { locale: "en-us" }
        CRISP_WEBSITE_ID: "e0201fca-1e59-4f30-9d00-8c37aa18293e"
      ▶ Cli_Data: Object { nn_cookie_ids: [], ccpaType: "gdpr", js_blocking: "1", … }
      ▶ DialogsManager: Object { widgetsTypes: {…}, createWidgetType:
      createWidgetType(t, e, n) ↱, addWidgetType: addWidgetType(t, e, n) ↱, … }
      ▶ ElementorProFrontendConfig: Object { ajaxurl: "https://www.codenameone.com
      /wp-admin/admin-ajax.php", nonce: "08026aeeeb", urls: {…}, … }
      ▶ ElementsKit_Helper: Object { setURLHash: setURLHash(t, n, i) ↱, ajaxLoading:
```

Figure 8-12. *Console dir on a window object*

Counters are an important debugging tool. We often want to know the number of times a method was invoked or a line of code was reached. This is such a common use case; that it's coded into the console API. With `console.count()`, we can increment an arbitrary number every time that line is reached; the current count is printed to the console. We can also use `console.countReset()` to reset the counter back to zero. This lets us verify that an API isn't reached too often and validate assumptions. Figure 8-13 demonstrates the simple usage of these APIs.

Figure 8-13. *Console count and countReset APIs*

Grouping lets us collect related printouts together in a collapsible group to keep the output organized. We can place all the logs related to a specific method in a group to reduce verbosity. To start a group, use `console.group("GroupName")`; this opens a collapsible region with the given name. Every following printout will be a part of that group until you invoke `console.groupEnd()`, as seen in Figure 8-14.

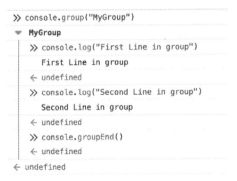

Figure 8-14. *Collapsible groups*

Monitor is a Chrome-specific feature that lets us monitor calls to a specific function. This is like adding a tracepoint (logpoint) on a method (function) breakpoint. We can invoke the function `monitor(functionName)` on any function. After that point, every invocation of the function will print its name to the log and the arguments it received. Invoking `unmonitor(functionName)` will remove the monitor and return us to the previous state. See Figure 8-15 for a simple example.

```
> function hello(name) { console.log("Hello " + name) }
< undefined
> hello("Shai")
  Hello Shai
< undefined
> monitor(hello)
< undefined
> hello("Readers")
  function hello called with arguments: Readers
  Hello Readers
< undefined
> unmonitor(hello)
< undefined
> hello("Again")
  Hello Again
< undefined
> |
```

Figure 8-15. *Monitoring and unmonitoring a function*

Similarly, Chrome supports the ability to monitor events using the `monitorEvents(object [, events])` and `unmonitorEvents(object[, events])` APIs. All events are logged to the console once we start monitoring events until we choose to stop with the `unmonitorEvents` call. The events argument is optional; it lets us reduce the volume of events we receive. I can monitor all window events using `monitorEvents(window)` or just specific mouseout events using `monitorEvents(window, "mouseout")` as you can see in Figure 8-16.

```
>  monitorEvents(window, "mouseout")
<  undefined
```

mouseout ▸ *MouseEvent* {isTrusted: true, screenX: 684, screenY: 668, clientX: 684, clientY: 550, …}	VM29178:1
mouseout ▸ *MouseEvent* {isTrusted: true, screenX: 621, screenY: 667, clientX: 621, clientY: 549, …}	VM29178:1
mouseout ▸ *MouseEvent* {isTrusted: true, screenX: 608, screenY: 665, clientX: 608, clientY: 547, …}	VM29178:1
mouseout ▸ *MouseEvent* {isTrusted: true, screenX: 537, screenY: 656, clientX: 537, clientY: 538, …}	VM29178:1
mouseout ▸ *MouseEvent* {isTrusted: true, screenX: 531, screenY: 655, clientX: 531, clientY: 537, …}	VM29178:1
mouseout ▸ *MouseEvent* {isTrusted: true, screenX: 521, screenY: 653, clientX: 521, clientY: 535, …}	VM29178:1
mouseout ▸ *MouseEvent* {isTrusted: true, screenX: 530, screenY: 650, clientX: 530, clientY: 532, …}	VM29178:1
mouseout ▸ *MouseEvent* {isTrusted: true, screenX: 601, screenY: 654, clientX: 601, clientY: 536, …}	VM29178:1
mouseout ▸ *MouseEvent* {isTrusted: true, screenX: 629, screenY: 659, clientX: 629, clientY: 541, …}	VM29178:1
mouseout ▸ *MouseEvent* {isTrusted: true, screenX: 688, screenY: 670, clientX: 688, clientY: 552, …}	VM29178:1
mouseout ▸ *MouseEvent* {isTrusted: true, screenX: 718, screenY: 677, clientX: 718, clientY: 559, …}	VM29178:1

```
>  unmonitorEvents(window)
<  undefined
>  monitorEvents(window)
<  undefined
```

resize ▸ *Event* {isTrusted: true, type: 'resize', target: Window, currentTarget: Window, eventPhase: 2, …}	VM29178:1
resize ▸ *Event* {isTrusted: true, type: 'resize', target: Window, currentTarget: Window, eventPhase: 2, …}	VM29178:1
resize ▸ *Event* {isTrusted: true, type: 'resize', target: Window, currentTarget: Window, eventPhase: 2, …}	VM29178:1
resize ▸ *Event* {isTrusted: true, type: 'resize', target: Window, currentTarget: Window, eventPhase: 2, …}	VM29178:1

Figure 8-16. *Monitoring and unmonitoring events*

Chrome can list all the objects created with a specific constructor or of a specific object type by using the `queryObjects` function. When we invoke that function with any object type, such as `Promise`, as we see in Figure 8-17, we can see the objects in the VM listed. This can work with a constructor to get only the instances created with the specific constructor.

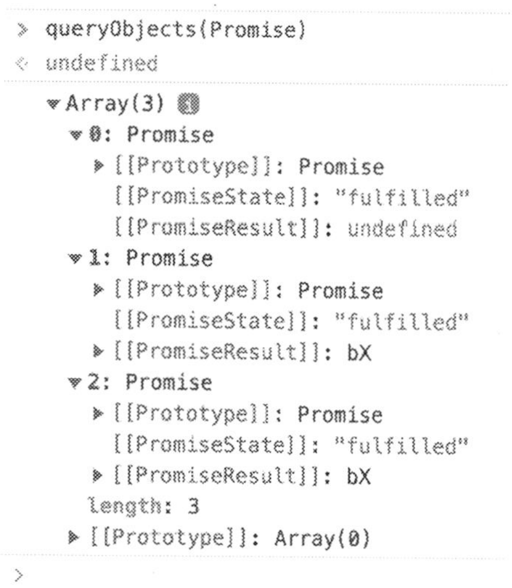

```
>  queryObjects(Promise)
<  undefined
   ▼ Array(3) 🔵
     ▼ 0: Promise
       ▶ [[Prototype]]: Promise
         [[PromiseState]]: "fulfilled"
         [[PromiseResult]]: undefined
     ▼ 1: Promise
       ▶ [[Prototype]]: Promise
         [[PromiseState]]: "fulfilled"
       ▶ [[PromiseResult]]: bX
     ▼ 2: Promise
       ▶ [[Prototype]]: Promise
         [[PromiseState]]: "fulfilled"
       ▶ [[PromiseResult]]: bX
         length: 3
       ▶ [[Prototype]]: Array(0)
>
```

Figure 8-17. *Querying objects in Chrome*

Networking

In Chapter 3, we discussed Wireshark, which is an amazing tool for observing network traffic. The tools within the browser exceed it for most common use cases and make debugging network performance and bugs stupid simple. Many problems express themselves in the frontend, either via the console or the network monitor. I'll skip the discussion of performance, since that is a subject so big it warrants its own book. In this case, I want to highlight tricks for debugging using these network consoles. The Firefox network monitor seen in Figure 8-18 is very similar conceptually to the Chrome network monitor in Figure 8-19. Both include nearly identical functionality and capabilities. Due to that, I won't demonstrate most functionality in both browsers.

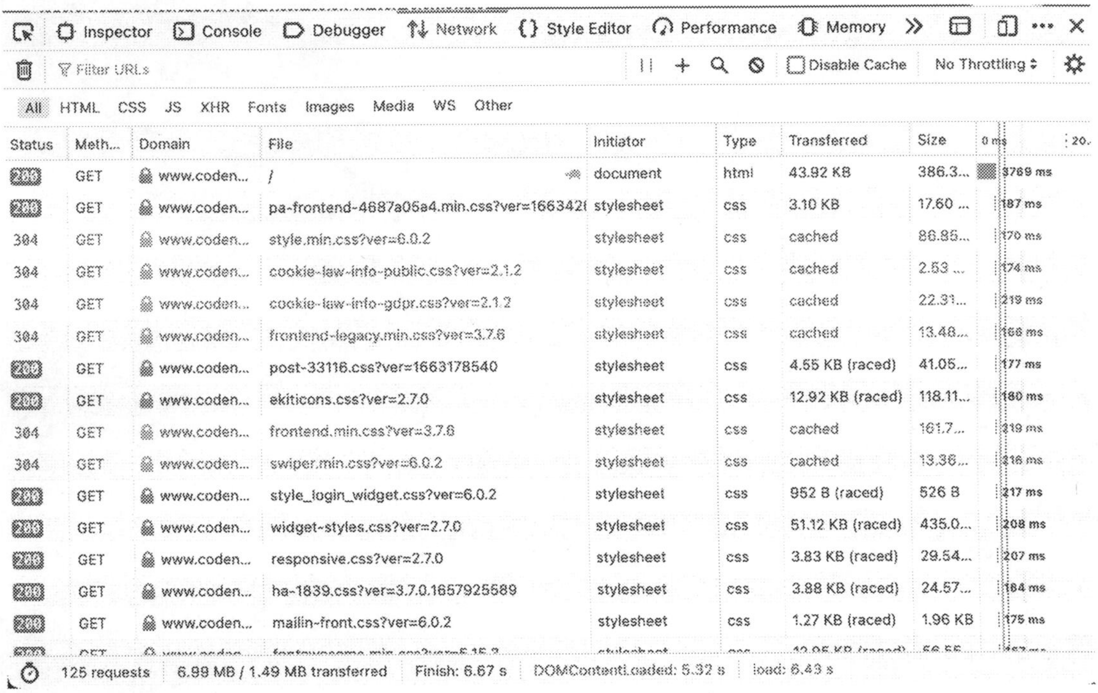

Status	Meth...	Domain	File	Initiator	Type	Transferred	Size	0 ms	20.
200	GET	🔒 www.coden...	/	document	html	43.92 KB	386.3...	3769 ms	
200	GET	🔒 www.coden...	pa-frontend-4687a05a4.min.css?ver=166342(	stylesheet	css	3.10 KB	17.60 ...	187 ms	
304	GET	🔒 www.coden...	style.min.css?ver=6.0.2	stylesheet	css	cached	86.85...	170 ms	
304	GET	🔒 www.coden...	cookie-law-info-public.css?ver=2.1.2	stylesheet	css	cached	2.53 ...	174 ms	
304	GET	🔒 www.coden...	cookie-law-info-gdpr.css?ver=2.1.2	stylesheet	css	cached	22.31...	219 ms	
304	GET	🔒 www.coden...	frontend-legacy.min.css?ver=3.7.6	stylesheet	css	cached	13.48...	166 ms	
200	GET	🔒 www.coden...	post-33116.css?ver=1663178540	stylesheet	css	4.55 KB (raced)	41.05...	177 ms	
200	GET	🔒 www.coden...	ekiticons.css?ver=2.7.0	stylesheet	css	12.92 KB (raced)	118.11...	180 ms	
304	GET	🔒 www.coden...	frontend.min.css?ver=3.7.6	stylesheet	css	cached	161.7...	419 ms	
304	GET	🔒 www.coden...	swiper.min.css?ver=6.0.2	stylesheet	css	cached	13.36...	416 ms	
200	GET	🔒 www.coden...	style_login_widget.css?ver=6.0.2	stylesheet	css	952 B (raced)	526 B	217 ms	
200	GET	🔒 www.coden...	widget-styles.css?ver=2.7.0	stylesheet	css	51.12 KB (raced)	435.0...	208 ms	
200	GET	🔒 www.coden...	responsive.css?ver=2.7.0	stylesheet	css	3.83 KB (raced)	29.54...	207 ms	
200	GET	🔒 www.coden...	ha-1839.css?ver=3.7.0.1657925589	stylesheet	css	3.88 KB (raced)	24.57...	164 ms	
200	GET	🔒 www.coden...	mailin-front.css?ver=6.0.2	stylesheet	css	1.27 KB (raced)	1.96 KB	175 ms	
200	GET	🔒 www.coden...	fontawesome.min.css?ver=5.15.3	stylesheet	css	12.05 KB (raced)	66.55...	167 ms	

⏱ 125 requests   6.99 MB / 1.49 MB transferred   Finish: 6.67 s   DOMContentLoaded: 5.32 s   load: 6.43 s

Figure 8-18. *Network monitoring in Firefox*

Name	Status	Type	Initiator	Size	Time	Waterfall
www.codenameone.com	200	document	Other	44.7 kB	5.13 s	
pa-frontend-4687a05a4.min.css?...	200	stylesheet	www.codename...	2.9 kB	232 ms	
style.min.css?ver=3.7.0	304	stylesheet	www.codename...	293 B	30 ms	
jquery.min.js?ver=3.6.0	304	script	www.codename...	397 B	30 ms	
jquery-migrate.min.js?ver=3.3.2	304	script	www.codename...	330 B	29 ms	
cookie-law-info-public.js?ver=2.1.2	304	script	www.codename...	329 B	29 ms	
v4-shims.min.js?ver=5.2.1	304	script	www.codename...	295 B	29 ms	
lord-icon-2.1.0.js?ver=3.7.0	304	script	www.codename...	299 B	28 ms	
mailin-front.js?ver=1660760232	304	script	www.codename...	313 B	29 ms	
paddle.js	304	script	www.codename...	406 B	52 ms	
pxiGyp8kv8JHgFVrJJLucHtAOv...	200	font	css?family=Rob...	(memor...	0 ms	
pxiDyp8kv8JHgFVrJJLm81xVF9e...	200	font	css?family=Rob...	(memor...	0 ms	
pxiByp8kv8JHgFVrLDz8Z1xlFd2...	200	font	css?family=Rob...	(memor...	0 ms	
pxiEyp8kv8JHgFVrJJfecnFHGPc...	200	font	css?family=Rob...	(memor...	0 ms	
pxiByp8kv8JHgFVrLGT9Z1xlFd2...	200	font	css?family=Rob...	(memor...	0 ms	
pxiByp8kv8JHgFVrLEj6Z1xlFd2J...	200	font	css?family=Rob...	(memor...	0 ms	
pxiByp8kv8JHgFVrLCz7Z1xlFd2...	200	font	css?family=Rob...	(memor...	0 ms	
KFOmCnqEu92Fr1Mu4mxKKTU...	200	font	css?family=Rob...	(memor...	0 ms	
KFOlCnqEu92Fr1MmEU9fBBc4A...	200	font	css?family=Rob...	(memor...	0 ms	

115 requests | 112 kB transferred | 8.2 MB resources | Finish: 6.74 s | DOMContentLoaded: 5.50 s | Load: 5.69 s

Figure 8-19. *Network monitoring in Chrome*

One of the biggest capabilities is the ability to re-issue a request. This is far more convenient than pulling out curl or postman since it allows us to modify an existing network operation and change some arguments. Firefox lets us right-click over any entry in the network monitor and select "Resend" to launch an edit window. We can now issue a custom request and change the parameters we pass to the request as shown in Figure 8-20. Both Firefox and Chrome support copying the request as a cURL command. You can find that capability under the copy menu in the right-click. This lets us reproduce an issue from the command line without going through the browser. You can also copy request headers and paste them into postman's headers section if you prefer working with it.

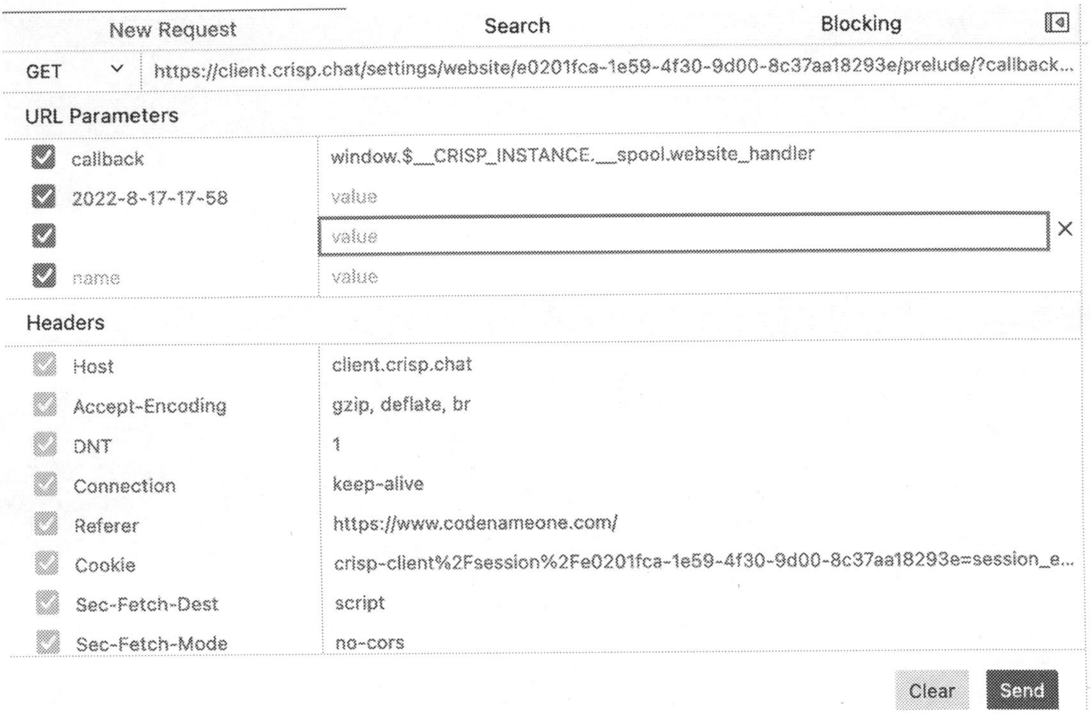

New Request		Search	Blocking	◁

GET ⌄   https://client.crisp.chat/settings/website/e0201fca-1e59-4f30-9d00-8c37aa18293e/prelude/?callback...

URL Parameters

☑ callback	window.$__CRISP_INSTANCE.__spool.website_handler
☑ 2022-8-17-17-58	value
☑	value ✕
☑ name	value

Headers

☑ Host	client.crisp.chat
☑ Accept-Encoding	gzip, deflate, br
☑ DNT	1
☑ Connection	keep-alive
☑ Referer	https://www.codenameone.com/
☑ Cookie	crisp-client%2Fsession%2Fe0201fca-1e59-4f30-9d00-8c37aa18293e=session_e...
☑ Sec-Fetch-Dest	script
☑ Sec-Fetch-Mode	no-cors

Clear   Send

Figure 8-20. *Resend a network request*

One of the most useful features in the networking toolchain is the throttling feature seen in Figure 8-21. With it, we can slow down the request speed to various predetermined speeds. This is wonderful for debugging performance-related issues, but it's also an important tool in debugging race conditions and problems that only occur in slower connections.

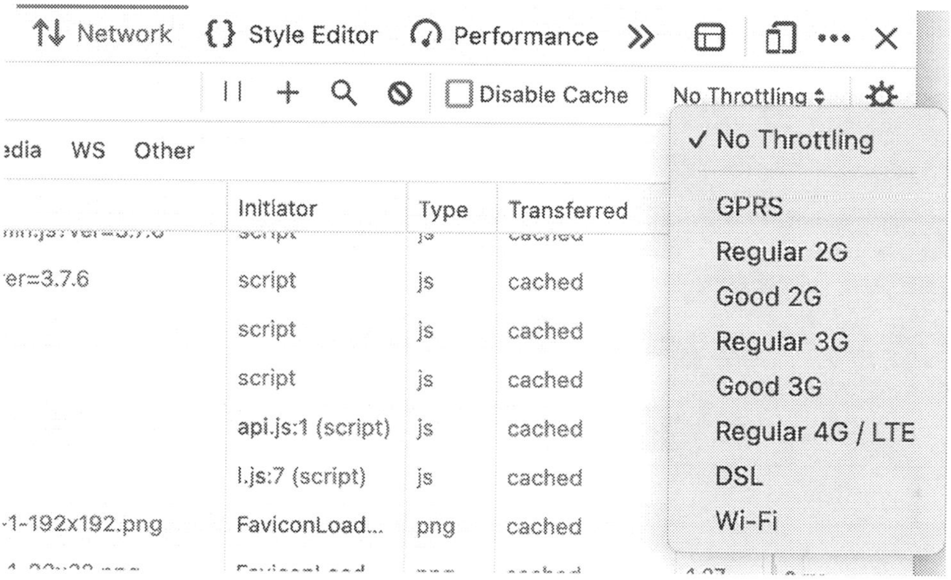

Figure 8-21. *Performance throttling options in Firefox*

Storage

One of the biggest problems in debugging an application is misbehavior specific to a device. This is often caused by local storage on the device that stores local cache or related information. A common workaround among frontend developers is the usage of incognito mode (a.k.a. private browsing). However, this approach has a few drawbacks:

- The state is shared between incognito windows. If you accidentally leave a private session open in one window and open another, the state will be kept, and it would be hard to notice.

- We might want to keep "some state" for convenience.

Both Chrome and Firefox include great support for managing storage in their respective developer tools. Firefox has a dedicated storage tab (see Figure 8-22), whereas Chrome includes everything in its application tab (see Figure 8-23).

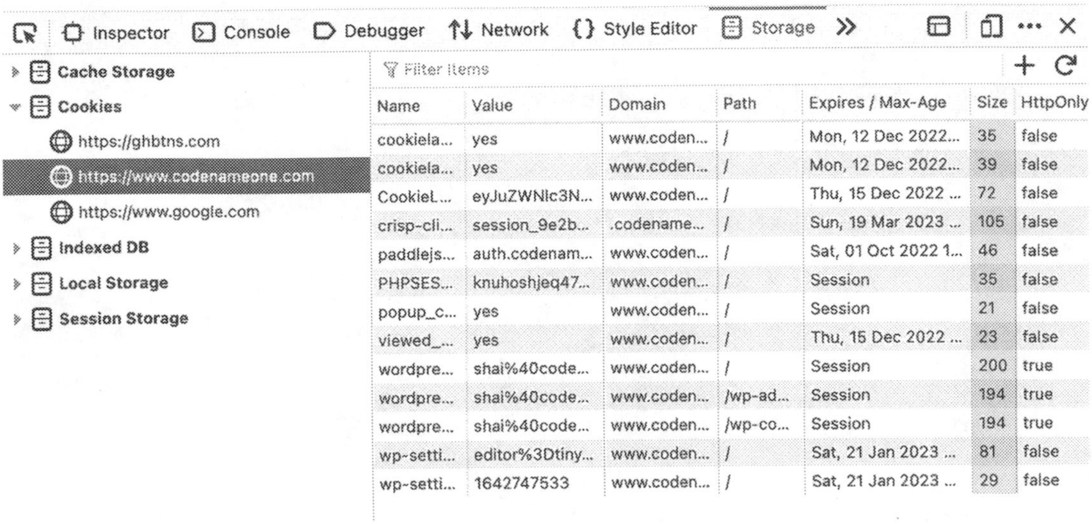

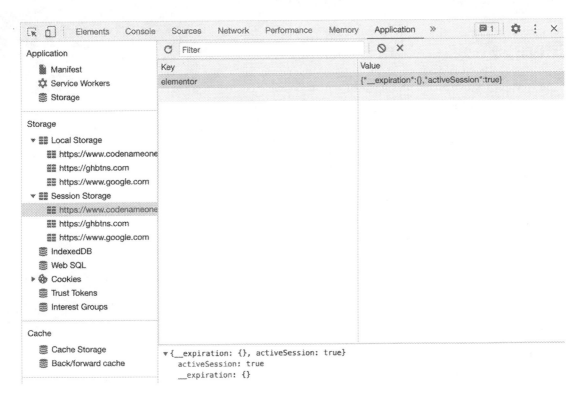

Figure 8-22. *Firefox storage tab*

Figure 8-23. *Chrome application tab with storage section selected*

The storage area lets us push debug information into storage to test specific edge cases. An end user can provide us with a local state from their browser which we can add locally. We can remove and edit individual elements from all storage types including cache.

DOM and CSS

Layout and style bugs typically stand out on their own and are typically separate from the fullstack issues. However, since we're discussing frontends so extensively, it makes sense to cover these issues as well. The inspect element view of the developer tools is possibly the most important feature within them. It's the default view and the starting point for most frontend work as seen in Figures 8-24 and 8-25. Notice that at first glance Firefox might seem more functional than Chrome. Chrome hides some of the features behind additional tabs, which has some benefits and some tediousness.

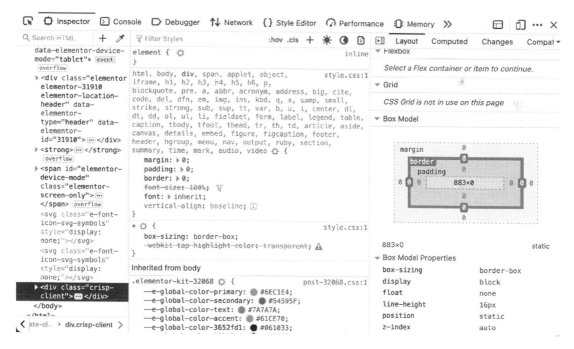

Figure 8-24. *Firefox's inspect element UI*

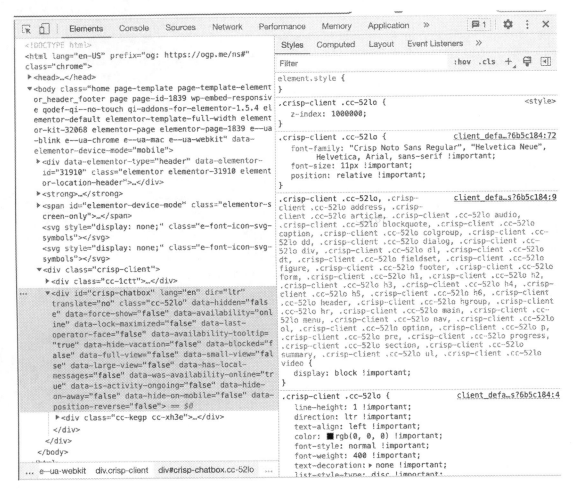

Figure 8-25. *Chrome's inspect element UI*

When we inspect an element, we can change everything about it and its CSS. The specific element is highlighted in the web view, and changes are applied instantly. This is an amazing tool for debugging CSS- and HTML-related bugs.

Every value within the inspector can be edited. We can also add new attributes and instantly examine their impact. This lets us experiment rapidly while tuning the actual code based on the results. One of the biggest problems developers run into is the specificity issue. The specificity issue is the situation in which changes we make to the CSS aren't applied. This can happen if a more specific selector is overriding the attribute we're trying to set.

We can detect this when inspecting an element's CSS. We would see our setting in strikeout mode and could scroll up to see the attribute that overrode our setting (see Figure 8-26). Once we understand the specific cause, we can edit our CSS rules to address that problem.

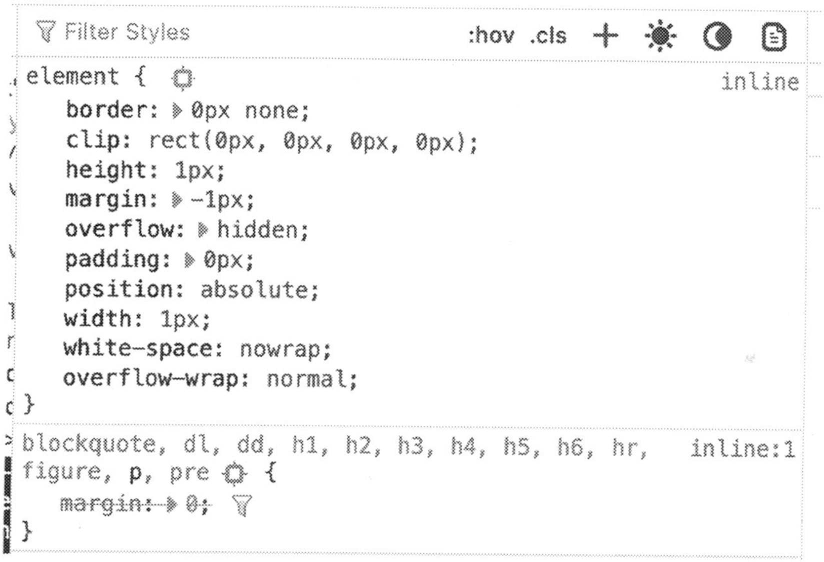

Figure 8-26. *CSS attributes*

Database Layer

Debugging database-related issues is a massive subject that is hard to cover in a generic debugging book. Issues are often very database specific,[3] and as a result, we need to make some wide sweeping generalizations about the database and caching layers. Common universal issues in working with a database include

- Connectivity issues.

- Query failure – This is a clear failure, so it isn't something we need to elaborate on.

- Invalid (corrupt) data.

---

[3] And OS specific, hardware specific, timezone specific, etc. But the database is a big deal.

Each issue category has its own set of approaches. I'll focus mostly on SQL databases, but everything said here applies to other database types as well. The solutions to some problems and syntax might differ, but the problems are similar. Notice I didn't cover consistency (ACID), concurrency, scale, locking, and similar issues. These are deep in the domain of databases. That's a subject for a dedicated book.

Caching is another source of issues; it's also one of the most important tools at our disposal. It can represent the difference between a high-performance scalable system and a slow clunky system. Unfortunately, it can also mean the difference between a reliable and a flaky system. When we run into problems, the cache is often the first thing we disable. Once we disable the cache, we might never enable it again. This is an unfortunate outcome. It means many developers don't benefit from this amazingly important tool. Debugging caching is too specific per tool, and it's hard to produce universally applicable insights.

Database Logic Layering

Before we delve into the problems and the solutions that we need, let's discuss general architectural choices that help debugging database issues. I'm a big fan of Object-Relational Mapping tools (ORMs), but I understand they aren't everyone's "cup of tea," which is fine. The important part is the isolation of direct database access within an abstraction layer that lets you inspect the seam between the database and your application. Such a layer should be fully mockable for the purpose of isolating database issues from application issues.

Assuming you use database caching (which you should[4]), its usage should be encapsulated within that layer for the same reason. This lets us use the standard debugger to test most database-related issues and lets us unit-test effectively. The database layer itself can be tested using tools such as datasource-assert,[5] which mocks the database.

Database Connectivity

Issues related to connectivity fall into the following common categories:

- Database resources – For example, a database runs out of available connections due to too many concurrent sessions.

---

[4] You should almost always cache, but there are exceptions. For example, StackOverflow discovered that caching their database didn't improve their performance.
[5] https://github.com/ttddyy/datasource-assert

- Networking issues – These can happen due to misconfiguration or connectivity problems.

- Race between containers – The database container might take longer to load than the application, and as a result, a connection won't form.

The latter ones aren't challenging. The former seems like an easy fix that doesn't require debugging. But this is a misleading premise. One of the most common fixes is to increase the number of resources allocated to the database, more connections, larger cluster, etc. While this is something that would be needed as the business grows, it's often done prematurely and leads to a vicious cycle of cloud spending.

A common source of resource depletion problems occurs because of bad cleanup code. When working with limited database resources, we must always handle failure and always clean up after a failure. This is a tedious work, and it's hard to detect sometimes. In the debugger for JVM languages, we can enable exception breakpoints on the SQLException and make sure every such exception is handled correctly.

Many resource depletion problems are caused by an errant feature that takes too long to release a database resource. Detecting and fixing these edge cases will solve the problem and increase performance. Detecting them is different for every database type but follows a relatively standard pattern.

MySQL[6] has an option to log slow queries. Edit the my.cnf file and set the following:

```
[mysqld]
long_query_time       = 1
log-slow-queries      = /var/log/mysql/mysql-slow.log
```

Once this is set, we can review the database log to see suspect queries and decide on a performance strategy to fix the connectivity issues.[7] An important bit of information in the log is the rows that were locked. If a query locks multiple rows for a duration, it can trigger a cascading effect where multiple queries need to "get in line" behind

---

[6] MariaDB has a slightly different process: https://mariadb.com/kb/en/slow-query-log-overview/

[7] Database performance is outside the scope of this book, but I would suggest reducing joins, tuning indexes, adding level 2 cache, reducing contention, etc.

it. Sometimes, the solution isn't to optimize the query, just to reduce its impact. PostgreSQL has a similar log we can use to detect such performance problems, which we can configure in the `postgresql.conf` file by setting the following:

```
log_min_duration_statement=500
```

This will log all statements that take up more than 500ms to perform; it might be a lot for a production database. Once we have the SQL statements, we might face two different problems:

- Understanding where the SQL came from – It might be challenging to understand the context in JPA, specifically which line of Java code relates to the SQL statement.

- Figuring out why this SQL statement is slow.

The latter can be understood using the SQL explain keyword which generates an execution plan for a query. This can help us understand what's going on when the query runs. I use IntelliJ/IDEA Ultimate which provides a visual interface to analyze database logs and query performance. There are many other visualization tools you can use, for example, *DBeaver*, etc.

Making the connection between the SQL that's executed in the database and a high-level ORM abstraction is challenging, especially since the database runs in a separate process and we can't follow the logging in the application server to the database log. This can be understood when we're running locally, but if we're in a production environment with a large codebase, finding the code responsible for a problematic query can be a needle in a haystack. Most tools like JPA support a verbose mode where they print out the generated SQL. Even when JPA does that, it doesn't connect the printed SQL to the line of code or even the thread that executes the SQL. This is a common problem for many SQL abstractions, and, unfortunately, there are very few solutions. One solution for JPA is JPlusOne,[8] which adds additional context. However, it also adds an overhead, so it might not be practical in a production setting. It might be useful for integration tests, though.

Having said all that, slow queries might be a misleading metric. A large volume of fast queries can often be worse for performance than one slow query. Such queries won't be detected by database logging since individually they would be fast. This is something

---

[8] https://github.com/adgadev/jplusone?ref=hackernoon.com

we can detect through our application logging and debugger. If one operation produces multiple queries, it might be indicative of a problematic operation. Unfortunately, I have no magic bullet for this, only vigilance.

Invalid Data

Bad data in the database is the bane of programmers everywhere. Proper database constraints are often challenging as they lack the same level of sophistication that we often require in the business layer. This can create a situation where code used to import or insert data into the DB might add invalid data. This data won't work when we try to view or edit it using another flow. Cleaning up the data in production is also a problem. Once the bad data is in the database, it's much harder to get it out.

How do we detect if a bug we're experiencing is due to bad data? Conditional breakpoints that verify assumptions can be very helpful here. However, since most such issues are specific to production, it won't be as valuable there. For this, we must log effectively so we can track such issues. Unfortunately, that's a problematic strategy since the log has different access restrictions when compared to the database, and we can't expose all data in the log. We can't query the log either. There are no simple solutions for this specific problem other than reviewing the data in the DB, logging extensively, and trying to get DB constraints right the first time around.

Consistent Databases

This isn't a bug, but rather a problematic concept that's prevalent when developing database applications. Kubernetes should have made deployment-specific issues a thing of the past. Unfortunately, even with Kubernetes, the difference between staging and production is still huge. Serverless deployments have made local environments and staging even harder to work with. In many regards, "modern systems" are harder to debug in comparison to systems defined a decade ago.

There isn't much we can do about serverless. But the problem is the usage of a different database for development and production, for example, HSQLDB for development and PostgreSQL for production. This made sense before the advent of docker. Thanks to docker we can run the same database in production and development. This is important for practicing debugging techniques locally that would be applicable when we need to address similar issues in production.

Summary

This chapter is about fullstack, but I spent most of it discussing the frontend and a bit of it discussing the backend. The reasoning is that we already understand the middle tier and discuss it throughout the book. But how do we bring this together as a coherent debugging process?

Moving a debugging session from the frontend to the backend through multiple layers of microservices and databases is challenging. There are several tools that make this harder, and I specifically avoided discussing them... up until now.

In the next chapter, we'll finally start discussing observability and monitoring. These tools let us gain insight into production systems, their performance, failure rates, and much more. Armed with these tools, we will be better prepared as systems scale further in the future.

CHAPTER 9

Observability and Monitoring

The future will be determined in part by happenings that it is impossible to foresee; it will also be influenced by trends that are now existent and observable.

—Emily Greene Balch

If you search the Web for the definition of monitoring and observability, you'll end up with almost as many definitions as there are results. Before we go into the nitty-gritty of textbook definitions, I'd like to focus on why we need these things at all. What purpose do they serve?

These tools provide actionable insight into our production systems. This isn't a new idea, but with the rising complexity we have due to containerization, orchestration, and microservices, these tools have become essential. It's rare to find a modern deployment that doesn't use several such tools. Tool vendors focus their sales, marketing, functionality, and documentation on the DevOps market, which makes the tools less "actionable" to the developer community. Some vendors have other niches such as Software Reliability Engineers (SREs), but the problem remains. The tools aren't developer friendly, and the tutorials are often obtuse from a developer's standpoint.

The functionality covered in this chapter warrants several books, and such books have been written. Most of them target DevOps and other demographics; developers need to understand these tools differently. For example, a DevOps would focus on the volume of data collected; how do you store it, transfer it, and analyze it? As developers, our debugging process takes place when these decisions were already made (usually).

© Shai Almog 2023
S. Almog, *Practical Debugging at Scale*, https://doi.org/10.1007/978-1-4842-9042-2_9

My goal is to give you cursory access to these tools so you can gain the most out of them as a developer to debug production. I hope that once you understand some of the power behind such tools, you'll pick up a dedicated book to dig deeper. I find that having a regimen of looking through dashboards daily helps me get a better sense of the system I'm maintaining – what gets used, what's performing badly, where failures are happening, and how it all fits together.

Theory

What is monitoring? The textbook definition[1] of monitoring is the process of collecting, analyzing, and using information that tracks our application. Monitoring assesses the health of the system by aggregating information so we can make informed decisions. Observability investigates the internal state of the system through logs, metrics, and traces.

Monitoring is the way in which we display and track information from many sources including observability tools. Monitoring and observability work together to deliver a cohesive view of our production environment. Most definitions of monitoring and observability refer to the three pillars of observability:

- Logs

- Metrics

- Distributed traces

We'll discuss those soon enough. Some definitions eschew this approach and look at the observability concept through the wider lens of our view into the whole system. Can you answer the core questions about your system in production or are you effectively blind?

My simplified explanation is that with monitoring we can see information about our system. With observability, we can ask interesting questions about the said system. For example, a monitoring system will show us how many HTTP errors occurred in the system; an observability solution will let us investigate the issue causing said errors. Both are complementary to one another.

---

[1] Note that I'm simplifying here. There's a mathematical basis for controllability and observability defined by Rudolf E. Kálmán. I think this is outside of scope for most developers.

A few additional concepts we need to know are telemetry, which is the process of collecting data from the observed systems, and alerting. Alerting is obvious; we can trigger an event based on an observed change. For example, if CPU usage is high, we can trigger an alert to the engineers so they can check the system. Another important set of tools are Application Performance Monitors (APMs). APMs are in effect profilers for production.

Note   In this chapter, I use the word application to describe the observed element. Notice that an application can be comprised of multiple isolated containers or processes and doesn't imply a single process.

Logs

We talked about logs in Chapter 4, but that was mostly from the developer perspective. When looking at logs from an observability perspective, we see a different picture of the same artifact. In this perspective, context, scale, retention, and proper metadata are the story.

It's no longer just a log that shows how the application behaved at a given time. It's now a collection of logs from all the instances of the app, connected to ongoing processes or events with associated information. In order to represent this effectively, common loggers support structured logging, which means the output is in JSON or XML format. That way, the observability tools can break down the log into its individual components.

Logs often encode within them a great deal of information. When we look at logs through developer tools, we see the information encoded for our convenience. As we can see in Figure 9-1, the structure of a single line can include many problematic aspects. The time value is very ambiguous in this specific log. Which year? Which timezone? The metadata typically appears mixed rather than segregated; we don't necessarily need to know the user ID or server URL for every request.

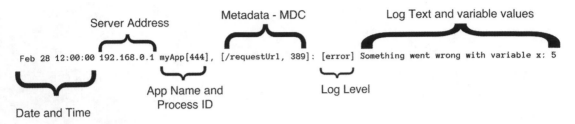

Figure 9-1. *Components of a log statement*

This is where structured logs make sense. Logs can use the less readable epoch time format for accuracy, while the user who views the log will see the more readable time format. The same applies for the other metadata. We might want to see logs dealing only with a specific user; we can use the metadata to filter that.

Monitoring systems can take that to a different level. By ingesting the logs, we can use the broken-down data to get insights on niche details without changes to our code. Log ingestion is the process of collecting the logs from multiple isolated processes and processing them for fast search. A monitor can measure error rates per user by reviewing the number of logs marked as ERROR per user ID.

Metrics

Metrics are measurements that give us a sense of the application's inner workings. They are often divided into three categories:

- Gauge – Displays a value at a point in time, for example, memory or CPU usage

- Delta – Measures the change between measurements, for example, increase in error rate

- Cumulative – Measures the change over time, for example, the total errors received in the past 24-hour period

Metrics can be custom created to fit the business needs and are a crucial part of our system view. They're an interesting diagnostic tool, but as a debugging tool, they're typically a stepping stone. We can identify potential problems via metrics, but usually fixing them requires more.

Distributed Tracing

Tracing is the thread that connects the pieces of a distributed system. It lets us follow the process across the container boundary while maintaining context. When an issue crosses the boundary between processes or containers, it's hard to follow along. Traces are comprised of nested Spans that together represent the entire request from start to finish.

The root Span contains an entire request within its hierarchy. Tracing tools can visualize the process as a flame graph or as a waterfall diagram that we can expand to follow through. This is similar to reviewing a stack trace for causality, but it's more elaborate since Spans are distributed and concurrent. For example, a future[2] can be a Span that would still remain under the parent Span. This provides essential context even for asynchronous operations. We will discuss this in more practical terms as we discuss OpenTelemetry.

Prometheus

Prometheus is an open source monitoring and alerting toolkit created by SoundCloud. Since its release in 2012, it has become the de facto standard for many monitoring needs. As a result, it became the second hosted CNCF (Cloud Native Computing Foundation) project after Kubernetes itself. The ubiquity, portability, simplicity, and performance of Prometheus keep it a popular option even a decade after its release.

I think the best way to explain Prometheus to developers is by explaining how it works. It periodically polls monitored resources and stores the information it retrieves. It then lets us query that information either via a visual UI or via an API.

This doesn't sound difficult at first glance, but the complexity abstracted by Prometheus is tremendous. It stores information in a time series, which means it can provide us with information relating to changes over time. For example, it can plot the CPU usage of all our servers over a period of time. It provides a query language we can use to extract the information we need as data or visualization. In Figure 9-2, we can see the CPU usage plotted by Prometheus in a widget. At the top of Figure 9-2, you can see the statement `rate(system_cpu_usage[1m])` which results in that graph.

---

[2] Asynchronous task launched by the current thread.

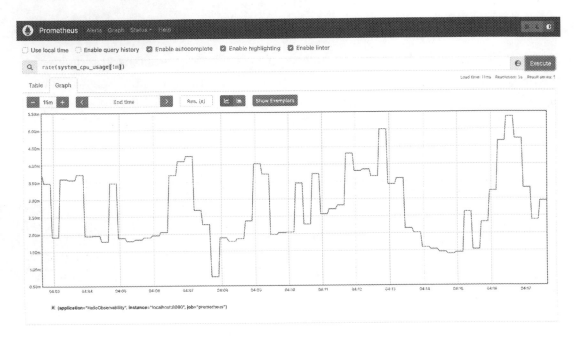

Figure 9-2. *Prometheus showing CPU usage over time*

When we configure Prometheus, we point it at a data source and give it the polling frequency. Many libraries and tools export data in the format expected by Prometheus, for example, Spring supports several different approaches that expose such data. This is important as we can expose JVM and application-specific data directly into the monitoring and alerting system. Good examples of metrics you can monitor are `jvm_classes_loaded_classes`, `cache_evictions_total`, `hikaricp_connections` (database connections), and many others. If you look back at Figure 9-2, you will see a button next to the "Execute" button. This button shows the list of metrics you can watch.

These are all very useful tools that provide an excellent bird's-eye view of the system. That's an important view as some issues can only be understood at that scale. However, you will notice that all we have discussed so far are capabilities of the container (or machine), JVM, and Spring. Capabilities of our application aren't listed here. When we want to track an issue or keep an eye out for a potential issue, application-specific metrics are the most important detail. Thankfully, Prometheus has no idea about any of that. Our application can export additional data, and our custom metrics will show up similarly to all the other listed metrics.

A common JVM framework for that is Micrometer,[3] which has the benefit of vendor neutrality. We can use it to export the metric we wish to observe similarly to an IDE watch variable. Unlike a watch, the value is observed in production and can be plotted over time. The following code shows a simple monitor for a failure when invoking an API. Using this type of code, we can track the number of errors when dealing with a specific API. This lets us pinpoint issues such as increased failure rates related to time of day.

```
private MeterRegistry registry;
private final Counter apiCallFailurerCounter;
private void initCounter() {
  apiCallFailurerCounter = Counter
            .builder( "api_call_failure_counter ")
            .baseUnit("errors")
            .description("Failures when invoking the API")
            . register(registry);
}
public void apiFailure() {
    apiCallFailurerCounter.increment();
}
```

Metrics are ideal for tracking performance and scale-related issues. They're not as great for accurate data since they're based on polling information. They don't track nuance well.

Grafana

Prometheus and Grafana are often mentioned in a single breath, even though they are distinct tools with different use cases. The overlap between Prometheus and Grafana is powerful. While Prometheus includes a basic UI, it's still very spartan. Grafana lets us create an elaborate dashboard with our metrics from multiple data sources. It integrates with many tools, but that's a subject for a different book.

The main value proposition in Grafana is the dashboard. We can include everything we need to know about our system into a single highly configurable dashboard. We can use a set of menus to create arbitrary dashboard widgets that perform metric queries

---

[3] https://micrometer.io/

and processing. Even better, there's a dashboard marketplace where we can reuse existing dashboards for common targets, for example, a dashboard for Keycloak which is a common authorization solution that lets you track things like successful logins in the past 24 hours. In Figure 9-3, we can see a simple dashboard for a Spring Boot application.

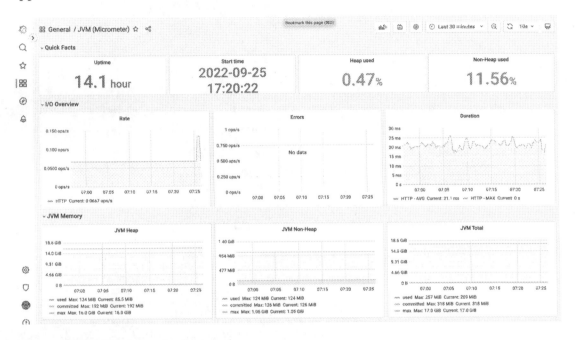

Figure 9-3. Grafana dashboard

I recommend backend developers always keep Grafana open. Explicitly check it twice a day, ideally in the morning. By familiarizing yourself with the dashboard, you instantly know how to recognize the "good" state of the application. When disaster strikes, you have a baseline in your head and a leg up on tracking it.

Furthermore, it's a useful tool for noticing issues before they become downtime. A small increase in error rate now might become downtime a week later. If we spend the time investigating and explaining now, we might avoid the full impact of the actual issue.

OpenTelemetry

OpenTelemetry is another CNCF project; it's a result of a merge between the OpenCensus and OpenTracing projects that preceded it. It's a massive project that includes observability agents and SDKs for sending observability data to the backend.

It's vendor neutral so third parties can create a backend that serves OpenTelemetry and processes the data. Multiple vendors[4] from the monitoring and observability fields have done exactly that.

Note that OpenTelemetry isn't a backend; it doesn't include one, although there are several that work with it. As a result, it can't be compared to Prometheus or similar tools. Ideally, we wouldn't even know we're using OpenTelemetry since the data collected by the agents would get delivered to our vendor-specific observability stack. The value of using it would be vendor neutrality, common functionality, and configuration. In Figure 9-4, we can see a tracing view from a vendor that uses OpenTelemetry. In this picture, we can see the nested spans, the root span, and the time each one of them took.

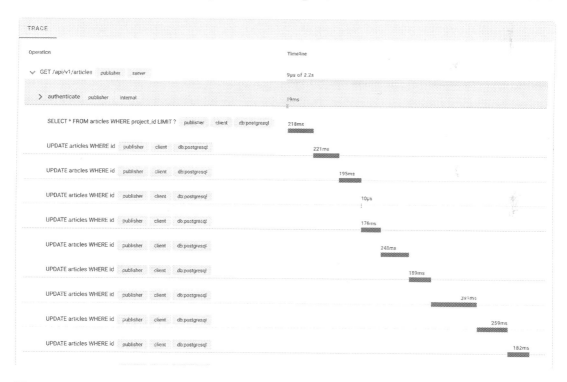

Figure 9-4. *Tracing span view in uptrace.dev*

As you can see from Figure 9-4, the spans run very deep into our application logic. Unlike monitoring information, which is very high level, practically public. This looks much closer to the type of information we would need while tracking an issue in detail. Naturally, we can't just publish this as a URL in our app for polling every 15 seconds.

---

[4] https://opentelemetry.io/vendors/

OpenTelemetry works very differently; we integrate it with platform-specific bootstrap code or parameters. Once bound, the telemetry information is sent directly from the agent to the backend. Agent is the term observability platforms use to define the library (extension) that sends information from your application to the observability backend. The JVM has support for agents with the `-agent`, `-agentlib`, `-agentpath`, etc., arguments. OpenTelemetry is implemented as such an agent when running on the JVM. When installed, the agent collects data almost seamlessly. The following code is the sample used in the OpenTelemetry documentation for adding an agent to a standard Java application:

```
java -javaagent:path/to/opentelemetry-javaagent.jar \
    -Dotel.service.name=your-service-name \
    -Dotel.traces.exporter=zipkin \
    -jar myapp.jar
```

As I mentioned before, if a call uses a future, a Span will be created seamlessly for that future and associated with the current span. If a web service is invoked via a known API, the OpenTelemetry agent will add details about the trace as HTTP headers. This will maintain the entire process even in a highly distributed microservice architecture, potentially spanning multiple nodes.

This raises some concerns as a request such as a database query might include personal information. Access to the observability tooling is probably not as restricted as access to the production database, so this might expose information that we weren't expecting. The automatic configuration includes sensible defaults to remove potentially risky information such as SQL statement values. We can override the defaults and include more (or less) data using the instructions in the guide.[5] In some cases, we would want more refined instrumentation and could use annotations such as `@WithSpan` to denote a span[6] that would start at each point.

An Observability Culture

Up until now, this chapter covered a small set of tools that we have at our disposal as engineers – at the very least, the tools we can request from the DevOps team. If I just list all the tools available with a short blurb, this might become the longest and least

---

[5] https://opentelemetry.io/docs/instrumentation/java/automatic/agent-config/
[6] https://opentelemetry.io/docs/concepts/observability-primer/#spans

interesting chapter of the book. There are **many** tools. They often have merit, value, and necessity. This is a rapidly evolving field, and even if we dedicated the entire book just to these tools and their capabilities, we might run out of space.

The tools are the first step in a culture of observability, automation, and the production cycle. In larger companies, there's a tendency to move a great deal of the production problems to the SRE team. This is problematic as the lessons learned in production lose some impact when passing through that filter. Engineers prioritize the issues they see in front of them.

To do that, we need to treat observability with the same urgency we give continuous integration and development processes. If our artifacts are broken, we won't have a working production environment. If we have no observability, we'll be blind to production disasters. With that in mind, we need to run observability exercises to simulate predictable failures and the way in which we can address them. We discussed this when talking about logs in Chapter 4. Observability and logging are like debugging in advance.

This might sound familiar to you if your company practices chaos engineering.[7] In such companies, there's a practice of chaos game day, where the "master of disaster" runs the team through an exercise simulating disastrous events to prepare for the worst.

There's a lot of overlap between these disciplines, and it makes sense to collaborate with such exercise and teams. But keep in mind that most production issues aren't disasters or failures. Most of what we deal with at the application level are bugs that we can't reproduce locally. They will cause a failure to the user; they are terrible. But they're usually more nuanced. We usually need a light hand on the wheel and deeper data from within the code.

Coverage

To understand the elements that we need to monitor, we need to first understand the types of failures we might expect. There are several common types of failures that are universal for typical web applications. Here are a few common ones:

- Resource exhaustion – Out of memory, storage

- IO failures – Bad disk, networking issues

- Web service failure – Problem in dependency

- Database corruption

- Security hack

---

[7] https://en.wikipedia.org/wiki/Chaos_engineering

Resource exhaustion and IO failure issues are probably covered by your DevOps team. If you have a good DevOps team, it's worth spending time with them, learning that process and aligning your conventions. Our team needs to collect all such potential risk factors. Then, for each risk factor, we need to describe what we would want to know to fix it.

For example, in the case of a web service failure, there would be many things we would want to know. A small sample of questions would be as follows:

- How many failures have occurred?

- Were there successful requests during this time?

- What error codes were returned and at what frequency?

- Are errors user specific?

- Are errors related to the location of the container?

Deciding

Now that we understand the type of problems that we might face in production, we need to design the observability infrastructure that we would like to deal with when running into such an error. The best practice is to have two sources of observability information. Observability can be expensive in terms of performance, storage, and costs. As a result, we need to keep a balanced approach and not log too much or include too many metrics. That's why I suggest keeping two observable elements. If it's only one, it can fail. If it's more than three, the overall costs can become prohibitive.

Let's go over the list from before and decide how we can address all of these:

- How many failures have occurred? – We can add a metric counter for every failure. We would have logs per failure, which we could query to find the number of failures.

- Were there successful requests during this time? What error codes were returned and at what frequency? – We can add a metric that tracks the response codes for every web request.

- Are errors user specific? – Logs should include user ID as part of the MDC,[8] which will let us summarize them per user.

---

[8] Mapped Diagnostic Context discussed in Chapter 4.

- Are errors related to the location of the container? – Logs and metrics include the source machine, which we can use to verify if the problem is specific to a machine.

Developer Dashboard

Many companies have multiple dashboards with Grafana or similar tools covering everything from the key performance indicators (KPIs) to system health. These dashboards are usually tuned for the needs of management, the DevOps team, SRE, etc.

Developers need their own dashboard with the values mentioned earlier. This should be the home page that we see every time we launch a new browser tab. These are the numbers and statistics that should be front and center for every member of the team. We should constantly look for anomalies and changes. Making this into a habit for the entire team changes the way we approach bugs and coding.

Summary

Observability and monitoring are enormous subjects that are covered by many books. I didn't even scratch the surface of this immense subject. But the nice thing is we don't need to know everything to make use of these tools as developers. We need to get a sense of how our application can fail and prepare for those scenarios using these tools. If we have enough coverage and preparation, it should include the information we need, even for a case that we didn't expect.

There are amazing observability and monitoring tools out there. While the tool of choice matters in some regards, the process of working with these tools is often similar. Unfortunately, most of these tools feel "out of place" for developers. We're used to our IDEs and code. These tools pull us out of that concept and introduce a new approach to debugging that requires a shift in perception.

In the next chapter, we'll talk about a new set of tools: developer observability. Some vendors call it the fourth pillar of observability, which it may well become. But for now, it introduces an observability approach that's designed for developers from the ground up. It takes concepts that are familiar to us from the world of debugging and applies them through the lens of observability.

CHAPTER 10

Developer Observability

The three most important aspects of debugging and real estate are the same: Location, Location, and Location.

—Richard E. Pattis

Production is the one thing that matters. Everything else we do is just preparation for production and fixing issues related to production. Despite the tremendously important nature of production, we have relatively limited tools to track issues there. When I say production bug, people always assume the worst – a crash. But a vast majority of production bugs are your typical day-to-day bugs.

When a bug occurs in production, we try to reproduce it locally, but we often can't do that. The next step is the logs and other observability tools we discussed in Chapter 9. But what do we do when the log that we need is hard to find, or isn't even there? What if observability doesn't give us anything to go on?

One solution is to add new logs, but this can take hours at best as we go through PR approval, QA, CI/CD, staging, and finally production. The point of real frustration is going through all of that and realizing you didn't log the right thing. Even with a fast CI/CD cycle, this can be very frustrating. It can also be costly as adding logs ad hoc can result in accidental overlogging.

Developer observability tools work similarly to traditional debuggers. However, they're designed for the scale and rigor of production. They are observability tools, but they're designed for developers and not for the DevOps team.

Before we proceed, I need to make a disclaimer. I was the first non-founder employee at Lightrun, which is a maker of a developer observability tool. I also served as a developer advocate at Lightrun. Note that the material that I cover in this chapter is vendor neutral and applies similarly to all tools. Some might differ on functionality, but the core concepts apply.

© Shai Almog 2023
S. Almog, *Practical Debugging at Scale*, https://doi.org/10.1007/978-1-4842-9042-2_10

What Is Developer Observability?

Developer observability is the fourth pillar of observability. It is a tool that lets us inject debug information into production code. This lets us instrument code as needed in a way that feels like a debugger. For example, we can inject a new log into production code while skipping the deployment cycle as shown in Figure 10-1.

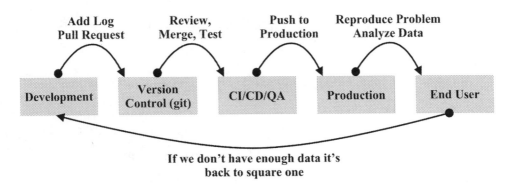

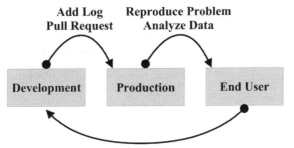

Figure 10-1. *Developer observability vs. the traditional approach*

Skipping the QA cycle and injecting capabilities into production sounds dangerous, and it is. That's why developer observability tools place restrictions on what can be injected, and some run the code in a sandbox. I'll discuss this further when covering the security aspects of developer observability.

There are two core properties of developer observability. The first is its on-demand nature. Observability doesn't require adding code or logic such as logs that require code changes. With developer observability, we can add an action without code changes or preparation.

The second property is that a developer observability action relates to the source code as the trigger. Typical observability tools work with spans, logs, endpoints, etc. These are either prebound to the application during compile time or are bound to elements exported by the application (endpoints). They are high-level abstractions. This makes sense; a DevOps or SRE doesn't necessarily know the applicable source code. Developer observability tools use source code lines as their reference and expect access to said code. When you add a log, you refer to a specific file and line number. This maps to the way developers operate and correlates to the way we work in a debugger.

Remote Debugging?

I discussed remote debugging and the problems it has in Chapter 6. I suggest reading that section again if you don't recall the details. To recap, here are the core problems with remote debugging:

- Insecure – Remote debugging protocols are fragile and insecure.

- Liable – Developers get full unrestricted access to the entire system, creating a security and privacy problem that can leave you liable.

- Breakpoints – Debuggers weren't designed for production. They break by default and can easily block a production server.

- Scale – We have many containers in production often in a cluster. Debugging across multiple server instances is problematic.

All of these are addressed by developer observability tools although not uniformly:

- Insecure and liable – I'll discuss both in depth in the "Security" and "Under the Hood" sections.

- Breakpoints – Developer observability tools have snapshots instead of breakpoints. They don't have features that stop the execution thread. Some go much further than that by sandboxing all operations and verifying code is read-only.

- Scale – Most tools let you place an action on a tag, which means a log can be added to a group of servers at once, not to just one server instance.

Basics

All developer observability solutions are comprised of these three components:

- Agent – We discussed agents in Chapter 9; the concept is very similar here. They are platform- and runtime-specific libraries that implement the core functionality of the tool.

- Backend – The agent communicates with the backend directly. This is an important architectural decision with multiple benefits; one of the most important benefits is keeping production hidden. We don't need to open a port in production for developer observability tools.

- Client – The client is typically an IDE plugin, a web interface, or a command-line interface. It interacts with the backend by sending actions to the agent. This lets us receive the results, if applicable.

To set up a developer observability solution, we need to install an agent (very much like the OpenTelemetry setup we discussed in Chapter 9). Once that is done, we can use the client to issue commands such as adding a log.

One of the big problems with remote debugging is scale. We want to place a tracepoint on a line of code, but it might never be reached if we have a cluster with multiple instances. A load balancer might send the request to a different machine, and we might make the false assumption that the line was never reached. This is a serious problem.

Developer observability solves this problem by introducing the concept of tags. Agents can be associated with multiple tags; as such, we can add an action to a tag, and all the agents associated with the tag will handle the action appropriately. For example, we can add a log to the "Production" tag which will add it to all the production servers. We can customize the tags and create them per group. A good example is an "Ubuntu-20" tag, which can help us test a problem that only reproduces on a specific OS version for our servers. Figure 10-2 shows two agents and one tag listed. The action added to the tag is implicitly added to both agents.

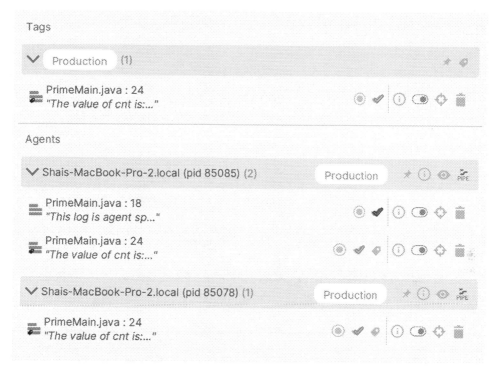

Figure 10-2. *Agents mirror the actions added to a tag*

Dynamic Logging

Dynamic logging is a remarkably powerful feature that masks a great deal of power under the hood. Log statements can be added to a specific line of code, and they can reference variables in context and sometimes even methods. Some developer observability tools will let us add a log such as this:

```
Value of variable is {varName}, I can do expressions {varname * factor}
invoke a method {obj.methodCall()}
```

We can write text, reference variables, perform expressions, and even invoke methods. In Figure 10-3, we see a log injected into a Java application where it prints the value of the variable cnt for every loop iteration. Once added, the log appears between the two lines without changing the line numbers.

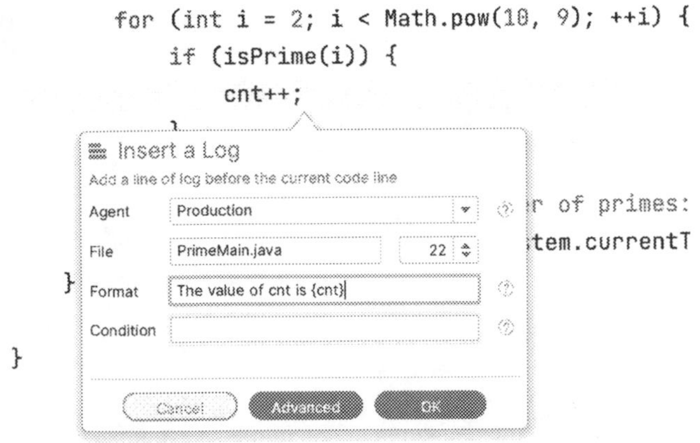

```
for (int i = 2; i < Math.pow(10, 9); ++i) {
    if (isPrime(i)) {
        cnt++;
```

Insert a Log
Add a line of log before the current code line

Agent   Production

File   PrimeMain.java   22

Format   The value of cnt is {cnt}

Condition

Cancel   Advanced   OK

r of primes:
tem.currentT

Figure 10-3. Adding a log to a line of code in Lightrun

Imagine adding a log dynamically to a file where logging is partial or missing entirely. This raises several questions, the first of which might be: How does this interact with the existing logging?

The answer is vendor specific and highly dependent on your configuration, platform, etc. It is possible to integrate the output of logs so they will appear as if you wrote them in the code. This is immensely valuable for some situations where you would like to read the log "in context" with other logs in the system. For example, say you have code that looks like this:

```
public String method(String arg, int otherArgument) {
    logger.info("Reached method {}, {}", arg, otherArgument);
    String resultFromOtherMethod = otherMethod(arg);
    return finalResult(resultFromOtherMethod, otherArgument);
}
```

The first log is obviously very useful, but I'd very much like to know the value of resultFromOtherMethod. I can probably inject a log that includes all the arguments in it but that would take up more CPU; I'm already logging the arguments, so this would trigger duplication. Furthermore, there might be logs from another method that might give further context. By adding a log between the return statement and the otherMethod call, we can get further insight.

Conditions

Logging can be very "noisy," for example, if a method is invoked frequently, we might end up with so many logs that our costs will balloon. It might also make the logs less readable. A good example is the case where a specific user is experiencing a problem with the system. These are the hardest bugs to reproduce locally since they usually depend on the production environment, specific production data, latency, and deployment.

We would want to add additional logging to debug this problem, but we don't want to go over the data for every user or pay the cost of logging for every user out there. The solution when debugging locally is conditional breakpoints. We can add a condition to a breakpoint, and it will hit only when the condition is met. In developer observability, all actions can use conditions, and it's a far more important feature than it is in local debugging. When debugging locally, we're the only users of the system; we get a reasonable number of logs. In production, we might have thousands of servers with millions of users. Imagine the amount of output we could add in such a scenario. Even for smaller deployments, the additional data can be overwhelming.

We can set a condition for any action, which means it will work for snapshots and metrics (both of which we'll cover later in this chapter). A very common condition is one that limits the action to a specific user account. That way, we can filter out the noise and see only the data that's applicable to the bug we're tracking. In Figure 10-4, we can see a conditional log that will only print out the data for a user matching the condition `Security.getCurrentUser().getId().equals("ID")`.

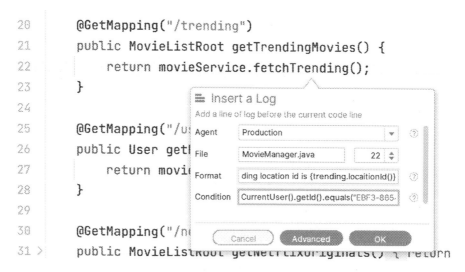

Figure 10-4. *A log with a conditional statement*

Collaboration

When we debug locally, it's a solo process. As we add actions in a developer observability tool, we make changes to the production, for example, by adding new logs. When a member of our team adds a log or any other action, it can be viewed by other members of the team. Some products support team segregation and privacy solutions, but when using features such as logging, we will inherently all see the changes from one developer.

Some tools support the ability to work as a team on an action. After a log is added, all members of the team can see it within the IDE integrated with the code. They can see the specific user that added the log and the details about that as we can see in Figure 10-5. Notice that the line count in Figure 10-5 skips over the log line since it isn't an actual code change.

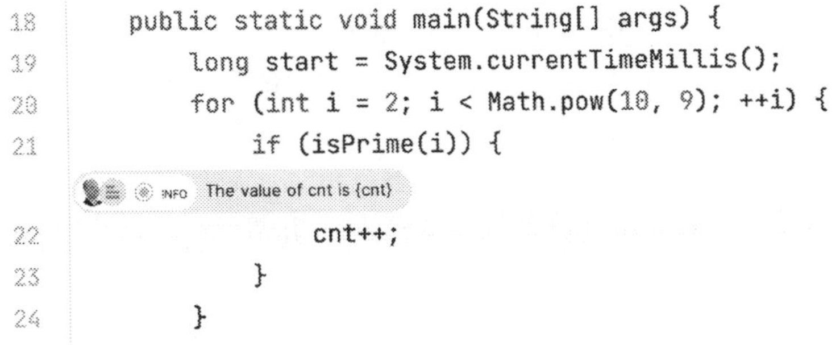

```
18          public static void main(String[] args) {
19              long start = System.currentTimeMillis();
20              for (int i = 2; i < Math.pow(10, 9); ++i) {
21                  if (isPrime(i)) {
        INFO  The value of cnt is {cnt}
22                      cnt++;
23                  }
24              }
```

Figure 10-5.   *A log embedded in the IDE UI*

In some cases, we would want to add logs as we track a specific issue, without disturbing our team. As I debug, I often add lines such as "methodX reached with value Y". Logs like that can be problematic, in terms of noise. There is also a case where a value we want to log is private, and we might not want it in the log. A good example is the user token; this might be something that can be used to impersonate a user. We might have policies that prohibit us from logging such a value. For such cases, we can pipe the output of an action or agent to a different location.

We can send all the logs from the developer observability tool to the IDE instead of the main application log. That way, they can remain internal within the team and reduce noise. Some solutions support user-level granularity for log output as well. In Figure 10-6, we can see logs piped into the IDE UI.

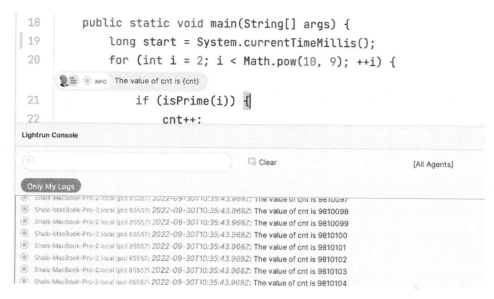

Figure 10-6. *Log output piped to the IDE UI*

Snapshots

Snapshots have different names in observability tools, specifically nonbreaking breakpoints or captures. They all mean the same thing; for convenience, I'll go with snapshots. The concept is identical in all the tools; it's a breakpoint stack trace, with stack values. There are some differences between snapshots and breakpoints:

- They don't stop the execution. In that way, they are more like tracepoints. They aren't interactive; we can't step over after they're hit.

- They only capture the state of a single thread.

- They have a size limit a very large stack might be missing some state.

In other regards, snapshots are a carbon copy of breakpoints. You can traverse the stack and see the call chain that resulted in the snapshot hit. We can see the stack frame variable states for every stack entry as shown in Figure 10-7. Variable values can include complex object states and hierarchies, but because the agent needs to transmit the snapshot data and needs to be efficient, there are limits. We'll discuss this in more depth when discussing the architecture of these tools.

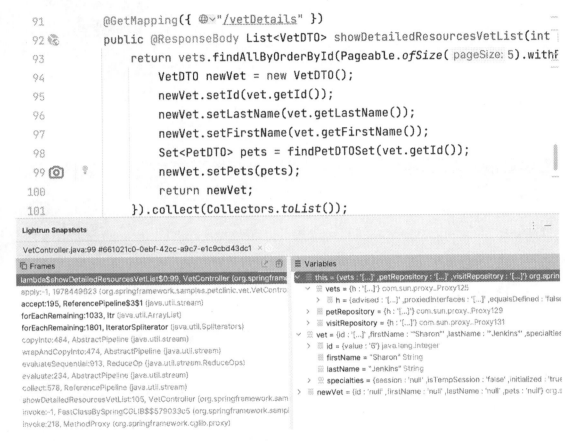

```
91          @GetMapping({ ⊕∨"/vetDetails" })
92          public @ResponseBody List<VetDTO> showDetailedResourcesVetList(int
93              return vets.findAllByOrderById(Pageable.ofSize( pageSize: 5).withF
94                  VetDTO newVet = new VetDTO();
95                  newVet.setId(vet.getId());
96                  newVet.setLastName(vet.getLastName());
97                  newVet.setFirstName(vet.getFirstName());
98                  Set<PetDTO> pets = findPetDTOSet(vet.getId());
99                  newVet.setPets(pets);
100                 return newVet;
101             }).collect(Collectors.toList());
```

Figure 10-7. *Traversing the stack trace in a snapshot looks like a breakpoint*

Working with snapshots is very familiar, but it takes some effort to get used to the lack of stepping over. There are some advantages as snapshots are nonblocking. Debugging concurrency issues is much easier because of the nonblocking behavior.

There are some major advantages to working with a snapshot over a breakpoint. We can add a conditional snapshot and go make a cup of coffee. We can even go home and come back the next day and have all the data we need to understand the root cause of a hard-to-reproduce problem. In one case, we had concerns that a newly discovered zero-day vulnerability might be exploited by users. We immediately added a conditional snapshot to the applicable line in the problematic file. This would trigger when a hacker would try to use the exploit and include all information related to the hack. Developer observability tools are read-only so we can't stop such a hack, but we would have everything necessary to mitigate if the snapshot was hit. It wasn't, but we tested it and verified it would have worked as expected.

Metrics

We discussed metrics in Chapter 9. I think they're wonderful. Profilers are great, but they only represent the performance of a local run. What matters is the user experience in production, and that can vary wildly due to latency, dataset sizes, etc. Typical observability metrics are high level. That's good for many cases, but sometimes it's hard to tell why the numbers are bad.

Let's say we see a spike in performance when looking at the observability data. It isn't consistent and doesn't necessarily tell us which line of code is at fault. It might be happening only to a subset of users who might be complaining. Traditional observability doesn't really help. My workaround for this used to be something like this:

```
public void slowMethod() {
    long startTime = System.currentTimemillis();
    // method body
    logger.info("slowMethod took: {}", System.currentTimemillis() -
    startTime);
}
```

I would deploy this to production, which was a great help but also tedious. I'd often need to redeploy this because the method invoked by the parent would trigger another method and so forth. This is the most accurate way to track such issues as a profiler impacts the performance of an application too much and is problematic in production.

Tic toc and method duration metrics are just that. You can apply them to an arbitrary block of code or a method (respectively) and measure the performance of that area. A tic toc measures the time between the tic (start of the measurement) and the toc (where it ends). A method duration is the exact same concept applied to an entire method and not a block of code. The nice thing about this is that we can apply such metrics as a conditional action. We can measure performance surgically only for a specific user. Some tools support outputting the results into Prometheus or other observability tools.

Another common issue is measuring fine-grained internal usage. When refactoring or migrating an API, we want to know which functionality is used and which isn't. We can instrument everything to our monitoring stack. But that's a hassle and requires planning ahead. It's hard to get answers for complex questions such as how many times are users from a spccific company reaching this line of code? Counters let us measure usage by incrementing with every invocation. We can bind a counter to a line, possibly conditionally, and get insight into usage.

Under the Hood

All developer observability tools are very similar in their basic architecture. Under normal conditions, I think some ignorance about the underlying architecture of a debugger is acceptable. The same isn't necessarily the case for a developer observability solution. These tools are deployed into production; we need to have at least a reasonable understanding of the risks and trade-offs we make when we install something in production.

I mentioned the division between the backend, client, and agent as we can see in Figure 10-8. But I didn't explain why that separation exists in the first place. Why can't a client connect directly to the agents? There are several reasons for that:

- A direct connection will require exposing the server addresses which will be risky.

- A developer would need to connect to every server which is a hassle.

- Agents can be made simple and almost stateless. This shifts complexity to the backend.

- Information collected by the agent can be stored even if the application crashes.

- Tags and related features can be implemented in the backend.

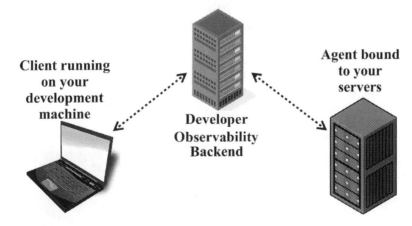

Figure 10-8. *Developer observability architecture*

There are many things that are very vendor specific within this basic architecture – the communication protocols; whether the client is an IDE, web UI, or CLI; and whether the backend server is hosted as a SaaS or on premise. All of those represent the differences between various vendors in this field.

Security

Security is probably the most important aspect of any production-grade observability solution. This is especially true in this case as debuggers are normally very vulnerable to exploits; a production debugger runs a risk. As such, the architecture is designed to minimize risk as much as possible.

Segregation

As we saw in Figure 10-8, the agent only communicates with the backend servers. Typically, an agent will send a request to the backend and receive a response. That means backend servers aren't exposed and can keep their IP addresses hidden from client machines. This is a crucial security measure when hardening a deployment.

This means that even if the developer observability platform is compromised by a hack, the hackers would still have limitations on what they can do. Even the backend server can't access the agents directly, only send them commands. Commands have limitations in scope.

To further enforce secure communication in all tiers, some vendors offer certificate pinning to harder communications. This is a feature that verifies the signature of the backend certificate to protect against a man-in-the-middle attack.

Accountability

According to IBM, 60% of security breaches in the organization are internal.[1] This is a major problem. Many developers have access to the logs, but very few have access to the database. If we log something bad or problematic (user passwords, credit card numbers, etc.), we might be in big trouble. This can be a problem whether someone tries to do this on purpose or accidentally. Luckily, some solutions exist.

Some developer observability tools support an audit log. This log tracks the operations that occur on the backend and the user that performed them. If a user tries to do something malicious, it will be logged. Such a malicious user will keep a digital trail behind.

---

[1] www.ibm.com/reports/threat-intelligence/

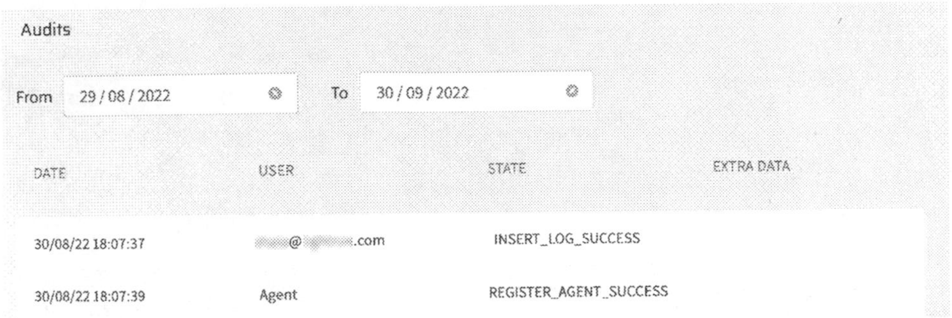

Figure 10-9. *Audit log*

Audit logs are great, and they work well for malicious intent, at least in retrospect. How do we prevent a mistake or even a malicious attempt? There are two common solutions. The first is Personally Identifiable Information (PII) reduction, which I mentioned briefly in Chapter 4. It's a niche logging feature which has gained special prominence in the world of developer observability.

The core idea is that some things should never be logged – credit card numbers, user tokens, etc. Some of these elements can be identified since they have a fixed pattern that we can recognize, for example, a Mastercard credit card has the pattern \b5[1-5]\d\d([\-\ ]?)(?:\d{4}\1){2}\d{4}\b as a regular expression. PII reduction lets us define such patterns and eliminate them from the log. This is especially important for developer observability tools where we can add a log without going through the code review process. Figure 10-10 shows the PII reduction UI of a developer observability tool.

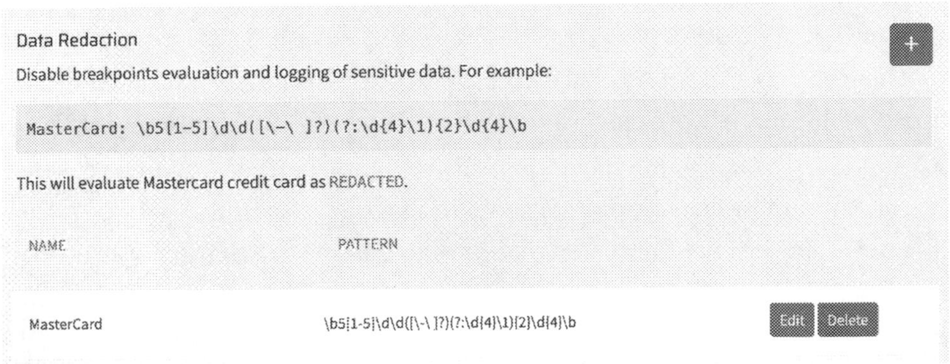

Figure 10-10. *PII reduction*

Usernames and passwords don't follow a pattern. The doomsday scenario would be a malicious developer on our team adding a log to the user login code, then logging all usernames and passwords. Such a person might be able to pipe all the information to their own machine. A person committing a breach could be caught thanks to the audit log, but administrators would need to know that they should look in the audit log.

Blocklists are there to prevent that situation from ever happening. We can block a pattern for a class or file name, then when a user tries to add an action in such a class, they will get blocked. When setting up a developer observability solution, this should be one of the first stops in the process. Figure 10-11 shows the setup of a blocklist.

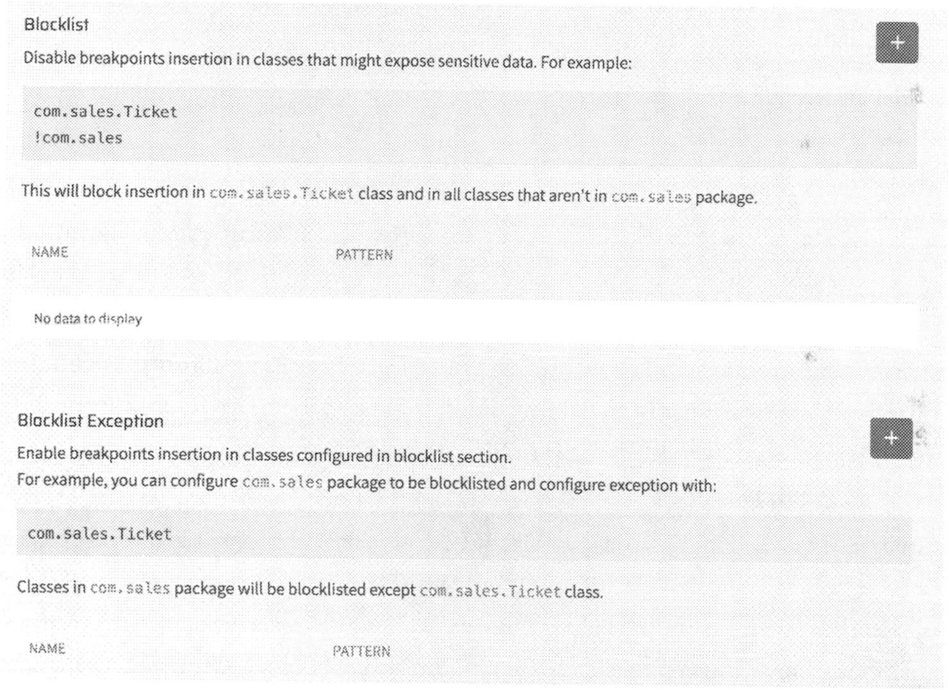

Figure 10-11. *Block list*

Agent

Agent security is even more important than backend security. A vulnerability in the agent can expose the servers completely. One of the first things I noticed when looking at developer observability log statements was the risk of method invocations. Why not add a log statement such as

```
Give Shai some sugar {transferCash(1000000, "shai@notmymail.com")}
```

This is a valid statement, and it would work by transferring money to my account, at least in theory, assuming the `transferCash` method is that simple. But some developer observability solutions have features to combat this vulnerability. The first is forcing read-only statements. This is difficult since read-only is sometimes ambiguous. Solutions like that will block some valid code. In my opinion, the peace of mind in read-only is worth the price of some false positives. Since `transferCash` will require a state change (even a network call), these solutions will fail.

Another capability is the sandbox. Some solutions offer the ability to run the code in a sandbox. That means the code won't be able to run malicious code. But this goes further; it means that code won't be able to consume too much CPU. It gets throttled. This solves a major concern when logging too much by mistake.

Summary

Developer observability is in its infancy relatively speaking. Additional tools and solutions are popping into the market and increasing the mindshare for these tools. I believe these tools will reignite developer interest in production. Back in the day, we used to work on the servers all the time; it's good that's no longer a requirement. But it's also a hindrance. When a user complains about a problem, we're often stumped. These tools become essential as debugging needs scale.

This chapter talked about the theory of developer observability; I'll discuss these tools more in the practical debugging chapters that follow. I think it's a tool that makes developers feel "at home" when compared to standard observability tools. But this isn't an exclusive situation. Both observability tools are needed for a complete production picture. The analogy I often use is that an observability tool is like the dashboard in your car and the check engine light. You can see everything you need as a driver. But when you take the car to the mechanic, they connect their own computer to analyze the engine. That's observability vs. developer observability. A high-level global view vs. localized highly detailed view for a specific professional.

The next chapter starts the third part of the book in which we will dive into more practical solutions for specific use cases of the debugger. Chapter 11 will discuss using the debugger as a learning tool to study new project source code and understand your environment.

PART III

In Practice

CHAPTER 11

Tools of Learning

The process of debugging, going and correcting the program and then looking at the behavior, and then correcting it again, and finally iteratively getting it to a working program, is in fact, very close to learning about learning.

—Nicholas Negroponte

I spent over a decade as a consultant. That was a tough job. I would arrive at a company as an "expert" and need to instantly prove myself under scrutiny. Imagine doing a job interview where the interviewer really doesn't want to hire you on a system you aren't familiar with. That's consulting. I was faced with codebases that were completely alien to me and had to solve problems that the people who knew the codebase in and out couldn't solve!

One of my secret weapons was the debugger. When I had to understand new code in a hurry, it was an amazing learning tool. As an instructor, I also use the debugger a lot; it lets the students see the actual implementation and understand everything. Stepping over the code and seeing variables change triggered the "ah ha moment" for many 101 students. Inspecting a complex data structure helped experienced developers struggling with grasping new concepts such as proxies in backend servers.

In this chapter, I'll discuss some of my tips for learning new code and understanding parts of the code you aren't familiar with. I hope that the next time you open a new project at a new job, the debugger will be your main companion.

Before the Debugger

Debugging is wonderful at illuminating the behavior of code at runtime and verifying assumptions instantly. It's sometimes clumsy at discovery as it's a fine-grained tool. When I first approach a project, I need to get my bearings, and the debugger isn't always ideal for that.

© Shai Almog 2023
S. Almog, *Practical Debugging at Scale*, https://doi.org/10.1007/978-1-4842-9042-2_11

In those situations, I usually open the UML diagramming capabilities of the IDE. As flawed as they are, I usually find them superior to documentation, which is frequently out of sync with the actual project code. IDE features such as "Find Usage" and "Go To Implementation" are often faster to use in the initial exploration.

In some extreme cases, I run the code with `strace` (which we discussed in Chapter 3), then as an exercise try to explain what the system does at any given time. It opens a socket to address X or reads file Y. This helps me understand how it works under the hood even without understanding the implementation. When I see something that I can't explain in the `strace` output, it's immediately an interesting exercise to follow in the source code.

Moving to a Debugger

These tools are wonderful for an initial lay of the land. They don't properly convey how things work in practice. A good example would be a generic interface that's invoked in the application flow. Which specific concrete implementation is invoked? It might be hard to tell without reading all the code and following the elaborate runtime flows. This is something we can easily determine in seconds with the debugger.

With a debugger, we can verify assumptions, see "real-world" usage, and step over a code block to understand the flow. We can place a breakpoint to see if a block of code was reached. If it's reached too frequently and we can't figure out what's going on, we can use a conditional breakpoint to limit the scope.

I make it a habit to read the values of variables in the watch when using a debugger to study a codebase. I then ask myself if this value makes sense now. If it doesn't, then I have something to study. Nothing teaches you more about source code than following a "mystery." If the value makes sense, then we clearly understand the source code, and we "win" either way. With this debugger, I can quickly understand the semantics of the codebase. In the following sections, I'll cover techniques for learning both in the debugger and in production.

Standard Debugger Techniques

I discussed most of these tools in the first chapter of this book. Most of the concepts and techniques we will go through aren't new, but some are. The context for tools and usage is different, and it's the main subject of this chapter.

Who Changes This Variable?

Many developers know about field watchpoints and just forget about them. "Who changed this value, and why?" is probably the most common question asked by developers. When we look through the code, there might be dozens of code flows that trigger a change. But placing a watchpoint on a field will tell you everything in seconds.

Understanding state mutation and propagation is probably the most important thing you can do when studying a codebase. A common question I have is "is this the only path that changes this field?". There are two ways I can verify that. The first is to use a tracepoint[1] with a stack trace as we can see in Figure 11-1. Notice that the stack trace checkbox is marked, and we only print it on field modification to avoid the noise of field access. I also print out the value of the field so we will have a context value to go with the stack trace. This way, I can review the output and instantly see which line of code changed the value of the field to a specific value.

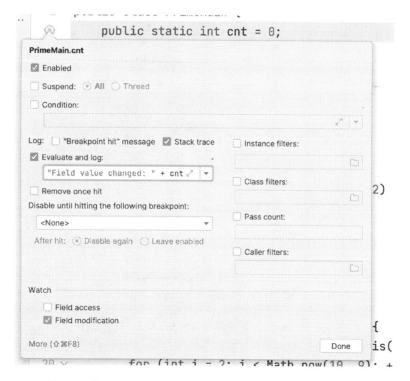

Figure 11-1. *Field watchpoint tracepoint with a stack trace*

---

[1] We discussed tracepoints (a.k.a. logpoints) in Chapter 1. They are breakpoints that don't suspend the current thread and can log or print the stack trace when the tracepoint is hit.

The second option is even more interesting. Say you have a field that's constantly accessed by one or two methods in the top stack which produce most of the "noise." You want to see if something else in the code might be triggering a chance to this field. For this, we can use the "Caller Filters" feature that you can see at the lower portion of Figure 11-1. Unfortunately, as of this writing, this functionality isn't supported for field watchpoints. However, if you have a setter method that encapsulates the field, you can use it on a breakpoint there.

When enabled, we can define inclusive and exclusive filters on the method that will trigger the breakpoint. An inclusive filter will allow us to stop only when the filter is applicable. An exclusive filter will block these methods and is the more useful case for this specific feature. In Figure 11-2, we can see a caller filter on a breakpoint; notice you can edit it directly or in the helper dialog that pops up when clicking the button next to the text field.

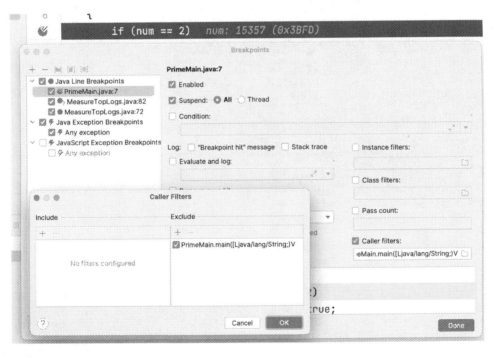

Figure 11-2. *Caller filter*

The syntax for the filter is a bit "odd" and takes some getting used to even if you have a deep background in low-level VM programming. Hopefully, JetBrains will expose a friendlier UI for this important feature in a future revision. For now, the syntax works like this.

Entries are separated by a space. Exclusive entries have the - character prepended in front of the word, for example, `-PrimeMain.main([Ljava/lang/String;)V`. Next is the package name, followed by the class name, followed by the method name. Within the brackets, we have the argument types listed with no separation, and after the brackets, the return type. The syntax for the arguments uses the JVM internal notation,[2] which you can see in Table 11-1. This is very counterintuitive to developers who aren't used to the syntax. There's no separation in arguments since all primitive arguments are a single character. All object arguments have a semicolon at the end anyway. There's no need for commas or spaces. The syntax for a class starts with the uppercase `L` followed by the fully qualified class name where the `.` character is replaced by the `/` character. Arrays are represented by prepending a `[` before the variable type.

[2] `https://docs.oracle.com/javase/specs/`

Table 11-1. *JVM Type Notations for Filters*

Java Type	JVM Notation	Sample
void	V	void myMethod()
		myMethod()V
boolean	Z	void myMethod(boolean b)
		myMethod(Z)V
char	C	void myMethod(char c, Boolean b)
		myMethod(CZ)V
byte	B	byte[] myMethod(byte b)
		myMethod(B)[B
short	S	void myMethod(short s, byte[] b)
		myMethod(S[B)V
int	I	void myMethod(int i)
		myMethod(I)V
float	F	void myMethod(float i)
		myMethod(F)V
long	J	void myMethod(long i)
		myMethod(J)V
double	D	void myMethod(double i)
		myMethod(D)V
class	L	void myMethod(MyObject i, int[] a)
		myMethod(Lcom/myPackage/MyObject;[I)V
[] (array)	[	String[] myMethod(byte[] b, MyObject[] a)
		myMethod([B[L com/myPackage/MyObject;)[Ljava/lang/String;

Note   The JVM was optimized for size. The class file format is no exception. The syntax for Java types is minimalistic to keep the size small. This is how class files represent method signatures internally.

Why Do We Need This Code?

As I step over in the debugger, I'm often stumped by blocks of code. Is this code even necessary? Do we even need that? This is very hard to answer as there might be wide-ranging implications. I sometimes comment out the code to try and see the impact, but this means restarting the debugging session, rebuilding, etc. That can be tedious and disruptive to my learning flow. A simpler solution is placing a breakpoint in that code and doing a return immediately (force return) every time we reach that block.

We can similarly use the throw exception option to trigger an exception in such a case. This is only useful for understanding code that might trigger such an exception and following the logic in a case of failure.

In both cases, we would want to understand the wide-ranging implications. Some of these we can see in the behavior of the application's functionality, but some are more subtle in the application state and in reachability. A field might be set to a value we don't want, or logic that might be "problematic" might be reached. We need to place breakpoints and tracepoints in those relevant areas to monitor for such implications.

Keeping Track

As we debug the code, it's hard to keep track of everything that's going on in our head, especially when we're learning and trying to keep everything organized. When we write code, we have multiple tools to keep track of everything: packages, classes, encapsulation, naming, etc. I might have one breakpoint that's related to one thing I'm trying to understand and another that's related to something else. I might have a variable value that I want to follow and another that I need to understand.

The debugger includes some tools that let us keep this all under control. Breakpoints can be collected into groups related to specific debugging sessions or processes as seen in Figure 11-3. We can enable or disable an entire group, so if we want to check something else for a while and get back to this session later, we can pick up right where we left off. When we create a group, we can give it a descriptive name that can help us understand why we created this breakpoint in the first place.

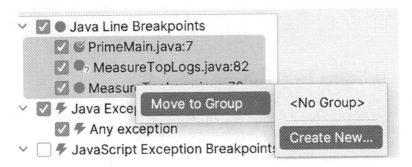

Figure 11-3. *Grouping breakpoints*

We can go even further and give every breakpoint a descriptive name that indicates its purpose as seen in Figure 11-4. This might seem unnecessary when we have a dozen breakpoints in place, but for sophisticated debugging sessions, that can become valuable. I often need to pause a debugging session due to a high priority issue. In these cases, I usually spend the time grouping and describing the breakpoints so I will have the context saved when I get back to the session later.

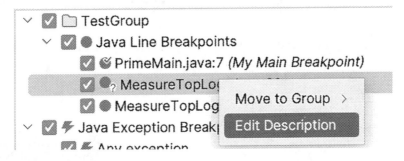

Figure 11-4. *Breakpoint descriptions*

I discussed object marking at length in the first chapter. They are one of my favorite features in IntelliJ/IDEA. We can use watch variables to keep track of values, but this only applies in the current scope; marking an object keeps track of it as we step through the entire application, so we don't lose track of the data. This is something I used to do with pen and paper as I was stepping through the code. This is a fantastic feature for learning and keeping track of the data.

Renderers, which we also discussed in the first chapter, are a remarkable learning tool. In many projects, I'm flooded with redundant information as I step over and view the watch. Objects have too many fields, and I want to focus on the main point of interest. For the learning session, I can create a custom renderer that only shows the variables I care about from the given object. This lets me understand what's going on immediately without expanding the object. If I do want to dig deeper, I can expand the object, but the quick view can tell me more by default. Figure 11-5 shows a simple renderer that shows the full name of the vet. I expanded the vet object on the right to show that I still have full access to the data if I desire that during the learning process.

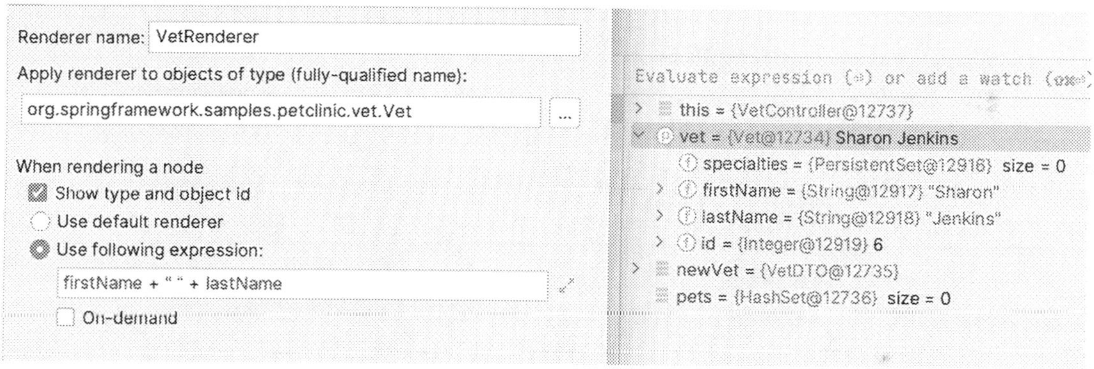

Figure 11-5. *Renderer*

What's Going On?

Context is very important when we're trying to learn. We have a global view of the classes through a UML diagram or just by looking at the code. But the flip side of that is the state. The variable values for instances in RAM tell us more about our understanding of the code than most other techniques. I discussed "Show Objects" in the first chapter; it's a remarkable feature. I also discussed object tracking with "Show new instances" which lets us see the stack traces that allocated the objects and helps us verify our assumptions related to the formation of the state.

By inspecting all the objects in memory, we can create a proper model in our mind of the application's runtime behavior. One of the cool things is that the object viewer respects the renderer settings, which lets us quickly scan a large set of objects. The main tool I use for object inspection is the filter field at the top of the dialog. It lets us narrow down the list to a more manageable size. Figure 11-6 shows a filtered list of Vet objects with a renderer applied to them.

Figure 11-6. Inspecting objects

Learning with Observability

Production is the most important thing to learn. Some systems can't be debugged properly locally. In such systems, observability solutions help us get our bearings in the code and state. I've discussed all these tools in Chapters 9 and 10, so I won't go too deep into the details. The beauty of using observability in this capacity is that it lets us understand how a system works in the real world.

Dashboard Exploration

A great way to start is to set up a custom dashboard and start adding metrics. Once you see the values for the metric, try to find the code that generates that metric. Code that generates a custom metric represents an area that's important. Otherwise, developers wouldn't have bothered generating said metric. There are some exceptions, such as metrics that are no longer relevant, so you need to first verify that data is coming through in the dashboard.

The dashboard gives us a bird's-eye view of the system and its high-level state. It's a way to get a feel of the "important information" in the system we're studying.

Log Pinpointing

Few things teach you more about a system than reading the log and reviewing the applicable code. Opening production logs and following through with the source code in hand is a powerful process. User flows are hard to understand in theory, but when we walk through with an actual user and understand a specific process, it clicks.

For this to work properly, additional metadata per log is very helpful. I would often need a way to isolate the logs related to a specific user and ideally metadata about the request. That way, I can reduce a specific flow, like a signup flow, to a readable set of logs that I can then use to understand the underlying code.

Learning with Developer Observability

I often stumble on an API call which baffles me. Do people even use this feature? This is something we can't always answer. With developer observability, we can add a log or a counter to resolve this question quickly. This can instantly inform us on the importance of a specific API.

Another important feature is log piping which lets us inject logs seen only by us; they won't be ingested by the observability stack. Make sure to send logging output to the IDE when debugging rather than keeping it with the rest of the logs. Otherwise, the experimentation and learning process might interfere with the regular maintenance of the system. When you add logs and things still aren't clear, a snapshot helps fill in the gaps by providing a stack trace and variable context.

Summary

Learning a new codebase is a challenging process regardless of our approach. Debuggers make this process more manageable and help us focus on the things that matter. Unlike other methods of studying code, debuggers help us focus on how the implementation works and program state in runtime. Nothing beats stepping over code with a debugger when you want to understand how it really works.

Understanding the debugger deeply helps us scale that process to learn large and complex codebases with elaborate state. Using external tools such as observability to understand the dynamics of the system helps cement the "big picture" as we're reading the code and going beyond the basic flows.

In the next chapter, we will discuss techniques and tools for tracking performance and memory issues locally and in production. I will discuss some of the tools available for that purpose, but I'll keep things focused on the debugger perspective.

CHAPTER 12

Performance and Memory

One accurate measurement is worth a thousand expert opinions.

—Admiral Grace Murray Hopper

In their groundbreaking book *Refactoring*,[1] Fowler and Beck tell a story of a slow performing system. All the experts gathered around to give their expert opinions on "what might be the cause." Profiling pointed at something that none of them suspected in the least. This is a familiar problem; we have preconceptions. Tooling doesn't. The reason for performance and memory problems often differs from our preconceived notions.

Profilers are amazing tools, but they aren't perfect. They grab a snapshot at a point in time. They disrupt the application and sometimes impact the result. They show the big picture and don't always reflect the detail. I've often faced a situation where RAM is taken up by byte arrays. This is problematic since many classes include byte arrays within them. It's hard to find the specific areas that should be optimized. The same is true for performance. The numbers are sometimes misleading.

In this chapter, we will review that thin line between the profiler and the debugger. After you run the profiler and get some results, this is how you make sense of it, by using it as a starting point for your debugging session. This is important since many performance and memory problems turn out as bugs.

---

[1] https://martinfowler.com/books/refactoring.html

Performance Measuring Basics

In this section, I'll discuss load testing tools, specifically JMeter.[2] I will skip profilers since that's a separate subject that deserves far more than a single chapter. I'll focus on the intersection points between profiling results and the debugger.

JMeter Overview

A load testing tool such as JMeter lets us invoke a feature repeatedly to simulate heavy load on a system. The typical setup for running a load testing tool is in the cloud, where load test servers send requests to a cloud deployment. This simulates real-world scenarios and doesn't starve the system of resources. That's the "right way" to use the tool, but it's also problematic.

There are two problems with this approach:

- It makes load testing inaccessible. If I need to set up cloud servers at a cost just to run a test, I'll do that infrequently (if at all).

- It makes debugging the load situation much harder.

Before we proceed, I want to be clear: setting up a test in the cloud is the right way to properly test load on the system. You should use that approach to assess the **real** bottlenecks in the system.

In this case, I'll run JMeter locally against a simple server; this will give me inaccurate results. That isn't a bad thing. Performance is like traffic. When we solve a bottleneck, we move the traffic jam to a new location. By running locally, we ignore large swaths of the stack. But the part we don't ignore is the code; the overhead we see in the code is often the most important overhead for us as developers and most applicable for this book.

JMeter lost some of its coolness factor to newer tools such as Gatling, but it's still a remarkably sophisticated solution. It lets us create test scripts and even record a session which it can later play back to the server with high intensity. For example, if we want to test a very sophisticated load process, we can set up JMeter as a web proxy to our browser and record everything we do on the website. It will generate a script based on that which we can run over and over on the load test.

---

[2] https://jmeter.apache.org/

Working with JMeter

JMeter works with test plans in which we define the requests we want sent. Ideally, one would run JMeter from the command line as part of our continuous integration process. It can fail a test if performance degrades or error rates rise, thus preventing a regression. But this is a different subject. We want to make a simple load test that we can use in conjunction with a debugger.

There are many ways to create a JMeter test; for simplicity, I often just use the import from cURL option as seen in Figure 12-1. This option pops up a dialog where we can paste in standard cURL commands, and a test plan is created for us implicitly. There are many other options such as recording,[3] which is another favorite of mine.

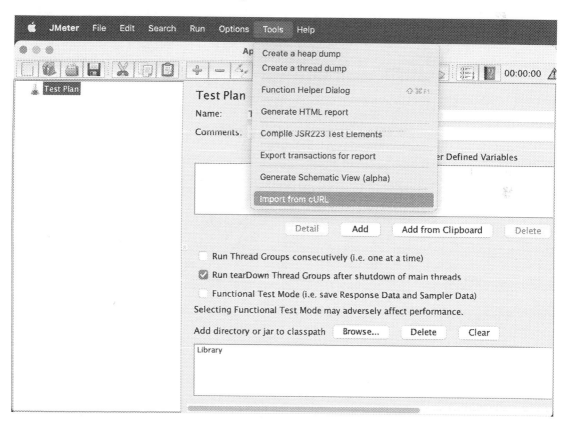

Figure 12-1. *Import from cURL*

---

[3] https://jmeter.apache.org/usermanual/jmeter_proxy_step_by_step.html

Once we do that, we can run the test against our servers; it will generate high-volume traffic, and we can debug the bottlenecks with this tool. It's important to set the result file name for the test plan as seen in Figure 12-2. Without it, the test results are lost, and it's harder to get insights on the execution from the JMeter side.

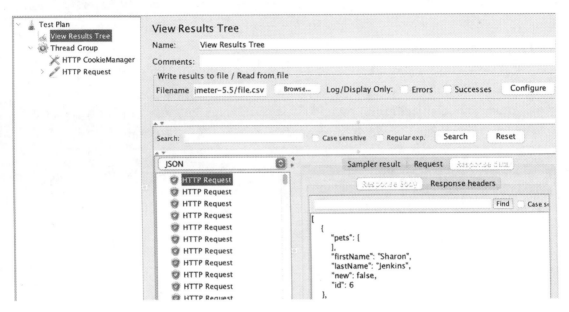

Figure 12-2. *Setting the results file is important*

With the *Tools* ➤ *Generate HTML Report* menu option, we can generate a visualization of this execution that we can use to understand what happened on the JMeter side as seen in Figure 12-3. I'll deal with the debugger for the rest of this chapter and use JMeter only to generate the load which we can subsequently test in the debugger.

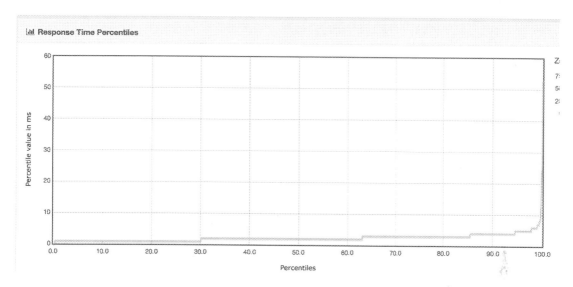

Figure 12-3. *The JMeter HTML report includes a cool throughput graph*

Basics of Profilers

I thought about adding a section about profilers to this chapter where I would have covered Java Flight Recorder (JFR) or a similar profiler. It's an interesting subject with many nuances. I eventually decided to skip that. There are many resources on using profilers; I don't have anything interesting to say about that.[4]

Understanding the output of a profiler is the interesting part. That's a bit of an art form mixed with familiarity with the code and UI of the profiler. There's black magic to that art form that I don't like. It's also something that I find hard to distill beyond:

- Look at the slowest method

- Dig into that method

- Dig deeper

That isn't helpful. Memory profiling is even more annoying. We get the type of the object (or primitive) that takes up RAM and need to find out where it's held. The tool sends us in a good direction, but it's missing the last mile. That's OK if you have deep familiarity with the code, it isn't ideal if you don't.

---

[4] www.baeldung.com/java-flight-recorder-monitoring

Debugging Performance

The debugger isn't great at measuring. It's a fine-grained tool that works best when pointed at specific metrics. But it can be used as a profiler. There are several tricks we can use to leverage the debugger as a sidekick to the profiler when measuring CPU performance.

A Hacker Profiler

You may recall I lamented about the lack of mutable state for tracepoints. That's indeed a huge problem. One of my favorite ways to do profiling is with simple code like this:

```
long time = System.currentTimeMillis();
// code
System.out.println("Total time: " + (System.currentTimeMillis() - time));
```

The advantage in this approach is in the localized nature of the benchmark. It doesn't have the impact of a profiler, and it measures just what we need. This is great when we're measuring a few calls to a method. But when running something like a JMeter test, we get a tremendous amount of data. In those cases, the profiler shines since it can show us great statistics. JMeter also has statistics, but they include the full round trip, not the details about the performance of the method and its degradation.

It's also inconvenient for iterative work. I usually move these a lot. If a method takes time, I move the top line inward to narrow down the problematic line or move this to a different method within the call chain to see if that method is problematic. This approach means I need to stop the server, add code, rebuild, and rerun everything. It's possible but tedious.

There's another way. We can log the time the method starts and the time it finishes. This isn't as convenient since we'll have to subtract the value ourselves, but there's a solution for that too. The naïve solution would be to add the tracepoint:

```
"Method enter " + System.currentTimeMillis()
```

We would also add the corresponding method exit. But this is problematic. Since we run the JMeter test with multiple threads, we might see two entries at once from two different threads. It would make things even harder. We also need the thread name in the tracepoint. Furthermore, even a short run will result in hundreds or maybe thousands of lines. How can we process such a large amount?

My solution is to use comma-separated values (CSV), which is a standard we use to represent tabular data. This means we can import the resulting data directly into any spreadsheet and run analysis on it. I can get the visualizations I want and instant calculations. The following code will generate CSV output when used in a tracepoint as shown in Figure 12-4.

```
"\"Enter\",\"" + Thread.currentThread().getName() + "\"," + System.
currentTimeMillis()
```

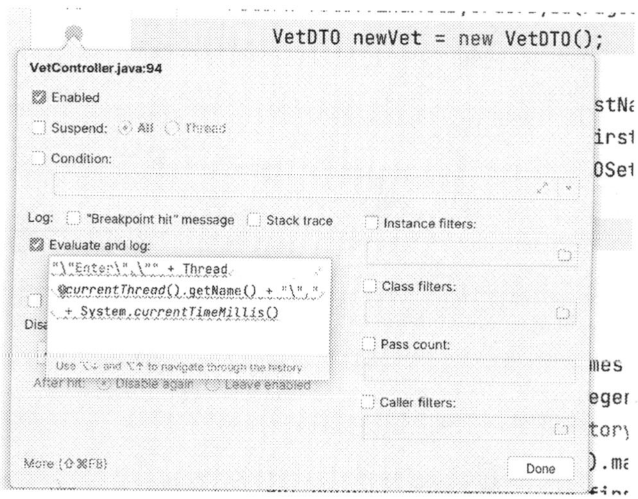

Figure 12-4. *Conditional tracepoint*

Alternatively, this can also be written using the `String.format()` syntax, which you can see in the following listing. As of this writing, the syntax with string concatenation is still faster than the corresponding `format` call. That's why I picked that approach. Code correctness isn't as important in a tracepoint expression.

```
String.format("\"Enter\",\"%s\",%d", Thread.currentThread().getName(),
System.currentTimeMillis())
```

Notice we need to use quotes to map the first two arguments so the spreadsheet will import the information correctly. Once this is done, I can import the resulting data into any spreadsheet and view it there.[5] In Figure 12-5, we can see a chart generated in a spreadsheet.

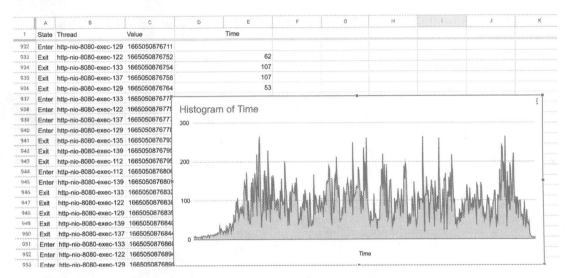

	A	B	C	D	E	F	G	H	I	J	K
1	State	Thread	Value		Time						
932	Enter	http-nio-8080-exec-129	1665050876711								
933	Exit	http-nio-8080-exec-122	1665050876752		62						
934	Exit	http-nio-8080-exec-133	1665050876754		107						
935	Exit	http-nio-8080-exec-137	1665050876758		107						
936	Exit	http-nio-8080-exec-129	1665050876764		53						
937	Enter	http-nio-8080-exec-133	1665050876777								
938	Enter	http-nio-8080-exec-122	1665050876775								
939	Enter	http-nio-8080-exec-137	1665050876777								
940	Enter	http-nio-8080-exec-129	1665050876778								
941	Exit	http-nio-8080-exec-135	1665050876793								
942	Exit	http-nio-8080-exec-139	1665050876795								
943	Exit	http-nio-8080-exec-112	1665050876795								
944	Enter	http-nio-8080-exec-112	1665050876806								
945	Enter	http-nio-8080-exec-139	1665050876809								
946	Exit	http-nio-8080-exec-133	1665050876832								
947	Exit	http-nio-8080-exec-122	1665050876838								
948	Exit	http-nio-8080-exec-129	1665050876839								
949	Exit	http-nio-8080-exec-139	1665050876846								
950	Exit	http-nio-8080-exec-137	1665050876844								
951	Enter	http-nio-8080-exec-133	1665050876860								
952	Enter	http-nio-8080-exec-122	1665050876894								
953	Enter	http-nio-8080-exec-129	1665050876896								

Figure 12-5. Tracepoint CSV imported into a Google spreadsheet and modified

To achieve this result, we first need to add a row to the top of the spreadsheet. This is important since the formula I describe as follows won't work without this. You don't have to add titles like I did in Figure 12-5, but it might be convenient. Next, we need to set the following formula in E2 to calculate the milliseconds:

```
=if(A2="Exit", C2-XLOOKUP(B2,$B$1:B1,$C$1:C1,0, 0,-1), "")
```

If you aren't used to spreadsheets, this might look a bit alien to you. Let's break it down; the = sign indicates a formula. It's followed by an `if` statement that tests if this is an entry or exit for the method. We only want the exit method. At the end of the `if` statement, you can see that a blank string is returned. This is indeed the case for the first row; since it will be an entry statement, the cell will remain blank.

The code in the middle is a bit more complex. This will only happen for rows that have the "Exit" label. In these rows, we subtract the current time from the last entry we have for the given thread. The `XLOOKUP` function searches the given cell range of cells

---

[5] You can find the Google Sheet I used for the screenshots here: https://docs.google.com/spreadsheets/d/1_3NJcqFnMaf98WtvZJKRyuw-bH1mZqHtOSIp3urFYOO/edit?usp=sharing

listing the thread name for the last occurrence of the current thread. It then returns the value of the cell in the following column (the one with the time). This formula would be simpler without the threading aspect. But now we have time in milliseconds which we can easily plot on a graph or use any other data analysis capability in the spreadsheet to understand.

The final step is to copy the formula all the way down for the data; spreadsheets automatically adapt the cell values that aren't preceded with the $ sign. As a result, the following line will automatically change to this:

```
=if(A3="Exit", C3-XLOOKUP(B3,$B$1:B2,$C$1:C2,0, 0,-1), "")
```

Notice that everything is adapted correctly. After applying the formula to the column, we can generate a chart based on the column to see everything plotted nicely. We can do so many things with the data and some basic understanding of spreadsheets. A simple trick is the sort function which we can apply to a new column using

```
=SORT(E2:E981)
```

This generates a sorted view of the data that we can then plot to generate the cool graph we see in Figure 12-6. I even added a trendline to show the degradation; it nicely highlights the edge cases where performance didn't keep up.

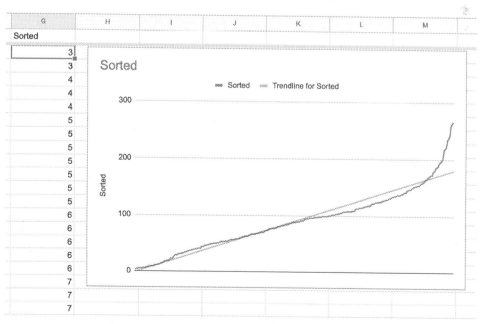

Figure 12-6. *Tracepoint CSV imported into a Google spreadsheet and modified*

Pinpoint Precision

Figure 12-6 shows a typical picture. Performance degrades in a "nice" clean fashion until it falls off a cliff. This is what we often see in a profiler, especially under load testing. Sometimes, this indicates a failure; usually, it indicates we crossed a threshold somewhere, but which one? What's failing in this case?

This is where developers start logging the hell out of the code, then running stress tests. This approach includes some major drawbacks:

- Logging is performance intensive and impacts the results.

- We need to compile every time and log a lot of data to understand what's going on.

- We need to comb through all that data to find that needle in the haystack. It's often not clear from the logs.

Wouldn't it be great if we could use a system like the tracepoints we discussed before and only stop when a method is in that top percentile of slow performance? Maybe even stop at a breakpoint so we can see the state after the fact? This requires surgical precision and is actually very easy to do. All we need to do is add one line as the first line of the method:

```
long startTime = System.currentTimeMillis();
```

Since no state is changed, you might be able to add this line and reload the app without restarting the running app. In IntelliJ/IDEA, you can do that using Reload Changed Classes as shown in Figure 12-7.

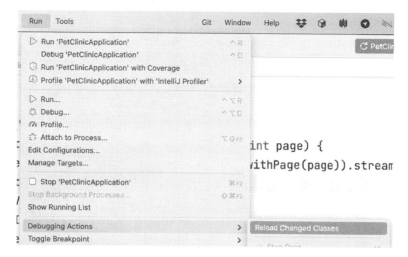

Figure 12-7. *Reload Changed Classes*

Once this is done, we can add either tracepoints or a breakpoint with a condition to match the outlier time value. For example, `System.currentTimeMillis() - startTime > 200`. This way, we can dynamically extract information about the slow performance and narrow down the impact area without restarting the execution.

Error Rates

A major reason for problematic performance peeks is simply due to errors. Exceptions are thrown, and as a result, buffers get flushed, and performance degrades. This is a perfect time to review the "Exception Breakpoint" section in Chapter 1.

We should define an exception breakpoint and review the errors that occur when we reach a high scale of requests. We can filter the exceptions to make sure we get only the relevant information.

Debugging Cache Misses

Caching is the most powerful performance-related tool in our quiver, whether it's in the CPU itself or from a remote database. Caching is the mechanism that tips the performance scale. It's also one of the hardest problems in computer science. I won't go into the various failures we can debug with caching (pollution, races, etc.) since this is a performance chapter. What I want to discuss is cache utilization.

When we access an element in the cache, there are two options: hit or miss. A hit is great; we have an element in the cache that we can return. A miss might be legitimate but might be an opportunity to improve the logic for the caching system. Unfortunately, these things are very hard to debug. The typical approach we use is to log cache hits and misses and then generate a chart representing this. Once we have that, we try to tune the code to improve utilization.

This is a tedious process. We discussed charting using a CSV and tracepoints in this chapter. The same technique can be applied to cache utilization with some minor tweaks. Let's say we have a cached object class that looks somewhat like this:

```java
public class CachedObject {
    private String identity;
    private Object value;
    private long lastAccessed;
    private int accessCount;
    private long creation;
    // class logic below...
}
```

Our cache has limited room. When we add an object to the cache, we often need to remove a different object. This is important to keep memory usage low but also to keep the size of the cache small. Searching through a smaller cache is faster. The value of the caching system is determined by our logic, the choice we make on which objects should be kept near. As you can see, there are many trade-offs we can take. We can remove the object whose `accessCount` is low, but that might not make sense if `creation` time is close; we might not have enough data. Maybe the object is accessed frequently for a short duration; in this case, `lastAccess` indicates the object is no longer used.

The thing we want to detect is an eviction followed by a miss for the same object. This is a clear case where we can improve the logic. Did we evict an object that we needed later? In this case, we can add a tracepoint in the code that evicts an object from the cache:

```java
"\"Eviction\",\"" + obj.getIdentity() + "\"," + creation + "," + lastAccess
+ "," + accessCount
```

We then add a similar rule to the cache miss logic where we log the identity value only:

```java
"\"Miss\",\"" + obj.getIdentity() + "," + System.currentTimeMillis()
```

The last argument is the one that matters. We can use the value of the miss time to check whether our logic could have been improved. For example, if the delta between the creation time and the miss time exceeds a threshold, this might be a legitimate miss. However, if the gap is shorter, we can conditionally highlight the problematic lines and review them individually in the spreadsheet.

We can implement this logic with a logger as well or with simple print debugging. The value tracepoints bring to the table is in conditionality and the ability to dynamically apply them to multiple eviction points. The fact that it includes zero overhead in production is a bonus.

Debugging Memory Issues

Memory corruption is a hard problem to debug without code changes; luckily, this isn't a common issue in Java. Our most common issue is memory leaks and overuse of memory. This is typically easy to profile as the tools explicitly list the objects in memory.

Note   There are other issues such as GC utilization and overhead. But those fall outside the domain of the debugger.

We discussed the memory capabilities of the debugger in the first chapter. It's a remarkable tool for gaining insight related to specific allocations and the current state of our application. The filter capabilities of the object view let us narrow down the objects and pinpoint a problematic entry.

But the killer feature is memory tracking (seen in Figure 1-14). This feature shows the stack trace associated with individual object allocations. We can zoom in on a specific line of code related to a wayward object and address the root cause of a problem.

Developer Observability and Performance

When discussing developer observability in Chapter 10, we discussed metrics. They are an amazing tool for typical production performance benchmarks. I suggest using them and ideally connecting them to your Grafana dashboards. Notice that most of the techniques I mentioned here can be used with developer observability and piped logs.

In this way, you can extract fine-grained profiling information from a production environment. The main drawback is that some high-volume data might be removed due to the sandbox. As such, the spreadsheet mentioned earlier won't work since it relies on a perfect match between the entry and the exit (there being an exit call for every method entry call).

Summary

Many books have been written about performance and profilers. You should pick one of them if you don't use a profiler on a semiregular basis. It's an amazing tool. But it's a blunt instrument when compared to a debugger. We need to use these tools in sync to approximate and then home in on the issue.

Spreadsheets are the unsung heroes of performance computing. They are amazing tools whose capabilities go well beyond the business world. By using formulas and smart analysis tools, we can get a level of detail that the best profilers can't possibly rival.

In the next chapter, we'll discuss security and common security pitfalls. Debuggers are amazing tools for hacking and hardening our infrastructure. There are many features we can leverage to find potential exploits as well as ongoing hacks.

CHAPTER 13

Security

We discovered in our research that insider threats are not viewed as seriously as external threats, like a cyber attack. But when companies had an insider threat, in general, they were much more costly than external incidents. This was largely because the insider that is smart has the skills to hide the crime, for months, for years, sometimes forever.

—Dr. Larry Ponemon

In my teens, we used to hack a lot. I wasn't a great hacker, but I was persistent. One of my first exposures to a debugger was the process of debugging a game's assembly code so we could understand and circumvent its Digital Rights Management (DRM).[1] This isn't a unique experience. Debuggers are some of the most powerful tools in the hands of malicious hackers. Debuggers explain the code and application state; they let us manipulate and inspect the application. They are the best possible tools to analyze and attack an unfamiliar system.

I recommend using dedicated tools to catch security issues early; we can't be too safe. However, the debugger is a security tool, and we should leverage its capabilities both to explore our weaknesses (as the hackers do) and to harden our defenses.

I chose to open this chapter with a quote about the risk from company internal attacks. 60% of security breaches are internal. Yet the vast majority of the security industry is aimed at that 40%. These internal breaches are far more severe than the external breaches. We need to pay attention to them.

---

[1] It was well over 30 years ago. Hopefully, the statute of limitations applies.

© Shai Almog 2023
S. Almog, *Practical Debugging at Scale*, https://doi.org/10.1007/978-1-4842-9042-2_13

Security Basics

Before we begin, let's talk about a few core terms and concepts related to security. The first and possibly more important term is *vulnerability*. A vulnerability is a weakness in our code or in the code we rely on. A vulnerability doesn't necessarily mean we can be hacked, but it does mean that this is a soft area that might be easy to attack.

An *exploit* is when a vulnerability can be used to perform something we shouldn't be able to do. To achieve an exploit, we might chain more than one vulnerability together. For example, a recent exploit used in Spring used an old vulnerability that got exposed again due to a new feature in Java 9. This provided developers with access to class object internals. The exploit then leveraged another vulnerability that allowed moving the log file and converting it to a JSP file. It could then run that JSP file and get code execution privileges. This was a *remote code execution (RCE)* vulnerability. These are usually the most severe issues.

Exploits are often creative and hard to follow. We can't predict exploits; we need to stop the vulnerabilities beforehand. This isn't enough since vulnerabilities are hard to catch as well. To make our systems secure, we need to *harden* them.

Hardening is a process of using defensive programming and deployment that would make it hard for an exploit to take root. Programmers can block features like serialization in Java. Admins can make containers read-only and use barebone containers to reduce the amount of potentially vulnerable code. There are many other concepts and terms related to security that we should know. But we won't discuss most of these subjects in this chapter as they would fill up an entire book.

An Example

This is all very theoretical. When I was a kid, we found out that the local 1-900 phone numbers had a corresponding local number you could dial for free. When they listed their numbers in the newspaper, they usually had a free local number for tech support. When they bought those phone numbers, they often bought many numbers in bulk. When buying in bulk, we usually get sequential numbers.

My friends and I inadvertently discovered the ID scanning vulnerability. We started dialing random numbers in the region of the tech support number, and we were able to dial into the 1-900 number for free. That's the exploit.

This isn't limited to 1980s enthusiastic teens. A few years ago, an upstart social network used numeric IDs to represent its users. They exposed this numeric ID in a URL to fetch the user details. Furthermore, they didn't even secure that URL. That meant one could just request URLs with numbers one by one and get all the user details. No restrictions to "friends," no authentication required!

A user ran an exploit and downloaded the entire list of users from that social network. Basic hardening would have verified that a user has the right to get the details of another user. It would have required authentication and would have limited the number of requests a single user could run. Security would have used a hash as the publicly exposed ID to stop a scanning attack like that.

Tips and Best Practices

Security is layered like an onion. A properly hardened secure environment will make an attacker work for the exploit every step of the way. Even if the attack succeeds, we will have more time to catch the attacker, and they will have less time within the system. For hardening, we need to first verify every identity and every permission. We need to limit what can be done, even by authorized users. We need to log everything in an administrator log; every operation and action must be trackable. If the worst thing happens and we are hacked, we need to understand exactly what was done to our system and how. An administrator log is the ideal way to keep track of everything that happens.

Restrictions on internal users are where even the biggest companies fail. Even when an attack is external, it would often impersonate an internal user when executing the attack. If internal users were limited in their abilities, the damage that the attack could do would be limited.

I strongly suggest using linting tools such as SonarCloud and ideally a security analysis tool[2] to track code issues and security vulnerabilities. There's absolutely no way to keep track of all the latest discovered vulnerabilities and notice elaborate issues.

Security Review

We can use the debugger to detect and verify some types of vulnerabilities. There are many types of vulnerabilities, and the list keeps growing. The debugger is a familiar

---

[2] https://owasp.org/www-community/Source_Code_Analysis_Tools

and dynamic tool that we can use for current and future vulnerabilities. The first thing we need to do in order to secure our system is understand how it can break. Once we understand the process of hacking the system, we can test whether it's secure. The debugger is perfect for that. The following are some common vulnerabilities and what we can do to detect and test them.

Injection

A well-known injection vulnerability is SQL injection, but there are many variations of this issue that we can discuss. The best place to start is with a simple example:

```
executeSql("select * from MyTable where id = " + id);
```

This code might seem innocent enough, but it's a huge vulnerability that was common in the early days of the Internet and, sadly, not extinct to this day. The ID can be anything. If I could set ID to ; DROP table users, that would be pretty unpleasant. The solution is to use prepared statements, validate input, and optionally use APIs like JPA which do those things for us seamlessly.

What can the debugger do to test injection style vulnerabilities? If we have suspect code, we can use the "evaluate" capability of the debugger to try various injection values to see if they indeed fail. But often, we don't have an immediate suspect. I would suggest using structural search[3] to find suspicious statements.

When we don't have an immediate suspect, we need to first validate that problematic characters don't get through. Does every variable that reaches the database layer go through the validate method? This is easy to test, but it does require code changes. Let's say we have a method whose validation code looks roughly like this:

```
public void validate(String value) {
    if(isSQLInjection(value) || isLogInjection(value) || isCSS(value)) {
        throw new InvalidValue(value);
    }
}
```

---

[3] www.jetbrains.com/help/idea/structural-search-and-replace.
html#to_search_structurally

We need to verify that every variable that goes into the database is either a variable we trust or went through the validate method. For this purpose, we can add the `whitelist` method which is blank by default. We would use it like this:

```
public static void validate(String value) {
    if(isSQLInjection(value) || isLogInjection(value) || isCSS(value)) {
        throw new InvalidValue(value);
    }
    whitelist(value);
}
```

Notice that we would also need to invoke that method on every hardcoded SQL value that we might pass. Then in the unit tests, we can mock the whitelist method with the following code:

```
private static List<String> whitelisted = new ArrayList<String>();
public static String whitelist(String value) {
    whitelisted.add(value);
    return value;
}
```

This is obviously a memory leak as we keep adding to the list without removing. I don't care about it for my unit tests. It might seem like a mistake, why not use a `Set` to avoid duplicates? I want the duplicates. I want a comparison of pointers (references) in this specific case, not an equality test. If I have two calls `validCall("X")` and `invalidCode(var)` where `var` is equal to `"X"`, I would want the first call whitelisted while the second one should fail. Notice that this isn't guaranteed in Java due to `String.intern()` semantics,[4] but this is the best we can do. Then we need to create a `checkInjection()` method:

```
public static boolean verify(String value) {
    return whitelisted.stream()
            .anyMatch(e -> value == e);
}
```

[4] https://stackoverflow.com/questions/10578984/what-is-java-string-interning

This is a bit obtuse due to the use of the == operator, simpler code would use the contains() method. At this point, our unit tests can mock the database and invoke verify for every argument received in the database layer. Only whitelisted values will pass. But we can check that quickly in the debugger using a conditional breakpoint. We can place such a breakpoint in the database driver code with the condition !verify(value). The breakpoint will hit for every entry that didn't pass through the validate method as seen in Figure 13-1.

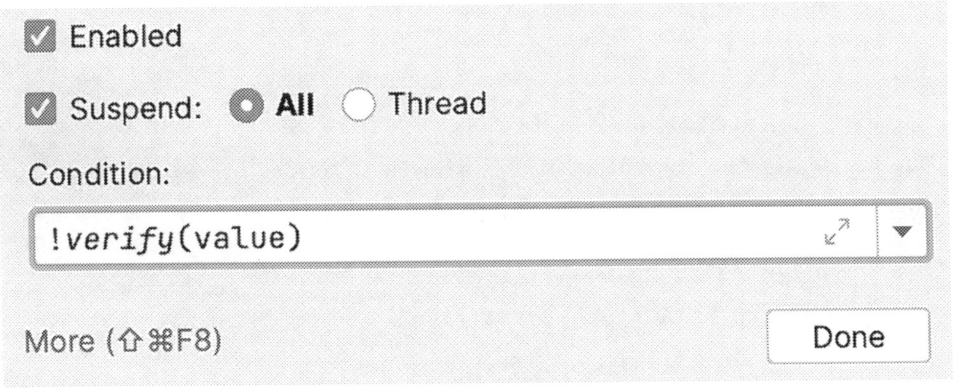

Figure 13-1. *A breakpoint that stops on unverified values*

ID Scanning

ID scanning is one of my favorite vulnerabilities as you might have noticed from my prior discussion. The knee-jerk reaction might be to remove the ID from the database. This might not be feasible for many cases. Performance of numeric IDs is often faster, but more importantly, changing the primary key at scale is a tremendous undertaking. It's entirely possible we can't change the ID.

If we can't replace numeric ID values with strings, we need to protect them. We should never return them to client code or alternatively block the client from accessing them at scale. These are things we need to detect in code. One of the most important concepts in security is restrictions on every layer.

A good example of that is a web UI that checks if you have permission to access a resource. A hacker would just circumvent the web UI. We need to check authority and permissions in every layer of the system. Otherwise, a bug or vulnerability in another layer can be used as part of an exploit. This might sound theoretical, but let's give a concrete example. Say we have a REST endpoint that returns the user details: /userDetails?id=numericId. The implementation of this method may be secure. But a new developer added a new endpoint /userCurrentLocation?id=numeric Id for the tracking app. This new endpoint wasn't properly secured.

A good implementation will still work since it will verify security in the implementation layer (business tier) and will fail there. We need to verify in tests that the business tier itself doesn't let us fetch an arbitrary user. But these sorts of tests are sometimes difficult to compose in an authentic way since the process of authorization is so deeply woven into the system. Do you have such a test in your project? Testing this from the debugger is much easier.

In the debugger, we can place a breakpoint in the database business layer code that fetches a user by its ID and add a condition that verifies the rights to fetch that ID. We can then use an unrelated business call with the debugger's evaluate feature to fetch a user for which we have no permission. We can see such a breakpoint in Figure 13-2.

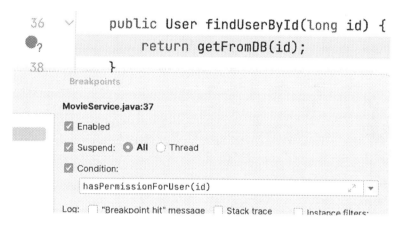

Figure 13-2. *A breakpoint that detects invalid scanning*

This is great, but what if someone is actively trying to scan IDs in your system? There are various tripwire solutions to trap such cases. These solutions are typically high level and would stop a scanner, but might stop legitimate usage as well. With developer observability tools, we can detect such misuse and pinpoint it to a specific account. We can't stop the actual scanning, but we can get all the details.

Detecting a scanning operation works in the same way as detecting a local breakpoint. We could add a conditional snapshot to the problematic line of code and increase the max hit count, so if multiple violations occur, we'll get additional data. In Figure 13-3, we can see such a snapshot on the same line of code. We could use a log at this point, but it wouldn't include as much data as we might want. This is valuable if we discover a scanning vulnerability and want to know if someone exploits it while we're working on a patch.

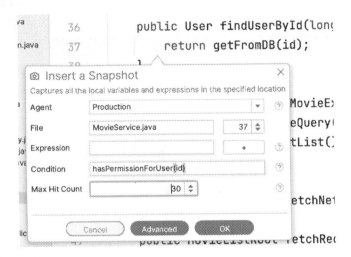

Figure 13-3.   *A snapshot to detect an exploit in progress*

Serialization Issues

I recently attended a talk by Brian Vermeer who labeled serialization exploits as "the gift that keeps giving." This is a well-known problem in the Java serialization specification; there are multiple attempts to fix those problems, but programming convenience, compatibility, and security are often at odds.

Serialization is problematic because it skips the constructor and lets us inject arbitrary state into the application. A single serialization vulnerability isn't necessarily a problem. It's hard to exploit one serialization issue. The problem is we have many serialization weaknesses and vulnerabilities in libraries and the JDK. Security researchers have created a tool[5] to generate serialization *payload* chains that you can use to attack a system. A payload is a package you can use to deliver an exploit. We can use `ysoserial` to generate a simple payload which includes a chain of classes that become an issue at the end. The following is a chain used to attack a vulnerability in ForgeRock:[6]

---

[5] https://github.com/frohoff/ysoserial

[6] https://portswigger.net/research/pre-auth-rce-in-forgerock-openam-cve-2021-35464

```
java.util.PriorityQueue.readObject()
 java.util.PriorityQueue.heapify()
  java.util.PriorityQueue.siftDown()
   java.util.PriorityQueue.siftDownUsingComparator()
    org.apache.click.control.Column$ColumnComparator.compare()
     org.apache.click.control.Column.getProperty()
      org.apache.click.control.Column.getProperty()
       org.apache.click.util.PropertyUtils.getValue()
        PropertyUtils.getObjectPropertyValue()
         java.lang.reflect.Method.invoke()
          TemplatesImpl.getOutputProperties()
           TemplatesImpl.new Transformer()
            TemplatesImpl.getTransletInstance()
             TemplatesImpl.defineTransletClasses()
              ClassLoader.defineClass()
               Class.newInstance()
               ...
               MaliciousClass.<clinit>()
               ...
               Runtime.exec()
```

This chain shows how a single read from an untrusted source can slowly escalate by nesting object types until we reach TemplateImpl which lets us load an arbitrary class file. Once we have that, we can load any class we want and own the system. This is an elaborate exploit, but since the related tooling is very powerful, even novices can construct elaborate chains and deliver an exploit payload.

There's a simple solution to harden systems against serialization attacks: serialization filter.[7] With a filter, we can whitelist the serializable classes and limit the surface of an attack vector. I recommend using a whitelist approach for any application. However, this isn't always an option. Some legacy applications might use serialization; I wrote such applications 20 or so years ago. Removing or even limiting serialization in such deployments might be untenable.

---

[7]https://docs.oracle.com/en/java/javase/17/core/serialization-filtering1.html

In these situations, we'd like to know our level of exposure to such attacks. The risk isn't so much from our code, but from the deep and elaborate dependency graph that comprises a modern application. This is actually a very simple process to test using the following code:

```
ObjectInputFilter.Config.setSerialFilter(new ObjectInputFilter() {
    @Override
    public Status checkInput(FilterInfo filterInfo) {
        return Status.UNDECIDED;
    }
});
```

We need to add this code to the entry point of an application,[8] then place a breakpoint on the return statement. This will unveil classes that are serialized, but that's something we can detect with a simple logger (which might be worth adding here). The main value in this approach is looking at the stack that leads to serialization calls. Go up the debugger stack and find the specific call. Is it possible that this call will load a class from an untrusted source? How does one reach this serialization call?

Internal Security

I mentioned before that 60% of all breaches are internal to the organization. Yet we spend most of the time protecting ourselves against external attacks. This makes some sense since internal "hacks" usually don't require sophistication. Most such cases are conducted via an open door. For example, a source code "theft" can simply mean copying the files to a USB thumb drive – hardly a sophisticated "hack."

There is a matter of data security though. A recent report on Twitter[9] indicated lax security, full access to all user information, etc. This is generally a bad practice more befitting a startup than a major corporation. We need internal security:

- Users have a right to privacy. Even if our company doesn't care about that right, it is enshrined in laws and regulations around the world. Gross negligence can lead to liability lawsuits.

---

[8] Notice that this code requires JDK 9 or newer.

[9] https://arstechnica.com/tech-policy/2022/09/senators-blast-twitters-alleged-security-failures-as-whistleblower-testifies/

- IP theft is a real problem, for example, Google sued Uber over IP theft.

- In the case of an external attack, internal protections will make it much harder to get away with any meaningful information.

Internal security is crucial and is mostly handled by administrators. As programmers, we often ignore that specific aspect of our job. There are a few things we can do in that area. Specifically, don't open holes, make sure to have an auditing trail,[10] and apply access restrictions. Not all of those apply to a book about debugging, so I'll focus on the few that do.

Don't Open Holes

Not opening a security hole sounds easy enough. Then we pass around a single universal key to the SSH of an AWS machine so we can debug something. Every permission granted for debugging should have an expiry date. The smaller the team that has access to these compute resources, the better.

As developers, we need to avoid remote debugging into production. As I mentioned before, this is a glaring security hole. We need to review every endpoint we open and try to limit information exchange. We need to limit what can be passed and how we accept data.

If we use a tool like developer observability, we need to review every potential hack and use blocklists aggressively. For example, if you use Keycloak for authentication, I would recommend blocking the entire `org.keycloak` package by default. It would make sense to block entire packages and individually whitelist specific packages. This is crucial as a malicious developer could add a log into the authorization code and steal tokens.

Refine Logging

I discussed logging in Chapter 4 but didn't discuss auditing. Auditing is the process of semantic transactional logging that tracks changes to a system. We can follow the audit log to understand the history of every change and associate it with the specific user that triggered it. An audit log isn't modifiable and can lead us down a breadcrumb trail in the case of a hack. Access to the audit log should be heavily restricted to avoid the risk of tampering.

---

[10] www.baeldung.com/database-auditing-jpa

The regular log should be minimized though. I even go so far as to recommend only logging warnings and errors. While many organizations properly secure the database, very few have the same restrictions on the log. We would see users who have no database read privileges but have full access to the log. It's very common to log user information and even tokens. A malicious person with access to the log can use such tokens for impersonation or even use private data to gain access in case tokens weren't logged.

Dealing with a Zero-Day

A *zero-day* is an exploit that no one knows about. That means a hacker could use it right now to gain access into any vulnerable system, and we would have no protection. Such issues come up occasionally and are instantly pounced on by hackers. There's a big market for such exploits in the criminal and government hacking sectors.

On Christmas of 2021, we received the gift of a major zero-day exploit: Log4Shell.[11] This was a vulnerability in Log4J which allowed variables passed to the logger to execute a JNDI query. The mechanics of the exploit were elaborate, but the concept was simple. Using a simple string, that would get logged in the server, could trigger an RCE. That's a terrible vulnerability that impacted an immensely popular third-party Java library.

As a sidenote, variables received from the client should pass validation beforehand. If this would have been the case, it's possible the vulnerability wouldn't have been exploitable. Unfortunately, that's rarely the case, and linters have only started warning about such risks in recent years.

When the exploit became known, there were still limited workarounds. Some of those initially suggested workarounds turned out to be incomplete. However, debugging worked. The flaw was in the `JndiLookup` class of Log4J 2.x. By placing a breakpoint in the class and triggering the vulnerability, we could inspect the impact firsthand. Notice that you don't need to have the source code of the class to do that. We also placed a snapshot on that class in production using Lightrun; this let us see if someone was trying to exploit the vulnerability.

---

[11] `https://snyk.io/blog/log4j-rce-log4shell-vulnerability-cve-2021-44228/`

Summary

Security is a subject of many books, and the awareness for various weaknesses grows stronger each year. Tooling is also improving to a level where it sometimes feels like a turnkey problem: "Install tool X and security will be solved." This is far from the truth. Improvements in security are essential to stop corresponding improvements in hacking. The sophistication of modern exploits is mind-boggling in some cases. The complexity of our stacks makes these attacks even more serious.

In that respect, a debugger is a simple security tool. It's generic, and as a result, it's often harder to see the vulnerabilities. But when we use it in concert with other tools, it's an essential piece of the puzzle. The attackers often use it because it shows us everything that's going on. It's the perfect sidekick to dedicated security tools and good developer policies.

The final chapter will cover strategies for dealing with real-world issues. We like to think of ourselves as unique, but debugging feels the same to all developers. We all feel stupid in the end, and most bugs are alike. In the final chapter, we'll go over some stories, strategies, and how we could do better.

CHAPTER 14

Bug Strategies

I realized that a large part of my life from then on was going to be spent in finding mistakes in my own programs.

—Maurice Wilkes

In the 1990s, I worked for a gaming company that built flight simulators for Electronic Arts. The founder of the company was a former air force pilot, so were over a dozen on staff. One of their core principles was that of a debrief. Not meetings, we had fewer meetings than any other company. A debrief is what pilots do after a mission is done, successful or not. It makes no difference. They get as much information as it's fresh in the pilot's mind.

Practicing debriefs in a tech company is just as valuable. It's painful, especially the parts where we relive the mistakes. But it's also crucial to debrief on success. There's always room to improve, and nothing is perfect. Unfortunately, the longer we wait with the debrief process, the memory becomes fuzzy. We miscalculate the amount of time we spend on everything and remember things differently. That's why it's important to take the time after a session and recount the process, even if it's only in your head. This helps us improve iteratively moving forward.

In this final chapter, I want to talk about our actual day-to-day debugging experience – what type of bugs we run into, how we address them, and the real-life stories behind them. I do this by revisiting bug stories from the past and debriefing on them. For every story, we discuss the good, the bad, and how we can do better in the future. I'm recounting most of these stories from memory; I left details abstract since they don't make as much sense.

© Shai Almog 2023
S. Almog, *Practical Debugging at Scale*, https://doi.org/10.1007/978-1-4842-9042-2_14

The Impossible Database Entries

"This shouldn't be possible" was the first response from the engineer I was working with. We were looking at an SQL database table where values of some properties were null. "There's literally no pathway in the code where these values are null," he repeated.

These are the worst kinds of bugs; some users were reporting issues when working with the service. Upon review of the status, we found that specific entries that were added as part of the process had values set to null in the database even though they were always initialized to non-null values in the code. What could be going on here?

I was stumped. This is a problematic process to debug. The code that added these entries clearly sets the values. We reviewed the code together and went through all the motions. Back then, we didn't have developer observability tools, so I couldn't put a snapshot to check that. Because of that, we added log statements and redeployed. I wanted to look at the actual SQL going into the database to see what the hell was going on, but this was hard to produce in the production deployment, and it just didn't happen.

The code itself used JPA in J2EE to write entries to the database. In JPA, one would create an object, populate the fields with variables, and store them, for example:

```
entityManager.save(myUserObject);
```

This is very powerful and lets us assume that some basic database functionality is working. We saw that the entries were indeed inserted correctly, but in all the cases we looked at, there was no corruption. This led us to the conclusion that the problem only happens under very specific conditions. But what could those conditions be?

Because this only happened in the production environment and only happened erratically, we were very limited in the scope of our investigation. Since it didn't happen in development, adding logging to SQL wouldn't help. Doing that in production would have been impractical as it would have slowed performance noticeably and would expose private information in the logs. We were stumped and, back in that day, didn't have the tools to debug this properly.

My solution was to alter the database table. The table schema was created by JPA and defaulted to allowing null. By changing the database table and making the columns non-null, we would change the behavior to a fail-fast approach. This isn't ideal since users will experience an immediate failure. But it would instantly expose the problem. We ended up doing just that, and then it became a waiting game for the failure.

CHAPTER 14   BUG STRATEGIES

When the failure happened, it was now instantly obvious from the stack. The initial insert wasn't at fault. It worked exactly as expected; we wasted our time looking at the wrong area of the code. A different thread was updating the entry and did a fetch in a different transactional context. It had a partial entity in memory that overrode the changes.

Lessons Learned

The initial project should have used a fail-fast policy as discussed in Chapter 4. This is a great defensive approach and is important for reliability. This is something that I didn't have control over, but it was an important tool in discovery.

When we looked at the code, we quickly zoomed in on the store operation. I assumed it failed even though I knew it shouldn't. The rule of thumb is this: when you know code "can't do that," it probably really can't. There's something else going on. We should have spent more time investigating potential influences.

There were no tools to debug production which left us rather blind. This was before developer observability or similar tooling were available so we couldn't use that. But the company didn't have much in terms of a general observability stack either, only logging.

The project should have had better test coverage for failure situations. I don't recall the full setup in terms of integration tests, but I'm sure that good coverage would have revealed the problematic error handling before production.

The Seven-Minute Process

A major bank I was working with was working on a trading system. Directly connected to the stock market, it was supposed to modernize an old COBOL system with a new web-based architecture – the latest and greatest Java Enterprise Edition + HTML. AJAX (JavaScript UI) wasn't around yet. Struts was a new idea.

As is common in such projects, months were spent on design. More than 40 programmers were brought in to actualize that design. A big team built a big and elaborate system that covers all the aspects needed for stock trading at scale. The contract for the contractor building the system stipulated many requirements. But one of the most important requirements was that a stock operation (purchase, sale, etc.) should take under one second.

On the development machines with no networking overhead, it took seven minutes!

249

This was unacceptable and ridiculous. It's a simple operation. Yes, it includes many steps, but it isn't decoding the genome. There are no inherent computational complexities or IO. What could be the problem? I was brought in to find the issue. People tried and had multiple fervent meetings on the subject. As I came in, I was bombarded with information I couldn't digest – theories, ideas, and references to internal systems. One thing became clear: no one ran a profiler; they were all guessing.

Eventually, I was given a desk and a computer to look at the code. It was a massive project. I quickly understood why no one profiled it; just getting the environment up and setting the profiler properly took me all day. Then running that took a while; by evening, I was looking at the numbers, and they were very clear. The top two performance hogs were two tiny inexpensive methods. What gives?

I checked who the authors of the methods were, and they were two guys with adjoining desks. After I showed them the profiler results, they looked at one another: "I thought you cached the results." It turns out each method was responsible for returning the content of a two-column lookup table. But one method invoked the other one. For every entry in one DB/2 SQL table, the other method ran the entire query on the second table and went through all the data as seen in Figure 14-1. By caching the results of one method, the runtime went down to seven seconds!

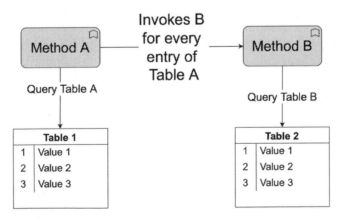

Figure 14-1. *For every entry in table 1, method B reads table 2 again*

Lessons Learned

Tooling is revolutionary and beats any theory. Work with facts and measurements. Do that iteratively. That company could have saved on my consulting fees by just running the profiler on a regular basis and structuring their project in a way that would make it easy to run the profiler. Don't waste time in meetings about theory when you don't have the facts in front of you.

Talk to your colleagues. Two guys were sitting side by side working in the same area of the code. Yet each assumed the other person was responsible for caching the results. Had they done proper code reviews, this is probably something they would have noticed. I would also suggest defining conventions for behaviors like caching, for example, `fetchMyElementCached(x)`, to indicate whether the method will keep data.

Going Bankrupt in PaaS

Our bootstrapped startup was in serious trouble. I was looking at a Google App Engine bill that had grown significantly overnight. If this billing continues, we will need to take down our product. There was no way we could afford this much in cloud spending.

Overnight charges started rising; we didn't deploy a new version of our application. The costs just kept rising. I had no idea what was going on. We were on gold-level support and contacted Google trying to get help. This was a complex process that required sending them our code, only to get the reply: "it's a bug on your side." That was a waste of money.

We kept trying while waiting for them. The first place to look is on the bill. Unfortunately, it wasn't itemized. Back then, App Engine only supported a Data Store API for persistence. This API was based on Google's Bigtable and was terrible. We used a JPA abstraction on top of it for compatibility and vendor neutrality. App Engine charges by operations, and it seemed the high cost was due to "datastore reads." In typical circumstances, you shouldn't read too much from the database and try to use caching as much as possible. We indeed used memcached which is a distributed caching solution available on App Engine. But somehow some calls were reaching the database.

Locally, we had no way to reproduce it as we couldn't tell how many calls were reaching the database. We didn't have a decent local environment for anything other than simple configurations and were ill equipped to deal with an issue like that. Adding logging would seem like a good option, but App Engine charges for logs and that would have sent our bill higher still.

This story has no satisfying ending. We made random fixes until billing went down. Because of the slow cycle of discovery, we had no way of knowing if a fix we made helped until we waited for the next billing update. We were blind. Shortly after that, we abandoned App Engine.

Lessons Learned

We need observability into production. We can't be constrained due to costs when it comes to that. We need a way to look at logs and debug. That's one of my biggest problems with serverless; it leads to the same exact problem, and I see many similar experiences online.

There are "good ways" to degrade services. When we debug, running out of resources is a problem I can debug. I can look at the resource and understand what's taking up the machine. Solutions that scale and charge based on that scale are impossible to debug. I can't put a breakpoint on Google's billing algorithm. The ability to debug locally or on staging is crucial; without those abilities, everything is at risk.

The Fast Network

Another situation of "that can't happen" occurred in a customer on-site deployment. Their application was failing but only when installed on-site at their offices. Because of the way everything was arranged, we had no stack or any way of knowing what the hell was going on.

I logged in to their system and ran everything remotely. It indeed failed. I proceeded to step over the code where it worked as expected. This is a classic race condition symptom, so I was already on the right track. Our application had several threads, but which one was responsible for this problem?

I moved the breakpoint around and used some tracepoints to narrow this down to the code that initializes the system. I found out that the networking code in that initialization code completed before the method finished. Networking was so fast it beat the speed of local IO and returned a result before the initialization code was done. This was so early in the bootstrap stages of the application I just didn't notice it.

Lessons Learned

That system didn't allow me to use a tool like *strace* (discussed in Chapter 3) to check the execution of the project. Had it allowed that, I might have seen the issue. The network operations were returning while the IO was still in progress. These days, I try to delegate more of that sort of debugging to customers.

There was a subtle reliance on the speed of the network in initialization code. It's an assumption that I made consciously, that local IO is faster than networking. I didn't give that assumption enough thought when writing the code, nor when I searched for the bug. During the assumption check phase (Chapter 2), I should have seen that.

The Missing Wing

We were working on a flight simulator for Electronic Arts. On the night before a big demo, we saw wings missing on some of our planes, only in release builds and under some circumstances. They would blink in and out inconsistently, and we had no idea why.

This was a huge C++ project that took a while to compile; we had no decent memory issue tracking tools and were effectively limited to guesswork. We ended up spending the night commenting the code out and seeing if the problem still reproduced. After all, debugging a release binary isn't practical.

It turns out that in a large method with multiple objects, one object was declared on the stack and returned by reference. This created a memory corruption that manifested itself in a completely different area of the code.

Lessons Learned

We did everything wrong here. We had no dedicated memory debugging tools. When working with an unsafe language, those are essential. We had no linting for the project; back then, linters were much simpler than they are today. I believe a modern linter would have instantly found that.[1]

We need to use tools that match the platforms we use. When we write native code, we need to use native unit tests to verify that code and need to use memory monitoring tools to fix issues in these languages.

---

[1] Probably with a rule like this: https://rules.sonarsource.com/cpp/RSPEC-946

The Microservice

I was working with a company as it was migrating to a microservice architecture. There was still a monolith somewhere along the way, but large portions of it were already migrated to independent services. They were experiencing some performance issues for a specific microservice.

Unfortunately, their observability stack wasn't great. They relied on a very basic dashboard and ingested logs for everything. I didn't have much to go on. I started by running the microservice and profiling it. I didn't see any obvious issues. Then I tested it in production with curl and got a similarly performant response. Another conversation with the manager clarified that this was an observation based on code that invokes the microservice taking a while to complete and showed me the relevant code. The code was written in Scala which I don't use, and it wasn't totally clear to me. I brushed it off and decided to try measuring in production under various circumstances. We also enhanced the logs with more parameters and tried to get more information.

As part of that investigation, I added logs both in the code that invoked the remote service and the service itself. Looking at the code, I noticed the timestamps made no sense. The other service started late. It seems that when one service invoked the other service, everything was delayed.

After a trip back to the manager, the picture became clear. An API gateway was used for the communication which was defined in a Scala function I didn't read into. This gateway had a queue configured to prevent taxing the microservice. Normal benchmarks didn't pick it up since the queue was wide enough, but when the system was used in production, the queue quickly filled up and caused noticeable delays.

Lessons Learned

Had I read the Scala code properly, I would have probably seen the problem before the logging. I should have put more effort into understanding what was going on.

Observability is always recommended; with microservices, it isn't an option. The complexity of the deployment requires a sophisticated monitoring and observability stack. With proper spans, we could instantly see the problem and would have understood everything.

Long-Run Fail

Tests find a lot of bugs, but some of the hardest bugs to track happen under intense stress. A system to deal with those issues is to run a heavier set of tests that can take all night to run. These tests try to simulate intense system load with the intention of stretching it to its limits. A test can run for ten hours and can produce so many logs it would be impractical to download them to our local machine. When it fails, we need to understand why it failed, and the log was our only clue. Normally, failures are to be expected. But as our system stabilized, we found out that crashes still happened occasionally. The long run would sometimes pass, but often it wouldn't. Unfortunately, it would crash in different locations, and we had no way of telling what went on.

It did crash on resource depletion, specifically on running out of database connections. The obvious solution which we considered was to increase the quota of database connections, which did reduce the frequency of the problem but didn't solve it.[2] We were stumped; we couldn't use any tooling since this already took ten hours to run and wasn't consistent to begin with. To make matters worse, what would we point out tooling at? A failure to get a connection from the pool isn't the bug, that happened when the leak happened.

We decided to do something bold; we ran *jstack* (Chapter 3) from the generic code that handles the failure on the processes itself. We redirected it to an external file, so we won't have to download the entire failure log. We then committed to a branch and waited. The following day, we saw a large stack which showed 20 threads stuck on a monitor. It seems that we had a bad monitor in our WebSocket code that was blocking threads until it timed out. These threads had transactional context and a database connection in heavy usage, so the resources ran out.

It was hard to see in real-life scenarios since the WebSocket would restart itself after a timeout with no ill effects. But users might have seen lower responsiveness for some features. Fixing the monitor made that problem go away.

Lessons Learned

Long-run tests are hard to build; the pain during their development and execution pays back in dividends when we go to production. The lack of visibility in that environment

---

[2] Decreasing the size of the connection pool can also help in some cases by queueing connections.

is painful; we do have developer observability tools installed there, but in this particular case, I'm not sure if they would have helped.

Some time travel debugging tool vendors offer their products as solutions for such issues (learn about TTDs in Chapter 5). I haven't tried that myself, but I think that might be one of the best use cases for time travel debugging. I did try developer observability tools for such cases, and they do show promise, but it's still a bit challenging.

Summary

When I was interviewed for my role at Sun Microsystems, I was asked: What was a bug you made and how did you discover it? I started giving an answer about a bug made by someone else, and the interviewer stopped me. He wanted a bug I created. I don't normally black out, but this was one of those few times; I could only think of one bug, and it was stupid. I won't tell him **that**. I picked the arguably worse option. I said I couldn't come up with anything, but I know I made some. I got the job, but I still remember that frustration from two decades ago.

Most bugs are stupid in retrospect. We all spend too long chasing these stupid bugs. I'm no different; my bugs are just as stupid. Practice and sharing reduce the time we spend chasing stupid bugs. Following the path and techniques we discussed in Chapter 2 can help here. The tools outlined in the other chapters can help with the hard bugs.

I hope you enjoyed this book as much as I enjoyed writing it. I hope it will improve your debugging experience, and I thank you for reading it all the way through. I would love to hear from you on Twitter[3] and on my blog.[4]

---

[3] https://twitter.com/debugagent
[4] https://debugagent.com/

APPENDIX A

Resources

Sometimes it pays to stay in bed on Monday, rather than spending the rest of the week debugging Monday's code.

—Dan Salomon

We covered a lot of ground in this book, and to do that, I had to rely on many great resources. Here are some of the resources I relied on and a few resources I created that you could use. There are many companies and great resources out there, but I chose to focus on people only. Otherwise, this section could be bogged down.

Other People

These are some amazing people who write about debugging:

- Julia Evans writes a lot about debugging. She's an amazing visual teacher. I highly recommend her tutorials covering *strace*. I suggest following her Twitter account at @b0rk. Also, check out her blog at jvns.ca and her ezine at wizardzines.com.

- Andreas Zeller wrote a debugging book and went on to create a great website on the subject at debuggingbook.org. He's also on Twitter as @AndreasZeller. His approach is more academic than mine.

- Dominik Seifert is the creator of Dbux, which is an open source time travel debugger, currently supporting JavaScript on VS Code. He created some interesting tutorials on the subject and blog at dev. to/domiii.

© Shai Almog 2023
S. Almog, *Practical Debugging at Scale*, https://doi.org/10.1007/978-1-4842-9042-2

My Resources

You can read things I write and follow me in the following channels. I speak at conferences on a regular basis and have many online lectures:

- debugagent.com
- twitter.com/debugagent
- github.com/shai-almog
- talktotheduck.dev

Index

A

accessCount, 230
Accountability, 201–203
Administrator log, 235
Agent, 184, 192, 193
Agent security, 203, 204
Annotations, 24–27, 184
Antagonism, 29
API gateway, 142, 254
Application Performance Monitors
      (APMs), 177
Arrays, 16, 18, 22, 86, 211, 219
Asynchronous stack trace, 11, 12
Asynchronous tools, 41
Auditing, 243, 244
Audit log, 20–203, 243
AWS Lambda, 136

B

Backend, 51, 143, 145, 182, 184, 192, 200
Back-in-time debuggers, 109, 111
Bankrupt in PaaS, 251, 252
bitesize.d, 60
Blocklist, 203, 243
Breakpoint descriptions, 214
Breakpoints, 213
    asynchronous stack trace, 11, 12
    conditional, 8
    exception, 7, 8
    field, 7
    line, 6

    management UI, 8
    method, 6, 7
    suspend state, 9, 10
    tracepoints, 9, 10
Breakpoints grouping, 214
Bug fixing cycle, 98, 99
    create test, 98
    find bug, 98
    fix bug, 98
    run code, 98
    run test, 98
Bugs, 29, 101
Buildg, 133
Byte arrays, 219

C

Cache utilization, 229, 230
Caching, 124, 169, 170, 229, 230
Caller filter, 210
C++-based scheduling tool, 35
Chaos engineering, 185
checkInjection() method, 237
Chrome JavaScript debugger, 148
Chrome network monitor, 161, 163
Classic race condition, 252
Client, 192
Cloud computing, 105, 116
Cloudflare, 145
Cloud Native Computing
      Foundation (CNCF), 124, 179
Cloud neutral, 124

© Shai Almog 2023
S. Almog, *Practical Debugging at Scale*, https://doi.org/10.1007/978-1-4842-9042-2

Remote debugging (*cont.*)
    port 5005 on localhost, 128
    problems with JDWP, 130
    VS Code, 129
Replay debugger, 113–115
Resource depletion, 171, 255
Resource exhaustion, 185, 186
Resource starvation, 45–46
resultFromOtherMethod, 194
Resume-Driven Development (RDD), 123
Rubber ducking, 50

S

Sandbox, 204, 232
Scala code, 254
Secrets, 132, 133
Security, 245
    accountability, 201–203
    agent, 203, 204
    exploit, 234
    hardened secure environment, 235
    hardening, 234
    hash, 235
    linting tools, 235
    production-grade observability
        solution, 201
    RCE, 234
    restrictions, 235
    segregation, 201
    vulnerability, 234
Security breaches, 233
Security hole, 243
Sentinel, 60
Serialization, 234, 240–242
Serialization attacks, 241
Serialization *payload* chains, 240
Serverless debugging

competing vendor-specific tools, 135
debugging strategies, 136
feature flags, 141, 142
idempotency, 137
Lambda function in IntelliJ/IDEA, 140
local debugging, 138–141
as an oxymoron, 136
performance, 135
scaling, 135
staged rollouts and canaries, 142
staging and dev environment, 137
Serverless deployments, 135–137, 173
Serviceability Agent (SA), 74
Seven-minute process, 249–251
Show Objects, 18, 215
Snapshots, 77, 195, 197, 198
Software Reliability Engineers (SREs), 175
SonarCloud, 235
Sophisticated debugging sessions, 214
Sophisticated deployments, 142
sort() function, 227
Source code theft, 242
Spreadsheets, 226, 227, 231, 232
SQL abstractions, 172
SQLException, 171
SQL statement, 184
Stack trace, 6, 10, 11, 25, 26, 41, 44, 111, 155, 179, 198, 215
Stack trace checkbox, 209
Standard debugger techniques
    code necessity, 213
    keep tracking, 213–215
    mutation and propagation, 209–211
    UML diagram, 215
Storage, 26, 123, 132, 136, 165, 167
strace, 57, 102, 252
    DTrace, 62
    Java, 65

Printed in the United States
by Baker & Taylor Publisher Services